TEXAS PUBLIC BUILDINGS OF THE NINETEENTH CENTURY

PUBLICATION NUMBER TWO

The Texas Architectural Survey

SPONSORED BY THE

AMON CARTER MUSEUM OF WESTERN ART

AND THE

SCHOOL OF ARCHITECTURE,

THE UNIVERSITY OF TEXAS AT AUSTIN

Texas Public Buildings
of the Nineteenth Century

Photographs by Todd Webb

Text by Willard B. Robinson

Foreword by Drury Blakeley Alexander

PUBLISHED FOR THE AMON CARTER MUSEUM OF WESTERN ART
BY THE UNIVERSITY OF TEXAS PRESS, AUSTIN AND LONDON

The Amon Carter Museum was established in 1961 under the will of the late Amon G. Carter for the study and documentation of westering North America. The program of the Museum, expressed in publications, exhibitions, and permanent collections, reflects many aspects of American culture, both historic and contemporary.

Library of Congress Cataloging in Publication Data

Robinson, Willard Bethurem, 1935–
    Texas public buildings of the nineteenth century.

    (The Texas architectural survey, publication no. 2)
    Bibliography: p.
    1. Architecture—Texas. 2. Architecture, Modern—
19th century—Texas. 3. Texas—Public buildings.
I. Webb, Todd, illus. II. Title. III. Series.
NA730.T5R62   720'.9764   74-578
ISBN 0-292-78006-0

CONTENTS

Contents

FOREWORD

The publication of *Texas Public Buildings of the Nineteenth Century* brings to completion the primary objective of the Texas Architectural Survey. In 1963 the officers of the Amon Carter Museum in Fort Worth invited the School of Architecture at The University of Texas to participate in a survey of the historic buildings of Texas. As the first survey of its kind in the state, it produced an inventory of Texas's architectural heritage that served as the basis for two publications, the first being *Texas Homes of the Nineteenth Century*. These books present in photographs and documentary text a selection of the most representative examples of the historic buildings of Texas.

In this second volume Professor Robinson's carefully documented text and Todd Webb's informative photography will promote the wider objective of the Survey in continuing to stimulate the interest and concern of the public in the preservation and enjoyment of a significant part of our heritage.

DRURY BLAKELEY ALEXANDER
Professor of Architecture
The University of Texas at Austin

PREFACE

This is the second and final volume publishing the results of the Texas Architectural Survey, a joint project to catalogue definitive architectural examples of the nineteenth century by the Amon Carter Museum of Western Art, Fort Worth, and The University of Texas at Austin. The first volume, *Texas Homes of the Nineteenth Century*, by Drury Blakeley Alexander and Todd Webb, appeared in 1966. Published in this and the earlier volume are photographs taken in 1964 of extant public buildings in Texas.

Progress has been as unkind to the architectural heritage of Texas as it has been to the historic buildings of other states. In such large cities as El Paso, Dallas, Fort Worth, and Houston, innumerable significant buildings have disappeared before the ball of the wrecking crane. Even since this survey, the Galveston County Courthouse, illustrated with photographs herein, has been razed, and others have been threatened.

While progress must continue, it is indeed unfortunate that so many significant buildings have disappeared without first being systematically recorded. In 1934 and 1936 the Historic American Buildings Survey, in collaboration with the American Institute of Architects, the National Park Service, and the Library of Congress, recorded with photographs and measured drawings a large number of structures. Two and a half decades later, Eugene George, Jr., directed a survey from Austin. In 1966, I supervised an HABS project in Jefferson. Subsequently, surveys were conducted in Galveston and San Antonio. In addition, the Texas Historical Survey Committee has marked many important buildings throughout the state. However, even with all this effort, numerous important extant structures remain to be accurately documented. While some architecture recorded by other surveys appears in this volume, it is intended that many additional examples will appreciably expand the factual and visual record of historic Texas architecture. It is hoped that the text will set the buildings in perspective with respect to their times and circumstances, rather than treating each structure as an isolated subject, as often happens in graphical surveys.

The text and drawings are not confined to extant buildings, but are intended to communicate the entire spectrum of the nineteenth century. Without mention of certain subjects, several important building types, examples of which no longer stand, would be missing, thus resulting in an incomplete work. Consequently, discussion of bygone structures, some of which are not illustrated with photos, is included.

In this study of public architecture, an equitable geographical distribution has been attempted, but it must be remembered that large areas of Texas were yet undeveloped as late as 1900. For example, Lubbock, now a city of 150,000, in 1899 was an isolated and unincorporated town of 293; Amarillo, now with 128,000, in 1900 was a small settlement only slightly larger than Lubbock. The greatest concentration of examples is logically from the regions that were well developed by the turn of the century.

It is my belief that architectural history based solely on visual evidence is incomplete. During the last quarter of the nineteenth century, there was a wonderful public pride in architecture. Because of this esteem, new buildings embodied many aspirations, which may not be apparent in their physical form: they were symbols of progress, expressions of culture, emblems of permanence, and, to the people in a community on a lonely frontier, they even expressed hopes for the future. Therefore, the true significance of nineteenth-century buildings cannot be fully appreciated by viewing them through twentieth-century glasses; rather, it is necessary to explore romantic points of view that were quite unlike pragmatic attitudes that prevail today.

To convey the spirit of the times, as well as to document information, newspapers and other firsthand accounts have been freely drawn upon in the text. Probably the most energetic promoter of every town was the local press. In addition to stimulating outside interests in economic development, newspapers had a strong impact on the cultural character of communities. The power of the pen was used to influence a receptive public on matters of taste, to agitate action on new buildings, and to promote community improvement. Articles on architecture, describing famous buildings both in the United States and abroad, were numerous. In addition, reporters wrote critically as well as descriptively and lauditorily on local architecture. These writings all were a part of the architectural setting of the century.

In the preparation of this volume, I am indebted to numerous people. My thanks go to Mitchell A. Wilder, director of the Amon Carter Museum of Western Art, for the opportunity to undertake this study. Dr. Ronnie C. Tyler and Mrs. Margaret McLean, both of the Amon Carter Museum, provided help and information. Miss Gertrude L. Smith, my cousin, provided much assistance with the manuscript. My appreciation also is due to Miss Sue Barr for her conscientious typing. Finally, my most sincere thanks to Margaret, my wife, for her endless patience and assistance.

WILLARD B. ROBINSON
Texas Tech University
Lubbock, Texas

TEXAS PUBLIC BUILDINGS OF THE NINETEENTH CENTURY

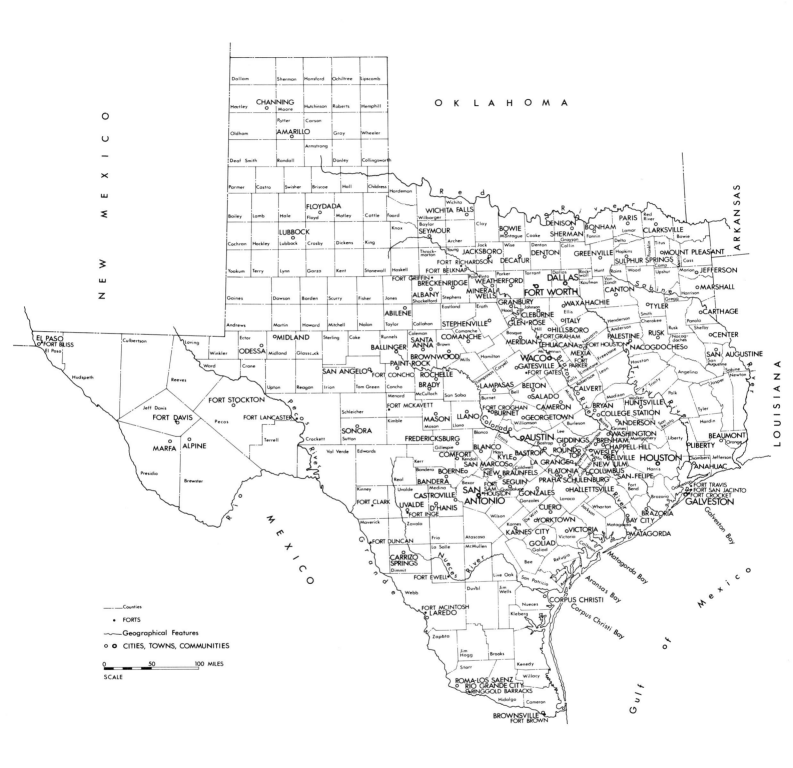

OKLAHOMA

NEW MEXICO

ARKANSAS

LOUISIANA

MEXICO

Gulf of Mexico

Dallam | Sherman | Hansford | Ochiltree | Lipscomb
Hartley | CHANNING○ | Moore | Hutchinson | Roberts | Hemphill
Oldham | Potter | Carson | Gray | Wheeler
 | | AMARILLO○ | Armstrong | |
Deaf Smith | Randall | Donley | Collingsworth
Parmer | Castro | Swisher | Briscoe | Hall | Childress
Bailey | Lamb | Hale | FLOYDADA○ Floyd | Motley | Cottle | Foard
Cochran | Hockley | LUBBOCK○ Lubbock | Crosby | Dickens | King
Yoakum | Terry | Lynn | Garza | Kent | Stonewall | Haskell
Gaines | Dawson | Borden | Scurry | Fisher | Jones
Andrews | Martin | Howard | Mitchell | Nolan | Taylor | Callahan

Red River

Wichita
WICHITA FALLS
Wilbarger
Baylor
SEYMOUR○
Archer
Throck-morton
Young JACKSBORO○
FORT RICHARDSON●
FORT BELKNAP●
FORT GRIFFIN●
BRECKENRIDGE○
ALBANY○
Shackelford
Stephens
Eastland
ABILENE○
STEPHENVILLE○
COMANCHE○
Comanche

Clay
Montague
Cooke
DENISON○
SHERMAN○
Grayson
BONHAM○
Fannin
Lamar
PARIS○
Red River
CLARKSVILLE○
Bowie
BOWIE○
Wise
DENTON○
Denton
Collin
GREENVILLE○
Hunt
Hopkins
SULPHUR SPRINGS○
Franklin
Camp
Titus
MOUNT PLEASANT○
Cass
Morris
JEFFERSON○
Rains
Wood
Upshur
MARSHALL○
Harrison
Gregg

Palo Pinto
WEATHERFORD○
Parker
Tarrant
FORT WORTH●
DALLAS●
Dallas
Rock-wall
Kaufman
Van Zandt
CANTON○
Smith
TYLER○
Cherokee
Rusk
RUSK○
Panola
CARTHAGE○
Shelby
CENTER○

MINERAL WELLS○
GRANBURY○
Hood
Johnson
CLEBURNE○
GLEN ROSE○
Somervell
Erath
Bosque
HILLSBORO○
Hill
Ellis
WAXAHACHIE○
ITALY○
Navarro
TEHUACANA○
MEXIA○
Henderson
Anderson
PALESTINE○
Freestone
NACOGDOCHES○
Nacog-doches
SAN AUGUSTINE○
San Augustine
Sabine
Newton

MIDLAND○
Sterling
Coke
Runnels
BALLINGER○
Brown
SANTA ANNA○
Coleman
Mills
MERIDIAN○
McLennan
WACO●
FORT GRAHAM●
FORT PARKER●
Limestone
Leon
Houston
Angelina
Jasper
Tyler
Hardin

EL PASO○
FORT BLISS●
El Paso
Culberson
Loving
Winkler
Ector
ODESSA○
Midland
Glasscock
Upton
Reagan
SAN ANGELO○
FORT CONCHO●
Irion
Tom Green
Concho
PAINT ROCK○
ROCHELLE○
BRADY○
McCulloch
San Saba
FORT McKAVETT●
Menard
MASON○
Mason
LLANO○
Llano
FORT CROGHAN●
BURNET○
Williamson
GEORGETOWN○
Burleson
BRYAN○
COLLEGE STATION○
ANDERSON○
Grimes
Madison
Walker
HUNTSVILLE○
Polk
Trinity
Robertson
CALVERT○
Milam
CAMERON○
Bell
BELTON○
SALADO○
LAMPASAS○
Lampasas
Coryell
GATESVILLE○
FORT GATES●
Falls
BEAUMONT○
Orange

Hudspeth
Jeff Davis
FORT DAVIS○
Pecos
FORT STOCKTON○
Reeves
Ward
Crane
FORT LANCASTER●
Crockett
Terrell
Val Verde
Edwards
SONORA○
Sutton
Schleicher
Kimble
FREDERICKSBURG○
Gillespie
Blanco
BLANCO○
Hays
AUSTIN●
Travis
Bastrop
BASTROP○
GIDDINGS○
Lee
ROUND TOP○
WASHINGTON●
WESLEY○
BRENHAM○
CHAPPELL HILL○
Washington
Montgomery
Liberty
HOUSTON●
Harris
LIBERTY○
Chambers
Jefferson
ANAHUAC○

MARFA○
ALPINE○
Brewster
Presidio
PECOS River
RIO GRANDE River
COMFORT○
Kendall
BOERNE○
Kerr
Real
BANDERA○
Bandera
Medina
CASTROVILLE○
D'HANIS○
FORT INGE●
UVALDE○
Uvalde
Kinney
FORT CLARK●
Maverick
Zavala
Frio
Atascosa
LA GRANGE○
Fayette
FLATONIA○
PRAHA○
SCHULENBURG○
NEW ULM○
COLUMBUS○
BELLVILLE○
SAN FELIPE○
Austin
Colorado
HALLETTSVILLE○
Lavaca
Fort Bend
BRAZORIA○
Brazoria
Galveston Bay
FORT TRAVIS●
FORT SAN JACINTO●
FORT CROCKETT●
GALVESTON○
SAN MARCOS○
Caldwell
Guadalupe
SEGUIN○
NEW BRAUNFELS○
Comal
FORT SAM HOUSTON●
SAN ANTONIO●
Bexar
GONZALES○
Gonzales
CUERO○
De Witt
YORKTOWN○
VICTORIA○
Victoria
BAY CITY○
MATAGORDA○
Matagorda
Matagorda Bay

FORT DUNCAN●
La Salle
McMullen
CARRIZO SPRINGS○
Dimmit
FORT EWELL●
Webb
Duval
Live Oak
San Patricio
Bee
KARNES CITY○
Karnes
GOLIAD○
Goliad
Refugio
Aransas Bay
Aransas

FORT McINTOSH●
LAREDO○
Zapata
Jim Wells
Nueces
CORPUS CHRISTI○
Kleberg
Corpus Christi Bay

Jim Hogg
Brooks
Starr
Kenedy
Willacy
ROMA-LOS SAENZ○
RIO GRANDE CITY○
RINGGOLD BARRACKS●
Hidalgo
Cameron
BROWNSVILLE○
FORT BROWN●

Counties
● FORTS
Geographical Features
○ ● CITIES, TOWNS, COMMUNITIES

0   50   100 MILES
SCALE

Spanish Colonial and Mexican Architecture in the Texas Region

IN EVERY HISTORICAL PERIOD of any or all people of the world, architecture appears to have expressed the life and times of the society that produced it. Through the functional types of buildings that were erected and through the spatial relationships between them were revealed essential material and spiritual aspects of a people's life. In the design of dwellings and edifices intended for fulfillment of the mundane existence was reflected the nature of their secular existence; in the temples dedicated to their God or gods was mirrored the character of their religious convictions. Relative values as to these aspects of life were then expressed by the form, opulence, and beauty of the necessary structures. In communities the functional and visual relationships further suggested values through the spontaneous or planned zoning of various activities and through the formal emphasis of the most important works.

In a particular geographical area, the times of a people were manifested in techniques of construction. The manner in which various natural and manufactured materials were assembled to provide shelter re-

vealed the level of advancement in that people's building art. These developments in technique were apparent in the architectural traditions that evolved and were passed from one generation to the next.

Prior to the evolution of efficient systems of transportation and expedient methods of disseminating knowledge, architecture spontaneously reflected the region through the materials that nature provided for construction and through the configuration of forms developed for protection from wind, moisture, and temperature extremes. Consequently, indigenous buildings erected on smooth, grass-covered plains differed from those on rough, tree-covered hills; shelters built to insulate against the bitter cold in the north differed from those erected to shed rain and to protect against the hot rays of the sun in the south. In pioneer times all structures set up in response to common limitations and requirements usually possessed similar attributes of style. Particularly in primitive regions, very few contrasts were apt to be found.

In any wilderness, settlement and the advancement of civilization were accompanied by an orderly adaptation to the natural environment. However, with progress, conflict was inevitable. In America, therefore, successful colonization depended upon the ability to develop works for defense to secure life and property. The forms of such buildings were determined by the types of warfare that were encountered and, like shelters from the weather, by the types of materials that nature could provide.

Interestingly, in the Texas country, in developing both protection from the weather and security from adversaries, indigenous architecture did not result in any universal techniques or styles. This was a land of climatic and geological contrasts, settled by people with diverse backgrounds and traditions.

During their explorations and early attempts at colonization in Texas, the intrepid Latins struggled against a rough and often inimical wilderness. In the unfamiliar environment, their destiny was vitally influenced by the land, as well as by relations with natives and other nations. In addition to geology and climate, the geographic features of each particular region influenced the outcome of efforts to master the country. The natural highways that pioneers traveled —in times of both peace and war—and the locations for their first settlements were largely determined by the configuration of the land and by bodies of water.

In 1519, when exploring for the first time that coastal section of the Gulf of Mexico belonging to the present state of Texas, Alonzo Alvarez de Piñeda sailed along a chain of narrow islands and peninsulas that protected the shore line of the wide Gulf Coastal Plain, on which scarcely a stone was to be found for building or any other purposes. Indentations into this level alluvial plain were formed by Galveston, Matagorda, and Corpus Christi bays, each of which received water from a principal river: at the first of these was the mouth of the deep Trinity River, the second received the clear Colorado, and the third was the terminus of the rapid-flowing Nueces. Although rafts or sand bars restricted access at river mouths or bay inlets, all these bays and rivers were navigable.

East and southwest of these Piñeda passed through the vicinities where the Gulf received the Sabine River and the Rio Grande, both of which were destined to be of political importance. The former eventually became a part of the eastern boundary of the Lone Star State, while the latter ultimately was recognized as a national border line through terrain that ranged in contrast from the dry, mountainous Big Bend country to the productive lands of the lower Rio Grande Valley.

Other early explorers observed the texture and color of the forests and prairies. Although they were not interested in remaining long, they viewed the unstable surface building materials and occasionally saw places that exposed the durable rock that the subsurface would yield.

In 1534, nearly six years after he was stranded in his attempt to reach Mexico from Florida on a crude barge, Alvar Núñez Cabeza de Vaca began his odyssey from the proximity of Galveston Bay, where later would be discovered extensive clay banks for the production of brick. Traveling southwest along the coast, he crossed the Brazos River, the deep-red-to-umbercolored waters of which rushed from the north through forests of post oak and cedar trees. Shortly thereafter, en route to the Rio Grande, where the journey turned inland on the way to Mexico City, he crossed the Colorado River, the tributaries to which afforded many sites suitable for the development of water power in the hill country to the northwest. Beneath the surface of that region and areas to its north were vast layers of the limestone belt, light gold to white in color. To the west were deposits of Pecos sandstone in contrasting chromas of red—durable materials for monumental edifices of the future.

Five years after Cabeza de Vaca crossed Texas, Francisco Vásquez de Coronado and his army of conquistadors entered the treeless but grassy Panhandle region. In their disappointing search for the legendary Seven Cities of Cíbola, they crossed the seemingly endless Llano Estacado—a flat plain, broken occasionally by abrupt canyons and dotted with numerous small, round lakes. Excepting soil and grass, there was little enough for building indigenously in that region; but, for that matter, there would be little need for several centuries.

In contrast, the army of Don Hernando de Soto, traveling westward after the death of their leader in 1542, found East Texas to be lush with trees and

Spanish Colonial and Mexican Architecture in the Texas Region

shrubs. They passed through open forests south of the Red River, where the deep greens of the verdure formed rich counterpoint with the fertile red soil. South of this region was the Big Thicket, a densely wooded section with thick underbrush, and along the Sabine River were vast stands of lofty pine to provide considerable resources for the architecture of future settlers. To delight the eye, there were the magnificent magnolias accented with large white flowers.

Over a century later this same region was crossed by Frenchmen. After missing their intended destination—the mouth of the Mississippi—Robert Cavalier, Sieur de La Salle, and his party accidentally landed upon the shores of Matagorda Bay. Subsequent to setting up a defensive work called Fort Saint Louis (1686), they explored land to the north and east. Finally, an expedition set out overland to reach the Mississippi River. Passing far to the east of the Balcones Escarpment, scene of granite-producing igneous and marble-producing metamorphic geological activity centuries ago, the party sans the deceased La Salle passed near the eastern section of the fertile blacklands and crossed the timberlands of East Texas. Although these adventurers, like the Spaniards before them, observed the variety of resources on the surface of the land, they did not remain to capitalize on them.

The climate experienced by early explorers, travelers, and immigrants in Texas was as variable as the landscape. Summers in the eastern region were accompanied by heat, humidity, and heavy rainfall, all of which slowed physical activities. To the westward, humidity and annual quantities of rainfall gradually decreased until the climate in West Texas became semiarid—summers were characterized by clear skies; dry, hot days; and cool nights. While summers were sultry in the central, south central, and coastal areas, winters were mild and pleasant. In the far south the climate was semitropical, but in the Panhandle snow and sleet were not uncommon in the cold season, although these seldom remained long on the ground.

The various environmental regions of the state were also vexed by fearsome meteorological phenomena. In late fall and winter, throughout the state, settlers had to endure "blue northers," when the sky suddenly assumed a cold blue-grey hue and piercing winds were

followed by a rapid drop in the mercury. In West and Northwest Texas unpredictable and devastating tornadoes were constant threats during the spring and summer, and along the coast tempests of hurricane intensity would cause many to rebuild from time to time.

Just possibly in part, it was because of a stormy Gulf that La Salle had missed his intended destination. In spite of the fact that his attempt to found a colony failed miserably, he succeeded in arousing the Spaniards into action in the settlement of Texas.

Following the investigation of La Salle's fort by several expeditions, Spain determined to retard further encroachment on its eastern frontier by the establishment of missions.[1] In 1690—some eight years after the founding of Mission San Antonio de la Isleta, far to the west, near El Paso del Norte—soldiers and friars traveled "hand in hand" into the wilds of East Texas to establish Mission San Francisco de los Tejas and Mission Santísimo Nombre de María. Built with walls of logs, driven vertically into the ground,[2] these missions, like the others that had been previously located in Florida and other areas of northern New Spain, were intended to organize and Christianize the Indians and to subjugate them to the Crown, thereby firmly establishing the Spanish claim to the region. In theory, this effort was considerably more economical than employment of a military force. However, after only three years, disease and hostilities forced the short-lived crude shelters of these outposts to be forsaken.

Not until more than two decades later did the aggressive French again threaten the frontier with a new trading post, called Natchitoches, near the Red River, thus arousing renewed efforts at civilizing the eastern wilderness with the mission system. Among the new establishments, all built of vertical logs and

[1] In the colonization of the frontiers of Spain, the close relationship that existed between the Crown and the Church proved to be a great advantage. The missions were supported by the Crown; in return, the missionaries served the Crown, in intent, by holding land claims through subjugation of the Indians.
[2] Ernest Allen Connally, "The Ecclesiastical and Military Architecture of the Spanish Province of Texas" (Ph.D. dissertation), pp. 49, 62.

covered with either shingled or thatched roofs.[3] were the Missions San Francisco de los Tejas (1716) and Nuestra Señora de los Dolores de los Ais (1716) and the presidios of Nuestra Señora de los Dolores de los Tejas (1716) and Nuestra Señora del Pilar de los Adaes (1721)—destined to become the Spanish capital of the province of Texas until 1773. However, the East Texas missions experienced difficulties arising from the lack of neophytes, and most were either abandoned or transferred after a short period of operation.

The success of the early missions depended not only upon attracting receptive, sedentary Indians, but also upon the land and what it would produce. If the missions were, as intended, to become self-sustaining institutions, fertile land and life-giving water were mandatory.

In the regions where the San Pedro Springs issued from a layer of limestone and flowed into the San Antonio River, the missionaries discovered productive soil and terrain favorable for irrigation. Not only was the environment benign, but also this region was conveniently situated, geographically, to serve for the development of a supply base between Coahuila and the eastern frontier of New Spain. Under such favorable circumstances, by 1731 five missions had been established in the vicinity of the Presidio de San Antonio de Béjar (1718), near the site of the future city of San Antonio. Among these were San Antonio de Valero (1718), more famously known as the "Alamo," the scene of dramatic events in the Texas Revolution, and San José y San Miguel de Aguayo (1720), whose beauty has won for her the appellation "queen of the missions."

The San Antonio missions represented remarkable cultural achievements, which could have been accomplished only by stoic friars who were willing to endure danger and hardship with little material reward. Into a wilderness menaced by barbarous Apaches and Comanches, they journeyed to teach arts, crafts, and music to the natives. At first their activities were housed in rough shelters of logs, adobe, or grass, but,

as soon as the most basic architectural needs were fulfilled, dedicated hands were soon at work on permanent buildings—in several cases, at new and better sites. Using tufa and limestone, at each mission they erected a friary, granary, workshops, cells, kitchen, refectory, and church. In reaction to the hostilities of warlike tribes, it was essential to set up strong fortifications, comprised of walls and turrets with loopholes.

Artistically inclined friars were skilled not only in construction but also in decoration. As soon as functional demands were met, attention was turned to glorifying their most important work with ornamentation. As on all frontiers wherever it was possible, the style of art was that of the homeland—in this case, the Baroque and Churrigueresque of Spain and Mexico. At the church of Mission San Antonio (1744), although they may not have understood them, the neophytes, as well as the settlers in the area, must certainly have been delighted by the twisted column shafts, Classical entablatures, and statues of Saint Francis and Saint Dominic that were protected in niches beneath sculptures of sea shells. More opulent was the church at San José (1768), with its west front characterized by decoration inspired by scrolls, floral and conchoidal forms, and cherubs' heads, and with its famous rose window, carved by Pedro Huízar, descendant, it is said, of the architect of the Alhambra, world-famous stronghold in Spain.[4] Like the church at nearby Mission Nuestra Señora de la Purísima Concepción de Acuña (1731), these edifices were also structurally sophisticated. All three had naves that were spanned with barrel vaults, and Concepción had a dome, which was carried on a pendentive over the crossing of the cruciform plan—structural hallmarks of Spanish colonial architecture.

The wax and wane of mission prosperity occurred within the eighteenth century. The San Antonio establishments, as well as another to the southeast, Mission Nuestra Señora del Espíritu Santo de Zuñiga, commonly called La Bahía (1749), thrived through mid-century. Notwithstanding, due to circumstances beyond the control of the friars, their wealth and cul-

---

[3] Ibid., pp. 119, 146, 165. Also, see Henderson King Yoakum, *History of Texas from Its First Settlements in 1685 to Its Annexation to the United States in 1846*, I, 51.

[4] Works Progress Administration, *Texas: A Guide to the Lone Star State*, p. 351.

tural influence declined near the end of the 1700's. In the last decade, most were partially suppressed, and the land, tools, and livestock were divided among the Coahuiltecan Indians to whom, according to policy, the missions belonged. However, complete secularization did not occur until 1824.

Earlier, Spanish authorities had recognized that missionaries and their small military guards were incapable of firmly holding the land and directing its development. Therefore, in 1731, with the hope of founding the nucleus of Spanish civilian population, fifteen families, numbering some fifty-five colonists, were sent from the Canary Islands to establish the Villa de San Fernando de Béjar (San Antonio) adjacent to the presidio of San Antonio. Unfortunately, because of laziness, and perhaps because of conflicting interests between the friars and the settlers over tillable land, progress was slow and there was little prosperity.

When the Spanish settlers journeyed into the wilderness to establish towns, they carried with them definite instructions regarding layouts. From Spain planning was formally regulated by "Ordinances concerning Discoveries, Settlements, and Pacification," which King Philip II in 1573 had incorporated into the Laws of the Indies—originally started in 1512 as the Laws of Burgos and culminated in 1680 as the Recopilación. Ostensibly patterned after the writings of famous Roman architect and engineer Marcus Vitruvius Pollio (first century B.C.) and developed to ensure the establishment of towns in the New World that would be both functional and beautiful, these ordinances idealistically specified the configuration of open spaces and the relationships between the buildings.[5]

By ordinance, the center, or nucleus, of the community was to be the *plaza de la villa*. It was to be oblong, with a length one and a half times the width—proportions considered ideal for fiestas; moreover, it was to be in proportion to the population of the town, but no less than two hundred feet wide and three hun-

dred feet long. From this space, two streets were to emanate from each corner and one from each side. So that the buildings might protect the streets from cold breezes, the plaza was to be oriented with corners to the prevailing winds—also a precept of Vitruvius. Around the plaza would be arcades for the convenience of the merchants; and, for the beauty of the *villa* or pueblo, it was specified that all buildings, insofar as possible, should be uniform.

The authority of church and government was to be indicated by the position of buildings. "The temple in inland towns shall not be placed on the plaza but distant from it and in such a place that it may be separated from any building which approaches it and which has no connection with it. . . . In order that it may be better embellished and have more authority, it must, if possible, be built somewhat elevated above the ground in order that steps will lead to its entrance. Nearby close to the main plaza shall be built the royal houses and the council and cabildo house."[6]

Both the Villa de San Fernando de Béjar and the Pueblo Nuestra Señora del Pilar Nacogdoches were essentially laid out in conformance with the Laws of the Indies. Located some distance west of the Presidio de San Antonio de Béjar, a large rectangular plaza, to be surrounded by *portales*, formed the nucleus of the layout for San Fernando. On the northeast end of the plaza, which was oriented with the corners to the cardinal points, was a square for the temple, or church.[7]

Shortly after the town was laid out, it was removed to a site adjacent to the presidio. Although somewhat irregular, the new plat conformed to the concept of the original plan. The *plaza de la villa*, slightly irregular in rectangular form, was located near the *plaza de armas* but separated from it by the parish church. From each corner emanated the required two streets, although these were not perfectly true. Unlike the first layout, however—perhaps because it adjoined the presidio—the orientation of the plaza was close to the cardinal points.[8]

[5] See "Royal Ordinances for New Towns, etc.," in Zelia Nuttall, "Royal Ordinances concerning the Laying Out of New Towns," *Hispanic-American Historical Review* 4 (November 1921): 749–753.

[6] Ibid., p. 751.

[7] Plan of Villa de San Fernando de Béxar, *Archivo General y Público, México, Provincias Internas*, vol. 326, published in Herbert Eugene Bolton, *Texas in the Middle Eighteenth Century*, facing p. 6.

[8] The form of the embryo settlement of the Villa de San Fer-

The civil and military architecture along these plazas and streets, indigenous to the land near the end of the century, was plagued by poverty. Fray Juan Agustín Morfi reported the Villa de San Fernando de Béjar to be "a wretched settlement consisting of fifty-nine houses of stone and mud, and seventy-nine of wood. . . . dwellings were badly built and incommodious, few of them containing more than one room and all of them only one story."[9] The barracks of the military establishment, according to Morfi, were not fit for stables.

The character of the frontier settlement did not change perceptibly during the half century that followed. In 1817 the governor of the province reported that the official building he occupied was entirely uninhabitable.[10] Over a decade later, when the community belonged to Mexico, it was observed by José María Sánchez that the buildings, "though many are of stone, show no beauty, nor do they have any conveniences."[11]

Later descriptions elaborated on the Spanish colonial and Mexican architecture of previous decades that had not yet changed significantly. The town square continued to be surrounded on three sides with stone buildings, one story high with parapets, resembling fortifications.[12] The walls of other houses, many of which were damaged by cannon balls during periods of hostilities, were of sun-dried mud bricks (adobe) or of crooked poles planted vertically in the ground, the interstices of which were chinked and daubed. The adobe and wooden buildings were mostly

windowless, and the former were roofed with adobe, the latter with thatching.[13] In 1834 a traveler from the East, Amos Parker, wrote "St. [sic] Antonio, like all the Spanish towns, is composed of houses built of logs and mud, and makes a squalid appearance."[14] Conditions were no better in the Spanish town Villa de San Agustín de Laredo. As in the Villa de San Fernando, a central square formed the nucleus of Laredo, founded in 1755 by individual enterprise but not surveyed until 1767. After laying out the square, the surveyor, José Prudencio García, established the streets and divided the blocks. Lots twenty varas wide and forty varas deep were laid out, and land was set aside for a parish house, a jail, and a church.[15] But, typical of Spanish settlements in Texas for many years afterward, Laredo did not prosper. By 1789 the only durable buildings were a stone church, nine stone houses, and two houses of adobe; other buildings were *jacales*—buildings with walls of crooked stakes, plastered with mud—fenced by stone, adobe, stakes, or bulrushes.[16] Several decades later, Sánchez reported: ". . . the buildings are covered with grass; and the houses have no conveniences. A desolate air envelops the entire city, and there is not a single tree."[17]

In contrast, Nacogdoches was situated in a richly vegetated region. Its plan was also developed according to a predetermined order, but the buildings were also spontaneous products of the region. Laid out by Antonio Gil Ybarbo in 1780 and populated by settlers from the abandoned Pueblo Nuestra Señora del Pilar de Bucareli (1774)—which had also been laid out according to law—the town was platted around an oblong plaza, oriented with the long axis running east and west.[18] The streets providing communication to the plaza were regular and straight, which, according

nando, circa 1770, is indicated on a map in the British Museum, London, Add 17662t.

9 Report cited in Hubert Howe Bancroft, *The Works of Hubert Howe Bancroft*, vol. 15, *History of the North Mexican States and Texas*, part 1, p. 653. See also Fray Juan Agustín Morfi, *History of Texas, 1673–1779*, trans. Carlos Eduardo Castañeda, p. 92.

10 Antonio Martínez, *The Letters of Antonio Martínez*, trans. and ed. Virginia H. Taylor, p. 17.

11 José María Sánchez, "A Trip to Texas in 1828," trans. Carlos Eduardo Castañeda, *Southwestern Historical Quarterly* 29, no. 4 (April 1926): 257–258.

12 See Chester Newell, *History of the Revolution in Texas*, p. 147; William Bollaert, *William Bollaert's Texas*, ed. W. Eugene Hollon and Ruth Lapham Butler, p. 217; Ferdinand Roemer, *Texas*, trans. Oswald Mueller, p. 120; Frederick Law Olmsted, *A Journey through Texas*, p. 149.

13 J. C. Clopper, "Journal and Book of Memoranda for 1828, Province of Texas," *Quarterly of the Texas Historical Association* 13 (1909–1910): 70–71.

14 A[mos] A[ndrew] Parker, *Trip to the West and Texas*, p. 157.

15 Sister Natalie Walsh, "The Founding of Laredo and St. Augustine Church" (M.A. thesis), p. 91.

16 Seb Wilcox, "Laredo during the Texas Republic," *Southwestern Historical Quarterly* 42, no. 2 (October 1938): 88.

17 Sánchez, "Trip to Texas in 1828," p. 251.

18 John Forbes Map, University of Texas Archives.

to a later visitor, "make the place more agreeable."[19] On the west end of the town square there was a secondary plaza for the use of the church.

In the pine forests of East Texas, the buildings of Nacogdoches were of several materials, all indigenous. Although a trading post of stone (Old Stone Fort) was built near the end of the eighteenth century, most Spanish and Mexican works were of wood and earth. According to Amos Parker, "the Spaniards built a town of log houses; generally having the logs standing perpendicular at the sides and ends, and the space between them filled with mud; with chimneys made of the same materials."[20]

Around the turn of the century, the small amount of new Spanish colonial ecclesiastical work built in these towns had little of the distinction of the earlier mission churches. The Roman Catholic Church (1800–1801) in Nacogdoches was crude and impermanent. According to Parker, who described the building three years before it was razed, the edifice was "built in the true Spanish style, with perpendicular logs and mud; now falling to decay."[21] However, a stone work had replaced it by 1821.

The architectural accomplishments of the friars in the previous century were not without significance in the nineteenth. Although most of the missions had been partially or wholly secularized late in the eighteenth century and were completely suppressed early in the nineteenth, the churches at these missions continued to fulfill needs for the common worship. The San Antonio de Valero Mission church was used for services from 1801 until 1825; the church at San Francisco de la Espada apparently was used from the time of partial secularization until complete suppression in 1824.[22] In another section of the province, the buildings of the Missions La Bahía, Nuestra Señora del Rosario (1754), and Nuestra Señora del Refugio (1793), the last mission founded in Texas, continued to be attended by priests until the 1820's.[23]

In addition to these, with repairs and renovations, the church of Nuestra Señora de la Candelaria y Guadalupe, a stone building with a cruciform plan similar to the church of Mission San Antonio de Valero, begun in 1734,[24] served the residents of San Antonio until a new edifice was erected over it (1868–1873).

Other works of previous years became diversely functional, many being modified to suit the needs of the times. In San Antonio near the end of the Spanish colonial period, dilapidated houses, confiscated from rebels, were used as quarters and barracks for the military.[25] At the turn of the century the Mission San Antonio de Valero was also appropriated by the military; in 1793 it became a garrison, and in 1805 the friary was converted into a hospital. Then, in 1835, a memorable date for Texans, the San Antonio Mission (the Alamo) was converted into a fort by the Mexican general Martín Perfecto de Cos. When Texans occupied the Alamo after the capitulation of Cos, the sacristy of the church was used as a powder magazine; cannons were mounted on earthwork platforms; and, since the friars had designed their defenses for protection against only primitive weapons, not cannons, the enclosing walls were strengthened with masses of earth.[26]

On such new work as was undertaken, a shortage of mechanics slowed progress. In the Alamo city a new military prison, a two-story stone work with a shingled roof, rose slowly.[27] New barracks remained still unfinished in 1817 because there were no troops to complete the work.[28] In another instance, a projected construction at the Presidio La Bahía was never realized. In 1810 architect Don José Ma. Cavallo was to direct work on barracks, but there were neither masons nor peons.[29] The last Spanish governor, Antonio

[19] Sánchez, "Trip to Texas in 1828," p. 283.
[20] Parker, Trip to the West and Texas, p. 120.
[21] Ibid.
[22] Marion A. Habig, The Alamo Chain of Missions, pp. 70, 220–225.
[23] Kathryn Stoner O'Connor, The Presidio La Bahía del Espíritu Santo de Zuñiga 1721 to 1846, p. 74.

[24] However, the cornerstone was not laid until May 11, 1738 (see Habig, Alamo Chain of Missions, p. 259).
[25] Martínez, Letters, p. 56.
[26] See Frederick C. Chabot, The Alamo: Mission, Fortress and Shrine, pp. 38–39. This work was carried out under the direction of Green B. Jameson, who had been appointed engineer of the post and had submitted plans to the government for improving the fortification.
[27] Carlos E. Castañeda, Our Catholic Heritage in Texas: 1519–1936, V, 195–197.
[28] Martínez, Letters, p. 57.
[29] O'Connor, Presidio La Bahía, p. 95.

Martínez, saw the need to fortify San Antonio against the Americans in 1820, but there was simply no money for tools and artisans.[30]

In addition to the lack of men and money, political conditions in the province of Texas at the dawn of the nineteenth century were unfavorable to the building art. In 1803, after Spain had retroceded the territory to France, the United States purchased Louisiana with its controversial boundary, creating external pressure on the province. Abroad, confusion resulted five years later when Charles IV abdicated from the Spanish throne, leaving his kingdom in the hands of Napoleon Bonaparte, who shortly thereafter placed the crown upon his brother, Joseph. In New Spain, while emissaries from Joseph urged allegiance, some patriots supported fealty to the Bourbon family of Charles IV. Meanwhile, others determined to defy the despotism of Spain and become completely independent. Strife and destruction followed until freedom was won. During this time, destitution and misery prevailed according to historian Henderson Yoakum, who wrote, prior to 1822, that there was "rarely . . . a congenial spot for human happiness."[31]

Retarded by hostilities of the Indians, poverty, and civil conflict—conditions that resulted in only very limited building of military work—civilizing the wilderness had been slow while Texas was under Spanish control. It appeared that Spain wished to maintain a wilderness buffer on the northern frontier. Although she recognized the need to develop the land of the inner regions and to control the Indians, she allowed only Spaniards to settle in the territory. Because of insecurity of life in the wilderness, not many wished to emigrate. By the opening of the nineteenth century, only a few settlements existed.[32] According to a report made in 1820, the entire province contained a mere three thousand souls.[33]

After Mexico won independence in 1821, the doors were opened to immigration. The General Colonization Law specifically invited foreigners[34] by stipulating, "Foreigners of any nation whatever, and natives of this republic, can project the formation of new towns upon lands entirely vacant."[35] To assure good and loyal stock, only those who could prove themselves to be Catholic, who could show good moral character, and who would swear fealty to Mexico were to be admitted.

But even before Mexican independence, Anglo-Americans had had designs for the settlement of Texas. Moses Austin, in 1821, had won approval of his application for a grant of land from Spanish authorities to develop a colony. Although the enterprising Austin died shortly before his plan could be put into action, his son, Stephen F., assumed the initiative in promoting the colony. Despite the interruption of his efforts when Mexico obtained independence, he persisted in his plan and was finally awarded a grant for the settlement of three hundred families.

Subsequently, under the General Colonization Law, other *empresarios* received large contracts for settlement. Among these, in 1825 Green DeWitt was permitted a grant north of San Antonio for four hundred families; Martín de León opened a colony to the southeast with a small grant for forty-one families. The following year Joseph Vehlein obtained a contract to settle three hundred families, and David G. Burnet contracted for settlement of three hundred families in the southeastern part of the state. Hoping for a better material life, Anglo-Americans flocked into Texas to claim the offered lands. However, tension between the settlers and the government, antagonized by Anglo-American aggressiveness, compelled Mexico in 1830 to pass a law forbidding further immigration from the United States—a contributing factor, of course, to the Texas Revolution.

After Texas became a Mexican co-state with Coahuila, although remoteness from the seat of gov-

[30] Martinez, *Letters*, p. 331.
[31] Yoakum, *History of Texas*, I, 208.
[32] These were Villa de San Fernando de Béjar, Pueblo Nuestra Señora del Pilar Nacogdoches, La Bahía (Goliad), and Villa de San Agustín de Laredo.
[33] "Instructions which the Constitutional Ayuntamiento of the City of San Fernando de Bexar Draws Up in Order that Its Provincial Deputy May Be Able to Make Such Representations, Take Such Steps, and Present Such Petitions as May be Conducive to the Happiness, Development, and Prosperity of Its In-

habitants," trans. Mattie Austin Hatcher, *Southwestern Historical Quarterly* 23 (July 1919): 61.
[34] *Laws and Decrees of the State of Coahuila and Texas*, trans. J. P. Kimball, p. 127.
[35] Ibid., p. 215.

ernment and political turmoil continued to hinder development, officials attempted to rectify the weaknesses that had been inherent in the administration of New Spain. The intent of the General Colonization Law was to augment settlement and promote the arts and commerce. To encourage the immigration of mechanics of all kinds, building lots were to be given gratis for their workshops.[36] A small tax on each of these lots, along with those sold to other settlers, was to be applied to the building of churches, which, in turn, would further encourage immigration. Commissioners, appointed by the legislature, were given authority to select sites and found towns as soon as forty families were assembled in any instance.

During both the Spanish colonial and Mexican periods, as well as later eras, town sites were selected with regard to the natural resources that would favor commercial and architectural development. Locations surrounded by fertile farmland and lush pastureland were favored for the support of the inhabitants and their beasts of burden. Furthermore, if the community were to prosper, trade and communication were vital; therefore, sites adjacent to navigable rivers and at the crossings of natural roads of inland travel were desirable. No location could be considered satisfactory unless an adequate supply of natural building materials, such as tractable wood, clayey soil, and soft stone, was convenient.

During Mexican domination, although specifications were changed, the form of new communities continued to be regulated by law. The area, geometrical design, and use of spaces in each town were stipulated by the *Laws and Decrees of the State of Coahuila and Texas*. For each town, four square leagues, regular or irregular in area, were to be designated. Streets were to be straight and to run due north and south, east and west[37]—considerations that facilitated the equitable distribution of property. For the salubrity of the town, the laws specified that these streets were to be 20 varas (60 feet) wide. In the center of the town, there was to be "a square measuring 120 varas on each side, exclusive of the streets, to

be called the *Principal or Constitutional square*."[38] Around this nucleus, the streets were to form square blocks.

The function of several of these blocks was clearly specified. On the west, the block fronting the principal square was to be designated for municipal buildings. On the east, the block fronting the square was to be reserved for religious purposes. If a church was built there, this allowed the traditional east-west orientation, with the west façade opening onto the principal square. Then, in suitable places, were specified separate blocks for a jail, a market, and educational buildings. Finally, outside the town the burial ground was to be located.

Since farmers with extensive holdings were laying out new towns,[39] many new settlements appeared on the map of Mexican Texas. At first, most were hardly worthy of the appellation of "village," and many, such as Orozembo and Montezuma, later disappeared. However, many others ultimately prospered. Among the permanent towns founded during this period were Bastrop, laid out in 1830 by *empresario* Austin; Liberty, founded in 1831; Gonzales, founded in 1832; and Guadalupe Victoria, founded in 1824 but not laid out until 1832.

Representative of these Mexican towns, Gonzales was laid out according to decree with the Plaza de la Constitución as the nucleus. The adjacent block on the east was designated as the church square, and that on the west was set aside for municipal buildings. Although their locations were not specified by decree, the block on the north was reserved for the jail, and the one on the south as a military square.

The families that populated these towns during the third and fourth decades of the nineteenth century were small in number in comparison with the area they occupied and were primarily concerned with day-to-day survival. Those that immigrated during the 1820's brought into the province little more than was needed for a minimum existence in the wilderness. With so few numbers and meager advancement in commerce, there was little means with which to

[36] Ibid., p. 21.
[37] Ibid., p. 72.

[38] Ibid., p. 72.
[39] Mary Austin Holley, *Texas*, p. 59.

erect schools, churches, or other buildings for cultural or communal use. Since most efforts at construction were confined to the essential shelters—the habitations and works for defense—public building continued to languish during the Mexican period.

Yet, even though largely concerned with survival and town building, Texans did strongly express awareness of the need for cultural improvement. Responding to the concerns of the settlers, the Mexican government legislated for education. In 1829 a decree was issued providing for the establishment of schools in the capital of each state to "instruct pupils in reading, writing, arithmetic, the dogma of the Catholic Religion, and all Ackermann's catechisms of art and sciences."[40] These were to be on the Lancasterian plan, an efficient system of education conceived to instruct large groups of children of the very poor, as well as the children of those who could afford to pay.

Since obstacles to this plan were encountered, Texans petitioned later for public schools. Their grievances were answered in intent, if not in realization, by a decree that specified, "In all capital towns of districts, whose funds are sufficient for that purpose, primary schools shall be established within six months at furthest, wherein . . . the elements of geography shall be taught, and lessons given, moral and political, on good breeding."[41] Unfortunately, funds were lacking, and, ultimately, a paragraph lamenting the failure of the government to establish any public system of education was included among the grievances listed in the Texas Declaration of Independence (1836).

The delayed progress in education, as well as the poverty of the country, was reflected in the lack of school buildings. Although there evidently had been a building constructed explicitly for educational purposes in San Antonio in 1811—simply described as "a hall with a platform, with two doors and one window"[42]—activities were most often housed in existing buildings. Later, in fact, the Mexican government ordered for the use of primary schools in the capital towns the designation of the largest building that could be obtained for instruction and for the residence of the teacher.[43]

Despite these efforts, lack of wholehearted support retarded the maintenance of schools. When Col. Juan Nepomuceno Almonte visited Texas in 1834, near Brazoria he found that a schoolhouse erected by subscription was occupied by only thirty to forty students, that a lack of funds rendered the support of San Antonio's school impossible, and that a school in Nacogdoches was likewise poorly supported. Those colonists who were able preferred to send their children to schools in the United States.[44]

The story of church and civic architecture was similar. Although *empresarios* were expected to see to the erection of places of worship and to provide the trappings required for worship,[45] whether because of poverty or lack of desire, they did little in the way of fulfilling this obligation. Such needs as a slowly increasing population may have had for churches went unfulfilled for the most part.

The architectural destitution of San Felipe de Austin typified the poverty of the province. In 1830, there being no public funds, an ordinance was passed inviting citizens of the municipality to loan sums sufficient for the erection of a jail. Since there was evidently no money forthcoming, an official decree was later passed designating part of the taxes collected there for the construction of a town hall and a jail.[46] When Parker visited the town a short time afterward, the courthouse had been built, and there were two taverns,

[40] *Laws and Decrees of the State of Coahuila and Texas*, p. 127.

[41] Ibid., p. 215.

[42] "Inventory . . . of Schoolhouse and of the Furniture in It," made by Don Ygnacio de las Santo Coy, cited and translated in I. J. Cox, "Educational Efforts in San Fernando de Bexar," *Quarterly of the Texas State Historical Association* 6, no. 1 (July 1902): 50. In 1811, 855 pesos were given to Don Bicente Travieso to build a schoolhouse (ibid., p. 30).

[43] *Laws and Decrees of the State of Coahuila and Texas*, p. 215.

[44] Report of Colonel Juan Nepomuceno Almonte, 1834, cited in William Kennedy, *Texas: The Rise, Progress, and Prospects of the Republic of Texas*, pp. 436–440.

[45] Kennedy, *Texas*, p. 347. See also, for example, "Hayden Edwards's Contract," in Yoakum, *History of Texas*, I, 463, article nine: "He [the *empresario*] shall see to the erection of temples in the new *poblations*, and see that they be provided with ornaments, sacred vases, and other decorations, destined for Devine service."

[46] *Laws and Decrees of the State of Coahuila and Texas*, p. 183.

four or five stores, and perhaps twenty dwellings, but there were "only two or three good looking buildings in the place."[47]

Mexican architecture in other parts of the state was no more advanced. For example, a courthouse at Anáhuac, a town with about thirty houses in 1831, was only a small log building.[48]

But, while the Mexican government furnished little in the way of cultural or civic support for the colonists, it found resources for architecture that was necessary to oppress them. To control the illegal entry of persons and goods, military works and customs houses were set up at several locations, such as Tenoxtitlán (1830), Anáhuac (1830), Terán (1831), and Velasco (1830). At Anáhuac, located near Galveston Bay, was built a large structure, about 20 feet wide and 150 feet long, containing barracks, with officers' quarters and guardhouse at opposite ends.[49] Velasco was a post fortified by a wall, on a circular trace, 300 feet in diameter. The enclosure consisted of two rows of logs six feet apart, the space between being filled with sand from the excavation for a ditch. Inside, there were a customs house, space for soldiers' quarters, and, in the center, an earthen cavalier for a cannon.

Fortifications in the wilderness for defense against Indians, however, were the sole responsibility of the settlers. Those who worked the land along unfriendly frontiers fortified in a manner that recalled, and surely was patterned after, the civil settlers' forts in Kentucky, Tennessee, and Ohio—from whence many immigrants had come—such as Fort Harrod (1774), Fort Nashborough (1780), and Farmers' Castle (1789).[50] All these consisted of a series of log cabins,

one or two stories high, surrounded with a stockade. The Texas settlers' forts of the thirties were similar. Fort Houston, located near the Trinity River in the vicinity of Palestine, was described in 1840 as a work "150 by 80 feet, containing two rows of log houses, enclosed with pickets."[51] Fort Parker, Limestone County (1834), built by immigrants from Illinois and destroyed by Indians in 1836, likewise consisted of log cabins enclosed by a stockade. Coleman's Fort (or Fort Colorado) near Austin (1836) was similarly enclosed with a stockade with two-story cabins located on diagonal corners. At the *rancho* of Don Erasmo Seguín in the vicinity of San Antonio, a settler fortification (circa 1834) consisted "of a square, palisadoed round, with the houses of the families residing there forming the sides of the square."[52] Since these were wood structures, all were ephemeral.

Thus, unquestionably, architecture of the early part of the nineteenth century was indigenous to the land from which it sprang. It was a spontaneous expression that was earthy and rustic, with little pretension in regard to size or decoration. In forested areas structures were generally of logs; in other areas they were often of adobe or rough stone, although all three materials, if they were available, were often used in the same location. Since the pioneers were engaged in a continuous struggle for survival against the elements, the wilderness, and human enemies, there was little opportunity to glorify their work. Nothing was produced in the first four decades of the nineteenth century comparable to the San Antonio missions of the previous century. Since poverty prevailed, construction therefore fulfilled only the most basic needs for shelter, with existing works often being adapted to new uses.

Of those pioneer public edifices that were erected during Spanish colonial or Mexican years, few remain. The natural materials that were readily at hand and that were easily workable for building deteriorated rapidly. Consequently, unless constantly

[47] Parker, *Trip to the West and Texas*, pp. 174–175.
[48] *A Visit to Texas*, p. 116.
[49] Holley, *Texas*, p. 115.
[50] Built in Kentucky by James Harrod, located on a hill, and containing a spring, Fort Harrod's enclosure was rectangular, and the defenses were strengthened by three corner blockhouses. Neatly lining the interior of the south wall were seven log cabins and a log schoolhouse. Fort Nashborough, Tennessee, was on a similar plan. Farmers' Castle, Ohio, consisted of an enclosure within which were built thirteen two-story cabins, all designed with the second story cantilevered beyond the first, as in blockhouse construction. If the stockade should be carried in an attack, it appears that each house was capable of becoming

an independent stronghold. Living within the stockade, the settlers each day proceeded to the fields in groups.
[51] Edward Stiff, *The Texan Emigrant*, p. 108.
[52] From a journal of a group of immigrants, cited in Kennedy, *Texas*, p. 404.

maintained, most early pioneer work eventually succumbed to the elements. Of those that were made of durable materials, many burned or became victims of progress as communities grew. However, during the next two and a half decades, a more durable and sophisticated architecture would develop.

Public Buildings of Antebellum Texas

THE TEXAS REVOLUTION, as is inevitable in wars, set back the development of the country. On the land and on the architecture, anxiety and hostilities left their scars. For example, because of fear of the Mexicans, San Patricio was nearly deserted by its Irish settlers, while Nacogdoches was abandoned. The buildings of San Felipe de Austin and Gonzales were burned to ashes by Texans, and those of Harrisburg by Mexicans.

Immediately after the war, recovery was slow. Many parts of the country were devastated, crops were scarce, and the people were poor. There was little money and no credit, and, to add to the difficulties, the Republic of Texas was burdened with the problems of frontier defense against Indians and tensions with Mexico, both of which retarded expansion and population growth. All this naturally impeded the production of public buildings. Such works that were realized during those early years of the Republic were, as would be expected, on a small scale.

After Texas was annexed to the United States, an improved economy favored the building art. Upon award of $10 million by the United States for disputed land, the state was able to pay debts and to undertake the construction of new public edifices. Al-

though several poor cotton crops slowed progress temporarily, the end of the forties—the period of the Mexican War—and the decade of the fifties witnessed increased prosperity and a corresponding increase in public building. In addition, the expanding population resulted in the growth of existing communities and the speculative platting of numerous new towns.

Although wagons and steamboats laden with households had been bringing immigrants to the fertile areas of the state, at mid-century and several decades thereafter, Texas was yet long on land and short of people. In 1850, according to the U.S. census, there were only 212,592 people in the state—less than one person per each of Texas's 267,339 square miles. The largest city was Galveston with approximately 4,177, San Antonio had 3,488, Houston 2,396, and Austin only 629.[1] By 1860 the state population had nearly tripled to 604,215, but ten years later it was still considerably less than a million.

Only with the settlement of her vast lands and the development of her isolated communities could Texas make real progress. Farmers were needed to till the land, while mechanics, such as carpenters, bricklayers, blacksmiths, printers, and saddlers, were in great de-

[1] Frederick Law Olmsted, *A Journey through Texas*, p. 474.

15

mand to populate and build the towns. According to immigrants' guides, Texas was a great land of opportunity for industrious young men of good moral character.

From Europe and all parts of the Union came immigrants struck with "Texas fever." Germans came to settle in Bexar and Fayette counties and to form the communities of Fredericksburg and New Braunfels; in San Patricio County, near Aransas Bay, colonies of settlers from Ireland were developed; Castroville was founded by Frenchmen; and there were many who came from England, Poland, Austria, and Italy. In the southern states, the "G.T.T." (gone to Texas) written on doors attested to the destination of many Anglo-Americans. Texas thus became an amalgamation of heterogeneous nationalities, each group bringing its own culture. At mid-century, San Antonio, example par excellence of this mixture, was described as a "jumble of races, costumes, languages and buildings"[2]—a charming complex that exists yet today.

But, as immigration progressed and the population increased and the territory improved materially, some contemporaries were keenly aware of the need for corresponding cultural advancement. Melinda Rankin, an educator in Texas, emphasized this awareness when she wrote: "As a country grows in prosperity, moral and intellectual improvements must keep pace, and as these, at present, are of the onward march in Texas, no emigration is desired which has only for its object speculations of worldly interest to the exclusion of every other consideration."[3]

Closely associated with cultural progress were concepts concerning order in the physical environment. The Texans that read the tastemakers of the period appreciated the express role of architecture in the advancement of civilization and culture. Andrew Jackson Downing, an influential architect and landscape designer in New York, for example, wrote: ". . . a good house (and by this I mean a fitting, tasteful, and significant dwelling) is a powerful means of civilization. With the perception of proportion, symmetry,

order, and beauty . . . comes that refinement of manners which distinguished a civilized from a coarse brutal people. . . . when smiling lawns and tasteful cottages begin to embellish a country, we know that order and culture are established."[4]

The moral as well as religious values with which the life style of the cultured was imbued also implicated the influence of architecture. The level of artistic development in building was thought romantically to be a strong influence on virtue, and, conversely, the ethics of society were thought to be expressed by architecture. A convention of Congregational ministers and delegates questioned, who "can fail to perceive that the mere structural arrangement of the house of worship may have much, very much, to do in the formation or shaping of character of those who from time to time assemble within it?"[5] Closer to home, Miss Rankin, although a laywoman, expressed in her description of Texas in 1850 the significance of soul in nineteenth-century architecture when she related that a new Methodist church in Washington added "greatly to its [the town's] character in all its relations, morally, socially, and religiously."[6] Earlier, when relating the role of buildings in representing the attitudes of the times, a Houston reporter wrote: "*A Church* is more than a work of art; it is a symbol . . . of religion; a visible sign and setting forth of religious sentiment. Churches are the outward consecration of our cities, of our villages, of our country, of the world."[7] The fulfillment of moral and aesthetic needs through architecture required buildings for noble cultural purpose with character of form and finesse of detail to distinguish them from structures for mere utility.

To further the advancement of culture—which was accompanied by a corresponding appreciation for refinement in architecture—societies for the cultivation of the mind were formed in sparsely settled Texas. As

---

[2] Ibid., p. 150.
[3] Melinda Rankin, *Texas in 1850*, p. 15.

[4] A. J. Downing, *The Architecture of Country Houses*, p. v.
[5] Convention of Ministers and Delegates of the Congregational Churches in the United States, *A Book of Plans for Churches and Parsonages*, p. 29.
[6] Rankin, *Texas in 1850*, p. 148.
[7] *Telegraph and Texas Register* (Houston), September 18, 1839, p. 1. Unless otherwise apparent, all newspapers cited herein were published in Texas.

early as 1837, a philosophical society, "scientific and literary in character," was formed in Houston with Mirabeau B. Lamar as president. In 1848 the Houston Lyceum was chartered, and in 1850 a histrionic society was formed in Marshall for the purpose of affording a means of literary improvement. Throughout the century, numerous debating and literary societies sprang up, dedicated to the intellectual, moral, and social improvement of the members; philharmonic and thespian societies also rapidly increased in numbers, attesting to the culture consciousness of Texans.

Recognizing that enlightenment was essential to both the advancement of culture and the preservation of liberty, Texans looked ahead and stressed education. Although heavily debt ridden in the decade following the revolution, with the encouragement of Mirabeau B. Lamar, president of the Republic of Texas, provisions were made for public education. In 1839, Congress provided that each county be allocated three leagues of land for public primary schools. Subsequently, an act was passed granting an additional league for support of an academy or a high school, where classical literature and mathematics would be taught. In 1845 the state constitution specified that one-tenth of the annual revenues accrued from taxation be used for support of free schools. However, low state income, together with conflicting viewpoints on the nature of local financial support for schools, retarded developments in public education until the latter part of the century.

Major roles in education were also assumed by religious institutions. At Rutersville—early self-proclaimed Athens of the South—the first college of the Republic, Rutersville College, was opened by a Methodist minister and began advertising for students in 1840. Five years later, Baylor University, a Southern Baptist institution now located at Waco, was founded at Independence. Austin College, a Presbyterian school presently at Sherman, was established in 1849 at Huntsville. These private schools fulfilled needs for higher education until in 1876 the doors were opened at the Agricultural and Mechanical College of Texas—a tuition-free school in Bryan for training farmers, machinists, engineers, chemists, architects, and contractors—and in 1883 at the University of Texas,

a tuition-free school originally designed to educate individuals in either academics or law. The 1839–1840 Congress had begun the work for these state institutions when it provided fifty leagues of land for two institutions of higher learning.

Accommodating the material growth and accompanying the cultural growth of the Republic, new speculative towns sprang up like mushrooms. As under Spanish and Mexican domination, locations that possessed favorable natural resources were sought for new communities. To entice prospective buyers of lots, rival proprietors preferred sites that were near river crossings, that were surrounded by fertile land, and that were near abundant natural building materials. With these, successful town building was probable, although not assured.

Speculators zealously promoted their enterprises by advertising resources. The prosperity of LaGrange, proprietors said when advertising for immigrants, was certain; among the natural advantages were "an inexhaustible supply of the best material for building and improvements; pine, cedar, and other valuable timber can be procured within a convenient distance; and an abundance of the best quality of rock is to be found in the vicinity thereof."[8] In 1836 among the enticements to settle in Houston were spring water; inexhaustible quantities of pine, ash, cedar, and oak for buildings; and a projected water-powered sawmill.

It was his consideration for the importance of the role of natural resources for architecture in the success of founding towns that motivated John Boyd to urge the removal of the capital to his projected town of Tawakanah (Tehuacana) on the Navasota River. He advertised futilely that limestone was abundant on and below the surface, both for use as building blocks and for the manufacture of lime for mortar. Cedar was available nearby, large quantities of various hardwoods were within thirty miles, and clay suitable for the manufacture of brick was everywhere.[9] But all this bounty was obviously insufficient to win the removal of the capital from Austin.

While all proprietors advertised the practical advantages of their towns, some also stressed the aesthe-

8 *Matagorda Bulletin*, August 2, 1838, p. 1.
9 *Northern Standard* (Clarksville), January 19, 1850, p. 4.

tic element. Environs of fertile farmland, healthiness of situation, and "also the charm of romantic scenery"[10] were advertised for Colorado City, a town located a short distance above LaGrange but destined for oblivion. Beautiful natural scenery and landscape views of the surrounding prairie and Cross Timbers country were proclaimed among the advantages of Taylorsville, Wise County.[11]

To promote the sale of lots, land, in addition to the public square, was often donated for public use. For instance, in Columbus proprietors gave Colorado County three blocks of land, which were to be sold and the proceeds applied to the building of the courthouse and jail. In Nacogdoches, in 1837, four lots were donated for a university. Other promoters occasionally reserved lots for donation to churches and academies. In 1839 the act authorizing the selection of a permanent location for the seat of government, in addition to lots for a capitol, university, and hospital, specified that lots be set aside for churches, schools, and other necessary public buildings.

Following liberation from Latin control, Texas communities were no longer regulated in their planning by law, but by tradition and commerce. In the nineteenth-century county seats platted after Texas independence, public squares continued to be developed as the nuclei of communities, but the intent of their function was somewhat different from the Spanish colonial and Mexican squares. Rather than as open spaces, they were intended as sites for key civic buildings, such as courthouses, although jails frequently appeared at corners of the spaces. Instead of developing from Latin paradigms, the origins of this concept appear to be Anglo-American, reaching Texas through Tennessee and Kentucky from Philadelphia.[12] However, concepts on public squares were also brought to Texas by German immigrants, and a *Marktplatz* was included in the communities of Indianola, Fredericksburg, and New Braunfels.

In the typical county seat, the public square was traditionally the focus for community life, the stage for social intercourse among residents. On the square, political speeches were delivered; auctions were held; legal business was transacted; cotton, grain, and produce were sold; horses and mules were traded. A public square, crowded with buggies and laden wagons, was a certain sign of prosperity.

While the public square was a social center, motivations for monetary profit also gave impetus to the platting of towns around a central space. Businessmen were, of course, eager to establish their mercantile houses, livery stables, hotels, and bars in prominent locations. Since they would be near the center of activity, building lots facing town squares brought higher prices and, thereby, greater profits to land speculators. Because of adverse effects on the land values of surrounding lots, the public square, once established, could not be easily moved or have its community function changed.

To reinforce the authority of the public space, if the lay of the land permitted, squares were commonly located on eminences, such as at Marshall, which was established in 1841, and Decatur, the townsite for which was selected in 1856. This position elevated the temple of justice, emphasizing its role as a landmark in the county. From the country, the public space and courthouse were announced by cupola or tower looming above tree tops. Although they may not have been visualized by the town founders in the hill country, dramatic vistas were sometimes created when the view of a courthouse "unfolded" as it was approached.

Public squares in Texas were of several types (fig. 1). The most common was simply a centrally located block in a rectangular grid of streets, such as at Brenham and Waco. A variation of this type occurred at Fort Worth, Ballinger, and Brady, when two blocks of the grid were reserved as the square, thereby allowing the courthouse to be built on the axis of one of the streets. A more prominent space was created when the one-block square was centered on the axes of two

[10] *Matagorda Bulletin*, August 2, 1838, p. 4. Probably because of its proximity to LaGrange, the town did not develop on that site. Later, a community in Mitchell County was also named Colorado City.

[11] *Standard* (Clarksville), February 21, 1857, p. 3.

[12] See Edward T. Price, "The Central Courthouse Square in the American County Seat," *Geographical Review* 58, no. 1 (1968): 49–50; John W. Reps, *Town Planning in Frontier America*, p. 222. The first town plan in Texas that conformed to Anglo-American tradition was evidently San Augustine, laid out in 1833, several years before Independence (see George Louis Crocket, *Two Centuries in East Texas*, p. 105).

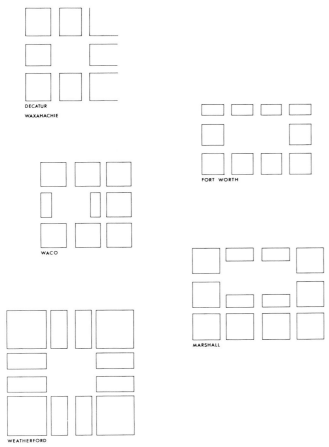

Fig. 1. Typical plans of public squares in Texas. (Drawings by author)

thoroughfares, terminating vistas from four directions, such as at Weatherford. A modification of the two-block square was developed at Marshall with the oblong space also centered on the crossing of two street axes. The form selected in each town appears to have depended entirely upon the inclinations of the founders.

Around the public square, unless limited by abrupt topographical features, the streets were platted in gridiron pattern, with approaches to the square from all directions usually receiving equal emphasis. The orientation of the grid was either to the cardinal points, as at Austin, or askew thirty to forty-five degrees, as at Houston, Dallas, and Fort Worth. This was true even when environs suggested irregular

street layouts. When rivers or hills were encountered, the grid was simply superimposed over the terrain.

During the early years of a community's development, the buildings that gave definition to public spaces were, of necessity, modest in scale and crude in construction. Typically, the embryo county seat consisted of a few small dwellings—which only occasionally received encomiums from travelers—a courthouse, and a jail. Several commercial establishments surrounded a square that was a dust bowl when it was dry and a quagmire when wet.[13]

Early adventurers in the Republic of Texas, in addition to descriptions of the land, scribed impressions of towns and public architecture. "LaGrange," wrote Francis Moore, Jr., in 1840, "contains about one hundred houses, including a courthouse and jail."[14] Another community, Brazoria, "contains a handsome courthouse, several large stores and many neat dwellings."[15] At about the same time, according to another author, Edward Stiff, there were in Houston public buildings consisting of "a market house, an arsenal, court-house, jail, two small theatres, the president's house, and the capitol. . . . The city contains twelve stores of assorted merchandise, six mechanics shops . . . and last, forty-seven places for selling intoxicating drinks."[16] Although these authors, among several others, provided no detailed descriptions of public buildings, ostensibly they were small log or rough frame structures.

Relative to the quality of early public buildings, George W. Bonnell wrote that those of Austin were "generally of a much better description than are usually built in new countries, and the improvement of the city has progressed with a rapidity heretofore unknown, even in this country. . . . A Presbyterian

[13] Early descriptions of town squares were not often favorable. For example, "Gonzales," wrote Frederick Law Olmsted during a visit near mid-century, had "the usual square of dead bare land, surrounded by a collection of stores, shops, drinking and gambling-rooms" (*Journey through Texas*, p. 237).

[14] Francis Moore, Jr., *Map and Description of Texas*, p. 64.

[15] Ibid., p. 53.

[16] Edward Stiff, *The Texan Emigrant*, p. 80. This capitol, a two-story frame building, was used from 1837 to 1839 by the Texas Congress. After the seat of government was moved to Austin, it became the Capitol Hotel; it was demolished in 1882.

church has been commenced, and I understand the Methodists have one under contract."[17]

Straightforward functionalism characterized most public architecture during the years of the Republic. The governmental buildings in the new capital city—removed from Houston to Austin in 1840—Bonnell wrote, were "not elegant, but very comfortable, and appropriate for a new government."[18] Built in 1839 and located on a hill opposite the president's house, the capitol, according to Moore, was "a large one-story building, about one hundred and twenty feet by fifty."[19] It contained two rooms, each about fifty by thirty feet, separated by a passage twenty feet wide. One of these spaces was occupied by the Senate, the other served the House of Representatives. According to another early traveler, Thomas Falconer, the public offices in Austin were simply "a series of detached log-cabins on both sides of the main street."[20]

In every region where large straight timbers were available, log buildings appeared throughout the Republic. Originally brought to the Atlantic Coast by various Europeans,[21] after which it spread westward and was later reintroduced into Texas by European immigrants, the log technique was used for virtually every building purpose, public and private. Unlike those of the Spaniards and Mexicans—and later the Germans[22] and French—who commonly built log walls with posts planted vertically into the ground side by side, Anglo-American techniques of construc-

tion employed fully hewn or undressed timbers, or, frequently, logs with only the vertical sides hewn flat, one upon the other horizontally, with various types of notched joints at the corners.

With this system of log construction, two basic cabin forms were frequently built in the Texas wilderness—the unipartite and the double cabin, the latter of which had evolved in the southeastern states in response to a hot climate. The former was a simple box, sometimes consisting of several rooms with earth or puncheon floors, usually covered by a shingled roof. The double type, commonly known as the "dog-trot cabin," consisted of two small apartments separated by a dog run, or breezeway, oriented to arrest the prevailing breezes. Both apartments and breezeway were under a common roof, and usually a porch was extended the length of the front. Doors from the apartments opened onto the breezeway.

In both forms of cabins were found accommodations for early travelers in the wilderness of Texas. Late in the 1830's a hotel located in the Red River country was found to be merely "a large log house, divided into two apartments, one of which was occupied as a cooking, eating, and sleeping room, the other . . . contained for sale, tomahawks, bowie knives, powder and lead, some Indian trinkets, and a quantity of whiskey."[23] The dog-trot cabin also sheltered many a weary adventurer. In East Texas, near San Augustine, Amos Parker spent a night "at a very decent looking double log house, having a wide portico in front, and a wide avenue in the centre . . . The house contained three or four rooms."[24] Farther south, the principal hotel in Brazoria was likewise a dog-trot cabin with a few windows "closing with wooden shutters and destitute of glass, with a place for a fire in the northern one [apartment] and a hole through the roof for smoke."[25] For lodging there, the traveler paid one dollar per day. Near mid-century, Frederick Law Olmsted, the famous landscape architect who journeyed through Texas, described this double log cabin type

[17] George W. Bonnell, *Topographical Description of Texas*, p. 65. Bonnell's description was written shortly after the town had been laid out.

[18] Ibid., p. 64.

[19] Moore, *Map and Description of Texas*, p. 130.

[20] Thomas Falconer, *Notes on a Journey through Texas and New Mexico in the Years 1841 and 1842*, p. 206.

[21] The technique of building log dwellings with notched joints was brought to Delaware in 1638 by the Swedes. However, it did not spread beyond there until the latter part of the seventeenth century. The English and Dutch built various forms of temporary shelters and then set up frame buildings in their earliest settlements, rather than log works, as is commonly thought (see Harold R. Shurtleff, *The Log Cabin Myth: A Study of the Early Dwellings of the English Colonists in North America*, p. 186).

[22] For example, see Ferdinand Roemer, *Texas, with Particular Reference to German Immigration and the Physical Appearance of the Country*, trans. Oswald Mueller, p. 229: "Most of the settlers . . . lived in huts, consisting of poles rammed into the ground."

[23] Stiff, *Texan Emigrant*, p. 114.

[24] A[mos] [Andrew] Parker, *Trip to the West and Texas*, p. 119.

[25] *A Visit to Texas*, p. 31.

as a characteristic accommodation in the rural areas of western Louisiana and of Texas.

In the settled areas, more picturesque, if not better, lodging was found. At New Braunfels, Olmsted found the Guadalupe Hotel (circa 1850) to be a neat building, reminiscent of Germany, with nothing wanting. Earlier, a visitor in Galveston found a good public house in the grounded "old Ohio River Steam Boat, Warsaw . . ."[26]

Among the early buildings to appear in new towns were those that were essential to the peace and protection of society. In new seats of government, county commissioners were obligated, as soon as practicable, to erect jails and courthouses. In civilizing the wilderness, from a material as well as symbolic point of view, these were of the utmost importance. Unless law and order were established in the wilderness, there was little hope for communities to survive and prosper. Demonstrating impulses to moral improvement, a substantial jail instilled confidence in justice and security from the lawless element. To stress this, the completion of a new jail was commonly advertised by proprietors when promoting their towns.

As with other frontier functional types, jails were commonly of logs, utilizing a variety of ingenious techniques to develop strength of enclosure. If the calaboose in Houston (1837) was built according to specifications, it was a twenty-four–foot square house of logs, hewn twelve inches square, and "neatly dovetailed, dowelled and pinned at the corners."[27] While the hewn logs, with precision joints at the corners, produced a stable structure, greater strength was possible with double walls of logs. For the Brazoria County Jail (1837), commissioners advertised for bids for a log building "44 feet long and 20 wide; two stories high; the two lower rooms to be 18 feet by 20, and to be built up with double walls, made of timber 8 inches thick, hewn square and dovetailed at the ends, and sufficiently apart to admit a log of 10 inches in diameter to stand upright between the two walls, and the walls to be filled in this manner; . . ."[28] The upper-

story walls were to be a single thickness of hewn timbers. This system of construction was adopted throughout the Republic and, later, the state.[29]

Over a decade later, a variation of the double-wall technique was used in the Bell County Jail (1854) in Belton, which consisted simply of two small rooms, one above the other, twelve feet square. The lower story had double walls of logs with upright iron slats bolted between, while the upper walls were a single thickness. The only access to the lower cell was through a trap door in the second-story floor.[30]

Like early jails, most of the first courthouses were also of logs. For Harrisburg (later Harris) County, a double log cabin (circa 1837) served as the first courthouse.[31] Later, the log cabin of John Neely Bryan (circa 1848) served as a county house for Dallas County for a brief period. The first Van Zandt County Courthouse (1850), if built according to specifications, was a log work "lined with boards . . . covered with four-foot boards nailed on, and a good puncheon floor, one door and shutter and one window and shutter."[32] For the first courthouse of Ellis County, in Waxahachie, the commissioners' court ordered "a log house, sixteen by eighteen feet in size, nine feet high."[33] The building was to have a door on each side and was to be built for fifty-nine dollars. While most of the early log courthouses have long since disappeared, the Comanche County building (1856)—a double log cabin—remains as an example (plate 1).

The log cabin of round or hewn logs—chinked with chips, rags, or mud, or covered with boards, and as-

[26] Stiff, *Texan Emigrant*, p. 149.
[27] *Telegraph and Texas Register* (Houston), October 21, 1837, p. 3.
[28] Ibid., December 6, 1837, p. 3.

[29] For example, in 1838, Liberty County advertised for bids for a two-story jail with outer and inner pens of one-foot-square hewn logs, with a twelve-inch space between to be filled with vertical square logs (see ibid., May 30, 1838, p. 1). Over a decade later, the jail for Van Zandt County was specified to be "out of post oak timbers ten inches square, to be ten feet square in the clear, double walls six inches between the walls to be filled by peeled timbers stood up endwise" (Commissioners' Court Minutes, Van Zandt County, cited in W. S. Mills, *History of Van Zandt County*, p. 18).
[30] George W. Tyler, *The History of Bell County*, ed. Charles W. Ramsdell, p. 145.
[31] S. O. Young, *A Thumb-Nail History of the City of Houston, Texas*, p. 52.
[32] Commissioners' Court Minutes, Van Zandt County, cited in Mills, *History of Van Zandt County*, p. 17.
[33] Commissioners' Court, Ellis County, Order for the Courthouse, cited in *A Memorial and Biographical History of Ellis County, Texas*, p. 78.

sembled with various techniques—belonged not to a particular era but to a stage of civilization. It was continuously used in Texas throughout the nineteenth century, serving during the formative stages of many communities.

Like most other buildings, the few churches built during the republican period and years of early statehood were frugal constructions. The same economical conditions that retarded the erection of other pretentious public works also slowed the building of new structures by various religious denominations.

Religious tolerance was not technically a freedom until shortly before Texas independence, when, although contrary to the Mexican constitution, the confederate state of Coahuila and Texas annulled the requirement for membership in the Roman Catholic religion.[34] Prior to this, while Texas was under the control of Spain and Mexico, church edifices were officially Catholic. After Texas emerged from under the despotism of Mexico, it would be over a decade before organization and prosperity would permit Protestants to erect noteworthy churches.

Although Anglo-Americans who settled in Coahuila and Texas were obligated to officially support Catholicism, early Protestantism came to Texas with immigration. According to the prominent historian Henderson Yoakum, "nineteen twentieths of the colonists of Texas neither observed nor believed in the religion prescribed in the Mexican constitution."[35] In the 1820's Baptist elders, Cumberland Presbyterians, and Methodist ministers preached in the state, and in 1833 a Baptist church was organized in Austin's colony, a Methodist church near San Augustine, and a Cumberland Presbyterian church in Red River County[36]—all before independence. Following the annulment of the religious requirement, a Presbyterian church was organized near San Augustine. Early in 1838 a Methodist church—the first Protestant edifice west of the Sabine River[37]—was begun; shortly thereafter an Episcopal church was organized and a building for worship erected in Matagorda.

Although the Protestant sects rapidly increased in strength during the years of the Republic and early statehood, criticism of the lack of religious edifices prevailed in many accounts. When they wrote prior to 1840, both Chester Newell and Edward Stiff reported that they knew of only one Protestant church in Texas—the Methodist edifice in San Augustine—and the latter of the two authors added, ". . . and few there are who enter that."[38] A visitor from England in 1840, when describing the towns of Texas, observed: ". . . though we find every town plentifully supplied with Pot-houses [bars], we see neither a church or sign of building one. When the inhabitants feel penitently disposed they have prayers in the Court House, or wherever is most convenient."[39]

The early buildings that served ecclesiastical purposes, then, evidently presented little that identified their religious role. In the wilderness, services were frequently held in the homes or on the porches of settlers or, for that matter, sometimes in a grove—the lack of identifiable church edifices did not express a lack of religion. In the capital city of Houston, the local paper announced in 1838 that Sunday-school meetings would be in the courthouse and preaching in the capitol.[40] Moreover, many of the early buildings that served primarily religious uses were quite domestic in character. Olmsted described a little Lutheran church near New Braunfels simply as "a small brown house with a turret and a cross."[41]

While a few churches built before mid-century in some towns may have had some distinction in form and decoration, the general appearance of many others apparently satisfied little from an aesthetic point of view. Melinda Rankin, at mid-century, wrote,

[34] "By the 10th article of the Law of the State of Coahuila and Texas, passed the 26th of March, 1834, it is declared that no person shall be molested on account of his religious or political opinions, provided he does not disturb the public order" (Mary Austin Holley, *Texas*, p. 181).

[35] Henderson King Yoakum, *History of Texas from Its First Settlements in 1685 to Its Annexation to the United States in 1846*, I, 233.

[36] Homer S. Thrall, *A Pictorial History of Texas*, pp. 738–742.

[37] Homer S. Thrall, *History of Methodism in Texas*, p. 53.

[38] Stiff, *Texan Emigrant*, p. 16.

[39] Francis C. Sheridan, *Galveston Island; or a Few Months off the Coast of Texas: Journal of Francis C. Sheridan, 1839–1840*, ed. Willis W. Pratt, p. 95.

[40] *Telegraph and Texas Register* (Houston), December 15, 1838, p. 4.

[41] Olmsted, *Journey through Texas*, p. 141.

Public Buildings of Antebellum Texas

"With the exception of those found in the cities and large towns, there are very few church edifices whose appearance manifests that taste and neatness which is desirable to see in buildings dedicated to so sacred a purpose."[42]

If there was little opulence in the ecclesiastical architecture of the 1830's and early 1840's, signs of economic and cultural advancement were apparent in the dignified appearance of other new public buildings in the following decade. During these years, an emerging prosperity permitted the erection of buildings that would finally fulfill aspirations for architectural dignity and grandeur. To meet these ambitions, the Classicism that was popular in the United States also proved to be appropriate for architectural expression in East and South Texas. Although the Anglo-American development of Texas occurred after the Classicism of the talented president-architect from Virginia, Thomas Jefferson, had reached its zenith in the East, several early structures in the Republic tardily reflected this southern influence.

The first Anglo-American buildings in which there were pretensions of elegance were evidently the courthouses. If built according to specifications, the front of the Liberty County Courthouse in Liberty (1844) was decorated with a door with an arched transom, and the courtroom with an arched window flanked by narrow rectangular windows on either side,[43] both characteristics of Jefferson's influence. Early republican seats of justice were often two stories in height. Unlike later courthouses, on the ground floor was the courtroom—an arrangement found in the early nineteenth-century courthouses of Virginia and North Carolina[44] built during Jefferson's era—

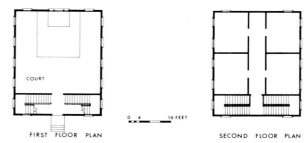

Fig. 2. Floor plans of Liberty County Courthouse, Liberty (1844). (Drawing by author, based on specifications published in the *Telegraph and Texas Register* [Houston], May 30, 1838, p. 1)

and on the second floor were offices. Liberty County's courthouse, specified to be a building of timber, "handsomely hewed,"[45] was to be thirty-two by forty feet, with a thirty-two–foot–square courtroom on the first floor and four offices of equal size on the second floor (fig. 2). The Harrisburg (Harris) County Courthouse in Houston (circa 1837), also a frame building, was thirty-six by twenty-four feet with court below and four offices above.[46]

While the development of distinctive Anglo-American architecture in the Republic had originated when Jeffersonian Classicism was on the wane, it began when the Greek Revival mode in the United States was waxing strong. The style became widely popular in Texas. In the towns that were established as commercial and cultural centers in the state—such as Galveston, Jefferson, Houston, and San Antonio—the affluent lived in houses with formal plans and prostyle porches; they worshipped in templelike churches and governed from Classical temples of justice, all in the Greek style.

After the introduction into America with English pattern books publishing architectural details discovered from Greek archaeology, this mode became fashionable in the East and the South after 1820, remained popular until about 1860, and reached Texas near the end of this era via Louisiana and the other southern states.[47] Continuing in popularity through

[42] Rankin, *Texas in 1850*, pp. 41–42.
[43] *Telegraph and Texas Register* (Houston), May 30, 1838, p. 1. In back of the judge's seat on the first-floor courtroom, the specifications stipulated: ". . . a large window, circular at the top, to contain 48 lights of 10–12 glass, with a small window on each side of the same 2 lights in width by 12 in height." The front door was "to be 4 feet wide by 7 feet high and, with a circular window on the top 3 feet high and of the same width of the door." In addition, the house was "to have 5 windows on each side and 2 in each end in both stories of 32 lights each of 10–12 glass, with double shutters."
[44] See Marcus Whiffen, "The Early County Courthouses of Virginia," *Journal of the Society of Architectural Historians* 18, no. 1 (March 1959): 6.

[45] *Telegraph and Texas Register* (Houston), May 30, 1838, p. 1.
[46] Ibid., October 21, 1837, p. 3.
[47] Talbot Hamlin, *Greek Revival Architecture in America*, pp. 213–233.

Fig. 3. City Market, San Antonio, Bexar County (mid-1800's). John Fries and David Russi, architects. (Photo from the Texas State Library, Austin)

Fig. 4. Magnolia Hotel, Seguin, Guadalupe County (mid-1800's). (Historic American Buildings Survey photo from the Library of Congress)

the third quarter of the nineteenth century—although there was little building during the Civil War and the Reconstruction—the Greek Revival style was given impetus in Texas by tradition and by cultural identification. Most Anglo-American settlers had immigrated from towns where that style was the mode of expression for public architecture. After they moved west, nostalgia assured the continuation of style, while the strength and harmony associated with it

provided a sense of permanence of civilization on an unstable frontier. In the regions of the state where the economy was dependent upon plantations, the formality of plan and composition that characterized this mode was certainly appropriate for a way of life that was similar to that in other regions of the South. Also stimulating appreciation for Classicism was the classical education that students received from academies and colleges, the buildings for which were also in Greek style (plate 2). All these influences, together with a strong desire for sophistication and distinction, assured the popularity of the Greek Revival in the Lone Star State.

In the 1850's, in areas where there was cultural sensitivity, Greek details and formal composition frequently appeared in hotels and other commercial buildings, as in the mid-nineteenth-century city market of San Antonio (fig. 3). At Jefferson, the Irving House (1854), now known as the Excelsior Hotel, was in the form of a large two-story frame house in the Greek Revival style. The Magnolia Hotel in Seguin (circa 1850), seven bays wide, was a two-story clapboarded block, with a heavy cornice and wide corner pilasters (fig. 4). The Stagecoach Inn at Chappell Hill (circa 1850), also a two-story frame, was yet another example of the revival of the Greek style—as elsewhere in the South, wooden construction of Classical buildings became a tradition in the forested regions of Texas, although masonry was also widely used.

The Greek was also considered an appropriate mode for ecclesiastical buildings, regardless of the denomination that the edifice served. In Marshall several characteristic examples appeared near mid-century. One of the earliest Protestant religious edifices in East Texas, the First Baptist Church (1849), was a wooden clapboarded structure with a Classical pediment and a belfry with Greek details. Also crowned by a rectangular cupola, the Cumberland Presbyterian Church (1853, razed 1883)—likewise built of wood— was a prostyle building with a typical Classical entablature. In Anderson the Baptist Church (circa 1850) had a Classical cupola and walls of fieldstone finished with plaster, which was scribed to imitate hewn stonework (fig. 5).

Although Classical details in simplified form were

Fig. 5. Baptist Church, Anderson, Grimes County (mid-1800's). (Historic American Buildings Survey photo from the Library of Congress)

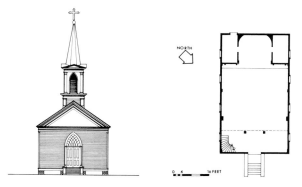

Fig. 6. Floor plan and northeast elevation of Immaculate Conception Catholic Church, Jefferson, Marion County (1869). (Drawing by author, from Historic American Buildings Survey)

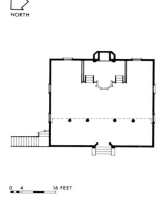

Fig. 7. Plan of Senai Hebrew Synagogue, Jefferson, Marion County (1876). (Drawing by author, from Marion County Deed Book, vol. L, p. 164)

easiest to model in wood, frame structures were susceptible to fire and decay; therefore, many congregations preferred to build permanent Greek Revival buildings with masonry. In Austin the First Baptist Church (1856–1857) was a two-story stone structure, eighty feet square, with flat roof and Classical details. Also built with brick walls was the First Methodist Church in Marshall (1860), an additional example of the monumental temple style (plate 3).

The popularity of the Greek Revival continued for over a decade after the war between the states. This was the mode of the Immaculate Conception Catholic Church in Jefferson (1869), a representative example of the traditional plan (fig. 6), although the lancets of the Gothic Revival indicated that the Greek had lost some of its force. As late as 1876 the Senai Hebrew Synagogue in Jefferson was built in Greek style but with round-arched windows (plate 4). However, the entrance to this edifice was unusual since it was placed on the short axis of a nearly square plan, thereby deviating from the common practice of being situated below the pediment (fig. 7).

Classical details and composition also characterized the antebellum courthouses that replaced the first temporary log shelters of the state. Whether of wood or brick, these appeared in the garb of the Greek Revival with articulated cornices, columns and pilasters in simplified Doric or Ionic order, and entries with

double-paneled doors, sidelights, and rectangular transoms.

The construction of new county buildings was given impetus by the state legislature. In 1852 an act was passed remitting county taxes that were collected for state financing to the counties to pay for new courthouses and jails. The duration of this allowance, originally specified for four years, was extended an additional two years. During this period a rash of county building occurred.

The mid-century antebellum courthouses—virtually none of which remain today—were mostly consistent in design. Following formal compositions, they were two-story blocks, approximately thirty-two feet high, on either square or rectangular plans. Usually the roof was hipped, and the whole composition was crowned and unified by a square or octagonal cupola. Located in the center of the public square, the courthouse generally had entries with Greek Revival details on all four façades—giving equal prominence to commercial property on all sides. Numerous examples of this courthouse type appeared as counties built permanent temples for Dame Justice. The second Harrison County Courthouse in Marshall (1851, razed 1888), popularly known as the "little Virginia Courthouse" after its paradigm, was characteristic (fig. 8). Surviving photographs reveal that the façades of the cubical mass were strongly articulated by wide pilasters supporting a heavy cornice. On one front, two Doric columns supported an attached balcony, from which public addresses could be made.

Square plans similar to the Harrison County Courthouse appeared frequently. The second Washington County Courthouse in Brenham (1852) was a plain brick cube with five bays on each side, crowned by an octagonal cupola. The advertisement for bids for the Jefferson County Courthouse in Beaumont (1854) called for a building thirty feet square with a frieze of two feet in width. Grayson County commissioners, in 1853, advertised from Sherman for a brick courthouse forty feet square;[48] and in 1856, before the seat of justice was moved to Fort Worth, the commissioners of Tarrant County, from Birdville, called for bids for a "courthouse to be two stories (thirty-two feet) high, and fifty by fifty feet, and finished off in plain style."[49] The plans of these seats of justice were typified by the second Van Zandt County Courthouse in Canton (1857–1859), an edifice of brick with "a neat brick entabular supported by four pilasters, one on each Corner of the house" (fig. 9).[50] Within this forty-foot square, the first floor was divided into four offices by cross corridors—a plan reminiscent of, if not ultimately inspired by, Andrea Palladio's Villa

[48] *Standard* (Clarksville), March 12, 1853, p. 2.
[49] *Texas Republican* (Marshall), May 10, 1856, p. 3.
[50] Commissioners' Court Minutes, Van Zandt County, vol. A, p. 244.

Fig. 8. Harrison County Courthouse, Marshall (1851, razed 1888). (Photo from *Harrison County Historical Herald*, December 1964; courtesy of the Harrison County Historical Museum, Marshall)

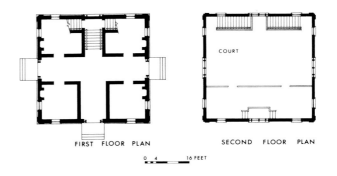

Fig. 9. Floor plans of Van Zandt County Courthouse, Canton (1857–1859). (Drawings by author, based on specifications in Commissioners' Court Minutes, Van Zandt County, vol. A, pp. 241–245)

Capra in Vicenza, Italy (1567), which was known in the United States through publications. The second story contained the courtroom, an arrangement of floors that was the reverse of the earlier Liberty County Courthouse.

While the square courthouse plan was common, it was not universal. The Smith County Courthouse in Tyler (1851) was a two-story brick edifice, seventy feet long and forty wide, with a square cupola.[51] For

[51] Albert Woldert, *A History of Tyler and Smith County, Texas*, pp. 16, 56.

the Red River County Courthouse (1852–1853), the first brick building in Clarksville, horizontal dimensions of forty-five by fifty-five and a cornice height of thirty-three feet were specified.[52] The first permanent Bell County Courthouse in Belton (1858–1859), designed by William Bock, was fifty by sixty feet, two stories, and built of limestone.[53] Thus, the simple rectangular plan was also popular.

The tradition of square or rectangular designs for these courthouses, often defined only by written specifications, was perpetuated by emulation. When planning for their new courthouse, commissioners often visited buildings in neighboring counties. Moreover, if they read the newspapers of the period, they were familiar with the architectural requirements that others published with advertisements for bids. Then, specifications were usually developed calling for a similar building, but with such modifications in size and detail as were appropriate for specific needs and budgets. For instance, when the Titus County commissioners advertised for bids on their new building (1858), they simply specified a "house, 40 x 55 feet— 2 stories high, 4 rooms below, and three above; the other work after the plan of the Court House of Red River county . . ."[54]

While the counties were assisted by the state in financing public buildings, the state had received from the federal government money that, in part, was used to build governmental buildings. As partial compensation for its cession of lands in the northwest—lands now in the states of New Mexico, Oklahoma, Kansas, Colorado, and Wyoming—$10 million was awarded to Texas. Early in 1852 the legislature appropriated $100,000 of this for the erection of a new capitol, and

Fig. 10. Texas state Capitol, Austin, Travis County (1852–1854, burned 1881). John Brandon, architect. (Photo from the T. U. Taylor Collection, Texas State Library, Austin)

$40,000 was designated for the erection of a land office.

The capitol (1852–1854), the design of which was credited to John Brandon,[55] was a fine Greek Revival monument, built of light cream-colored limestone (fig. 10). Located in Austin on an imposing eminence on an axis with Congress Avenue, the edifice was a large rectangular mass, 90 feet wide, 145 feet long, and slightly over 54 feet high. Complementing the visual repose of the Classical style, the base of the building was emphasized by rusticated stone, and the plain walls were surmounted with a Classical cornice. A portico, supported by four well-proportioned Ionic columns and approached up a broad flight of steps, relieved the austerity of the mass, and a cupola rose above the whole to unify the composition.[56]

---

[52] According to the agreement with the contractor, "it is to be 45 by 55, with a base of 3 feet; lower story 12 feet to the ceiling; upper story in which is to be the court room and two Clerks' offices, 15 feet from floor to ceiling; and these with the cornice will give the building an elevation of about 33 feet.—It will be handsomely finished throughout, with seats for the audience without the bar of the courtroom, rising from front to back. The walls are to be 18 inches thick" (*Northern Standard* [Clarksville], August 14, 1852, p. 4).

[53] George W. Tyler, *The History of Bell County*, ed. Charles W. Ramsdell, p. 147.

[54] *Standard* (Clarksville), August 21, 1858, p. 2.

[55] There was evidently some controversy over the selection of an architect for the building. Although there were plans submitted by several architects, the commissioners in charge of superintending the work reportedly rejected all and drafted their own (*Texas Republican* [Marshall], April 17, 1852, p. 1).

[56] According to the *Texas Almanac*, 1858, p. 90, the functions of the building were as follows: "Entering beneath the portico, there is a basement story containing twelve rooms, twenty by thirty feet, and fourteen feet high, on each side of a passage twenty feet wide, and running the entire length of the building. The floors are of solid oolite marble, inlaid with hydraulic cement. Entering the second floor, either by the portico or by a flight of steps from the basement, we find the Senate Chamber and Hall of the Supreme Court on one side of a side passage, the

It is noteworthy that the General Land Office (1856–1857) in Austin, built in a period in which details derived from ancient Greek architecture were so admired in fulfilling the desire for architectural integrity and beauty, appeared in a different style (plate 5). Designed by a German immigrant, Conrad C. Stremme—which certainly explains the departure from tradition—this was a massive work with round-arched openings, recalling the Romanesque architecture of Germany (plate 6). Although the character was different, orderly and balanced composition declared the universal admiration for stately expression, similar to the Greek mode.

While the Greek Revival came to the state with immigrants as a tradition, the federal government also contributed to the perpetuation of the mode. Consistent in style with federal work being done elsewhere in the United States, the Galveston Customs House (1858–1861) was one of the finest Greek Revival buildings in the state (plate 7). The exterior was well proportioned (plate 8), and the interior was enhanced by a stairway with delightful details (plate 9).

Although the architect of the original design of the Galveston Customs House, Ammi B. Young, supervising architect of the Treasury, in Washington, D.C., practiced as a professional, it is evident that most antebellum architects in Texas were actually master builders. They designed buildings, aesthetically and functionally, according to tradition and to simple needs of the owner, and then provided the materials and labor for construction. A master builder in Clarksville, Sidney B. Smith, who was called an architect, advertised: "Will contract for Public or Private buildings of any class, and will work in the best style."[57] In 1857 an advertisement of the architect for the Trinity Episcopal Church (1855) appeared in the *Galveston News*:

John DeYoung
City Surveyor, Draughtsman, Builder
and Real Estate Broker
Galveston, Texas[58]

Perhaps L. W. Lissenbee, of Mount Pleasant, was the epitome of the multitalented master builder. In 1860 the scope of his services was stated in one of his advertisements:

L. W. LISSENBEE
ARCHITECT AND CONTRACTOR
Mt. Pleasant, Titus County, Texas
WILL plan and make specifications for
the erection of public or private
buildings, in brick or wood, and will
contract upon the best practicable
terms.[59]

Among the works of Lissenbee were the Hunt County Courthouse in Greenville (circa 1855), the Titus County Courthouse in Mount Pleasant (1858), and the Bonham Masonic Institute (circa 1856). Builders like Smith, DeYoung, and Lissenbee evidently acquired their knowledge of the art of building from practical experience. Some, perhaps, increased their competence by studying architectural pattern books. Abner Cook, builder of the Governor's Mansion in Austin (completed in 1856), acquired experience in Macon, Georgia, then Nashville, Tennessee, before moving to Texas at the age of twenty-five to become one of the state's most famous master builders.[60]

The work of these master builders culminates the development of antebellum architecture. In the growing communities of the state, the quality of architecture had advanced in two and a half decades from a crude, indigenous type of shelters to sophisticated styles that fulfilled demands for permanence and artistic expression. However, indigenous and sophisticated architecture also existed at the same time; with Greek Revival buildings rising in the established towns, on the fringes of the civilized lands—where

---

Hall of Representatives occupying the whole of the other side. The Senate Chamber is sixty feet, and thirty-four feet high. . . . Each Legislative hall is provided with amply, but wretchedly constructed galleries, entered by another flight of steps, and on the same story is found the State Library Hall." The roof over each legislative hall was hipped, while the roof over the hall between them was flat. This edifice burned in 1881.
[57] *Standard* (Clarksville), May 1, 1858, p. 2.

[58] Cited in William Manning Morgan, *Trinity Protestant Episcopal Church, Galveston, Texas, 1841–1953*, p. 53.
[59] *Standard* (Clarksville), April 28, 1860, p. 3.
[60] G. L. Landolt, *Search for the Summit: Austin College through XII Decades, 1849–1970*, p. 86.

survival was a challenge in the face of hostilities and natural obstacles—architecture continued to be native to the region and buildings continued to reflect the level of cultural and economic development. On these frontiers of settlement, as well as on the political and military frontiers, military architecture would also play an important role and would likewise respond to the conditions of the environment and to specific requirements of function.

Plate 1. Comanche County Courthouse, Built in Cora, Texas; Now Located North of Comanche (1856)
Architect Unknown   Overall View

The first Comanche County Courthouse epitomized many log public buildings built throughout Texas during the nineteenth century. At first there was only one room, but a later addition created a double, or dog-trot, cabin. Hewn flat on two sides, logs were notched together at the corners, and the interstices between were filled with wood strips and daubed.

After the county seat was moved from Cora to Comanche, county offices were housed in numerous other structures before the turn of the century. In 1859 a new log courthouse was built with picket walls. After this second structure burned in 1864, county offices were housed in

commercial buildings around the square until the third courthouse, a two-story brick with round- and segmental-arched openings, was erected in 1873. Less than two decades later, yet another, more pretentious, temple was built.

Preserved with the first courthouse are the cornerstone and the statue of the Goddess of Justice—sans sword and scales—from the fourth, an edifice with Classical details constructed with sandstone from a nearby quarry. Designed by Larmour and Watson, this last nineteenth-century building was started in 1890 and razed in 1939.

Plate 2. Nacogdoches College, Washington Square, Nacogdoches, Nacogdoches County (1858)
Architect Unknown   Exterior View

Among the numerous fine buildings in the Greek Revival style in Texas was this building for Nacogdoches College, an institution that was established during the days of the Republic. The walls and the columns were brick, while wood was used for the entablature, the cornice, and the octagonal cupola. The designs of the entrance and openings were characteristic of the Greek style in the state.

The land on which the edifice stands was part of an earlier Mexican land grant that had been made for education. Located on the high school grounds, the building now functions as a museum.

Plate 3. First Methodist Church, 300 East Houston Street, Marshall, Harrison County (1860–1861)
Architect Unknown   View from Northwest

Originally named the Methodist Episcopal Church, South, of Marshall, Texas, the sanctuary was erected by Alexander Pope, masonry contractor, and Billington Smalley, woodwork and painting contractor. The foundation, walls, and columns were of hand-molded bricks.

The prostyle form and Greek Revival style created a monumental and stately work. However, the response of one contemporary critic to the unusually massive columns was unfavorable. According to his views, the building committee "must have come to the conclusion that four or five large chimneys in front of the building would add harmony of proportion."[1]

Numerous modifications have been made in the building since completion. In 1883 a gallery and fresco work were removed from the interior. After the turn of the century a belfry and a steeple were removed along with some details, such as the pilaster capitals. Since the building was recorded in 1936 by the Historic American Buildings Survey, the vestibule between the two center columns and the Georgian-style cupola have been added.

[1] *Texas Republican* (Marshall), May 4, 1861, p. 2.

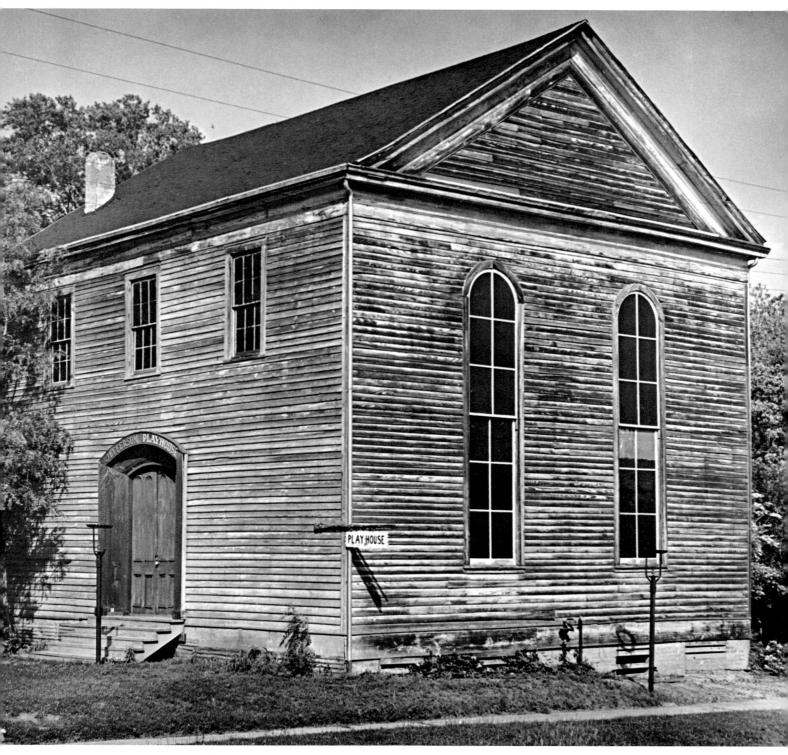

Plate 4. Senai Hebrew Synagogue (Jefferson Playhouse), Market and Henderson Streets, Jefferson, Marion County (1876)
W. F. J. Graham, Builder   View from West

In 1869, Father John M. Giraud purchased several lots for the Sisters of Charity of Saint Vincent de Paul. One of these lots was the site of a Greek Revival residential building, which for a brief period became Saint Mary's School. In 1874 the entire property was deeded to the Senai Hebrew Congregation of Beth-El, and two years later the synagogue was built adjoining the school.

The synagogue was built in Classical style. In Jefferson, as was often the case in regions where timber was plentiful, details as well as the structural framework were entirely of wood. The entablature—architrave, frieze, and cornice—was built up with wooden mold-

ings in a configuration that was virtually identical to those appearing on so many Greek Revival residences in East Texas.

On the interior the entry, sanctuary, and ark were centered on the short axis, thereby contrasting with most churches. At the back was a balcony supported by Doric columns. The walls and the ceiling were finished with tongue-and-grooved boards. Although the building is now used as a playhouse—setting for the reenactment of Diamond Bessie's murder trial each spring—only minor alterations have been made in the original fabric.

Plate 5. General Land Office, 108 East 11 Street, Austin, Travis County (1856–1857)
Conrad C. Stremme, Architect   View from Southwest

In 1836, to administer the public lands, an act of legislature created the General Land Office for the Republic of Texas. After Texas's admission to statehood in 1846, the comptroller was placed in charge of the construction of an edifice to house the records and activities of the office. The site for this building—to which records were moved from an earlier land office—was a hill near the Capitol.

The state was fortunate to secure the services of a talented architect. One-time professor of architecture at Dorpat, Conrad C. Stremme had been rewarded abroad for his abilities by the conferment of the title "Hereditary Nobleman," a Russian order.[1] With symmetrical composition and heavy sculptural gable parapets that reflected his European background, Stremme created a monumental and stately edifice. Heavy stringcourses, water table, and base visually strengthen the work.

Masonry was used throughout the building, which was designed as a fireproof structure. Exterior walls were two and a half feet thick, plastered on both sides, while those of the interior were two feet thick. A series of masonry vaults bearing on arches support the second floor, and a series of vaults bearing on iron beams support the attic.

[1] August Watkins Harris, *Minor and Major Mansions in Early Austin*.

Plate 6. General Land Office, Austin
View of South Door

Massive walls, contrasting with fine moldings, were distinctive features of the openings. The chamfering of the intrados of the arches produced a horseshoe motif, an interesting and unusual detail in nineteenth-century Texas architecture. The five-pointed star, symbol of the Lone Star State, appears in the design.

Through this door was a vestibule containing the main stair. Beyond, on the ground floor, were spaces for the land commissioner, school lands administration, book records, and Spanish land grants. On the second floor were spaces for drafting, translation, and transcripts. It was in the drafting room that William Sydney Porter, who wrote under the pseudonym "O. Henry," worked when he authored his short story "Bexar Script No. 2692."

In 1917 the land offices were moved to new quarters. The old building was subsequently assigned to the Daughters of the Republic of Texas and the Daughters of the Confederacy in Texas, which organizations maintain it as a museum. Among the items of interest on display is O. Henry's drafting table.

Plate 7. Galveston Customs House, Twentieth Street and Avenue E, Galveston, Galveston County (1858–1861)
Ammi B. Young and Others, Architects   View from Northwest

In 1857 the U.S. Congress initially appropriated $100,000 for the construction of a customs house, which was also to house a post office and a federal court.[1] The following year a contract was awarded to C. B. Cluskey of Washington, D.C., and E. E. Moore of Galveston for the construction of a three-story Greek Revival building, designed by Supervising Architect of the Treasury Department Ammi B. Young. In 1859—the year the work was to be completed—amid various protests against the plans, work was suspended and the building was redesigned. Although the name of the author of the alterations is now obscure, it was determined that the plan would be in the form of an H and that, instead of three stories, there would be only two. Then Cluskey refused to enter a new contract, after which it was awarded to his partner, E. E. Moore, who sold it to the firm of Blaisdell and Emerson of Boston.[2] Finally, the work was completed in March 1861.

Like many buildings in Galveston, the Customs House has sustained damages from the tempests, requiring numerous repairs. After many renovations, the building is still owned by the federal government and now serves as a federal court and a post office substation.

1 *Texas Almanac* (1858), p. 192.
2 Lawrence Wodehouse, "The Custom House, Galveston, Texas, 1857–1861, by Ammi Burnham Young," *Journal of the Society of Architectural Historians* 25, no. 1 (March 1966): 67.

Plate 8. Galveston Customs House, Galveston
View from Southwest

One of the finest Greek Revival buildings along the Gulf Coast, the Customs House was basically a structure of masonry and iron, the latter of which was shipped from New York. Walls were of brick, while the columns, cornice, balustrades, and window jambs and lintels were cast iron. Corrugated iron covered the roof.

Repose and dignity, appropriate for the expression of government functions, resulted from the formal composition of masses and openings and from the use of Classical features. In the original proposal, an Ionic colonnade was to have been used on the first story, Doric on the second, and Corinthian on the third. In the modified design, only the Ionic and Corinthian orders were retained. These were employed on the north and south façades and on the west portico. The heavy cornices at the roof and second floor—which were originally specified to be finished to imitate stone—emphasized the horizontal composition, while the balustrade handsomely terminated it.

Plate 9. Galveston Customs House, Galveston
Detail of Stair

On the ground floor of the building were the customs and post offices, the latter of which was entered through the west (Twentieth Street) portico. On the second floor, to which this stair provided communication from the north portico, was located the federal courtroom.

Like many of the exterior details, the stair was built with iron. Intricate detail, characterized by numerous perforations appropriate for cast-iron designs, produced a lacy appearance and created a graceful lightness.

Military Architecture

THROUGHOUT COLONIZATION AND SETTLEMENT of the Texas frontier, conflict and hostilities were ubiquitous. When not competing with each other, aggressive Latins and Anglo-Americans continuously encountered the natives. From the very beginning, Indians were considered liabilities in most attempts at civilizing the wilderness; only the Spaniards attempted to make them assets. In the days of the missions, the friars suffered many atrocities at the hands of ruthless Lipans, Apaches, and Comanches, but, undaunted and dedicated to Church and Crown, they continued their work, adapting to the exigencies of the times. The friars fortified their missions; the Crown provided soldiers, although often few in numbers, for the establishment and garrisoning of presidios.

Along a frontier that was sparsely settled and weakly fortified, the Indian problem persisted throughout Latin domination, and there was little improvement when Texas became, with Coahuila, a co-state of Mexico. When Anglo-Americans began settlement, the Mexican government provided meager succor to the remote frontier. In fact, in opening lands to immigration, the government intended that the settlers themselves would secure the northern frontier of Mexico. Although officials and colonists attempted to make treaties with the natives, depredations continued. Around 1835 the civil militia that had been formed was dissolved by Mexican decree, thus further increasing the danger from Indians.[1] Then, as if conditions were not bad enough, in 1837, Mexicans incited the Indians to plunder and murder.[2] In response, the settlers fortified themselves with stockades.

The years of the Republic witnessed no reduction in hostilities. The settlement of lands placed pressure on the Indians, who retaliated by frequently raiding the settlers. Consequently, late in 1836 the president of the Republic was empowered to order the erection of such works that might be necessary to prevent depredations. Two years later the legislature passed an act providing for the defense of the northern and western frontiers. This bill authorized a system of de-

[1] Henderson King Yoakum, *History of Texas from Its First Settlements in 1685 to Its Annexation to the United States in 1846*, I, 336.
[2] Ibid., II, 227.

fenses consisting of a military road from the Red River to the Nueces and a chain of forts set up at intervals along the road. These fortifications were to be built with stone, when available. However, there was uncertainty as to the best location of the road, and such works as were ultimately set up were evidently mostly or wholly of wood.

These works, along with several campaigns, still failed to check the elusive Indians. Texas frontiersmen must certainly have welcomed annexation to the United States, since they could then look forward to federal relief from the menace of the Indians.

However, frontier defense in the Lone Star State during the second half of the nineteenth century required more than the suppression of hostile Indians. In addition, it involved not only obligations to Mexico but also fears of attack by other nations. Therefore, frontier defense became essentially threefold in function: first, the defense of settlers and roads on the inland frontier; second, the protection of both American and Mexican communities along the Rio Grande from Indians normally residing within the state, which the United States had guaranteed by the Treaty of Guadalupe Hidalgo; and, third, the defense of the maritime frontier of the Gulf Coast of Texas against potential aggression of foreign powers—a problem in national security.[3] The provision for each of these broad functions required a different and specific type of military architecture.

By the time frontier defense in Texas became its responsibility, the U.S. Army had considerable experience with Indian suppression and control along a constantly moving frontier. Previously, in order to garrison soldiers for the protection of settlers and travelers, posts had been located at strategic points in the wilderness. At first, before Indian warfare was understood, these were projected to be strongly fortified, but, as the frontier and civilization moved westward, it was found that strong works for active defense were unnecessary. Since Indians rarely attacked a garrisoned post, fortifications were eliminated. Therefore,

to label the inland posts of Texas with the appellation of "fort" was technically a misnomer, since there were few or no fortifications. Rather than designating a fortified place, the term simply denoted either a temporary or permanent cantonment or barracks for accommodating several companies of men.

In Texas the Indians were stirred by desires to plunder, rather than by ambitions to wage a systematic war. Consequently, these wily equestrians, among the most fierce and savage in the West, waged a predatory kind of war. Against them, the infantry was totally ineffective, and even the cavalry found it difficult to punish them, since the character of the country often made chase difficult.

By mid-century, experience had proven that tactical warfare was largely without success against Indians; control was possible only with brute strength. In 1851 the secretary of war reported, "Experience has shown that the most effective way to protect our settlements is to overawe the Indians by a constant display of military force in their immediate neighborhood."[4] It was certainly this point of view that influenced judgment concerning the location of posts at mid-century. In 1849, after evaluation of the geography of settlement, a cordon of posts was established in advance of the pioneers, along a line extending southwest from the present city of Fort Worth. In this chain were Fort Worth, Fort Graham, Fort Gates, Fort Croghan, and Fort Inge.

While the general locations for these forts were determined by the relationship between the country occupied by Indians and the advancement of white settlement, specific locations were influenced by the terrain and natural resources needed by the post. Sites near water but with good drainage were essential for the health of the garrison. They should have either wood or coal readily available for fuel and should be near meadows to provide ample forage for the animals. Then, near the post, should be materials for building. Later, sites were sought near land that was suitable for cultivation. If any of these resources was

---

[3] The Mexican and Indian frontier was nearly two thousand miles long; the seaboard frontier was approximately four hundred miles in length.

[4] U.S., Congress, House, C. M. Conrad, *Report of the Secretary of War*, H. Ex. Doc. 2, 32d Cong., 1st Sess., 1851, p. 106.

missing, the expense of maintenance was considerably increased.

When establishing forts, the army journeyed into the wilderness with light firearms and tools, but most of the men had had little experience with the use of the shovel and ax. In the early years in the defense of the Texas Indian frontiers, the troops evidently spent more time developing skills of craftsmanship than marksmanship. When W. G. Freeman inspected the posts south of Fort Worth, as well as those along the Rio Grande, he reported that he "found military instruction invariably subordinated, perhaps necessarily, to learn the labors of the axe, saw and hammer."[5]

On the remote locations of those early frontier forts, shelters were expediently fabricated by the soldiers from materials immediately at hand or with light materials that could be easily transported. In each region, they generally built as others had before them under similar circumstances. Thus, *jacales*, adobe buildings, and log structures were common. Like the shelters of the early settlers, military architecture in the wilderness was indigenous to the land—the buildings reflected the state of civilization on the frontier on which they were built.

Originally, since it was known that the early posts on this inland frontier would be impermanent, only temporary buildings were authorized. In consequence of this situation, and the limited technical skill of the soldiers, only primitive techniques were employed. For example, at Fort Worth—a post that had been relocated because the first site was thought to be unhealthy—rough timber was the basic building material (fig. 11). The commanding officer's quarters was reported to be of "hewn logs—clapboard roof—leaky."[6] The company quarters, along with the mess shed and stables, was labeled as a "palisade work."[7]

built of logs, planted vertically side by side in the ground, recalling the colonial work of the Spanish in Texas and the French in other parts of the United States.

In the immediate vicinities of Fort Croghan, Fort Graham, and Fort Gates, timber was satisfactory for logs but not for being sawed into lumber. At the first two posts, squared oak logs were used for the more important buildings, while undressed logs were employed mostly for the service buildings. At Croghan, in 1851, the buildings consisted of "four double houses, two rooms each, built of logs, squared or faced, with common log kitchens for the officers' quarters. Buildings [were] all of oak."[8] At Graham the hospital and officers' quarters were of squared logs, roofed with shingles, while the commissary was evidently of common round logs, roofed with clapboards.[9] At Fort Gates the quarters for officers, laundresses, and muleteers were frame, covered with oak clapboards; the company quarters and hospital were "frames filled in with upright posts pointed and placed in the ground."[10]

Milled lumber for such items as jambs, sills, and joists was available only at distant points: for Fort Graham, it had to be hauled 120 miles; Fort Croghan, 90 miles; Fort Gates, 85 miles. Near all these forts, stone of excellent quality was abundant and would have been the most economical material, but there were no skilled masons, and orders prohibited permanent buildings.

The shelters at Fort Inge, one of the southern posts in this chain, were also flimsy and crude. In 1853 the men occupied quarters with walls of chinked upright poles and roofs of thatch.[11] Frederick Law Olmsted, when he visited the fort, described the shelters as "very rough and temporary, some of the officers' lodgings being mere *jacales* of sticks and mud. But all

[5] W. G. Freeman, "W. G. Freeman's Report on the Eighth Military Department," ed. M. L. Crimmins, *Southwestern Historical Quarterly* 53, no. 3 (January 1950): 312.

[6] Rough Plan of Fort Worth, Texas [circa 1850], Cartographic Branch, National Archives, Record Group 77, Drawer 148, Sheet 38½.

[7] Ibid.

[8] U.S., Congress, House, *Report of Lieutenant A. Jackson*, H. Ex. Doc. 2, 32d Cong., 1st Sess., 1851, p. 275.

[9] U.S., Congress, House, *Report of First Lieutenant N. C. Givens*, H. Ex. Doc. 2, 32d Cong., 1st Sess., 1851, p. 271.

[10] U.S., Congress, House, *Report of Lieutenant Haldeman*, H. Ex. Doc. 2, 32d Cong., 1st Sess., 1851, p. 274.

[11] Freeman, "W. G. Freeman's Report," p. 76.

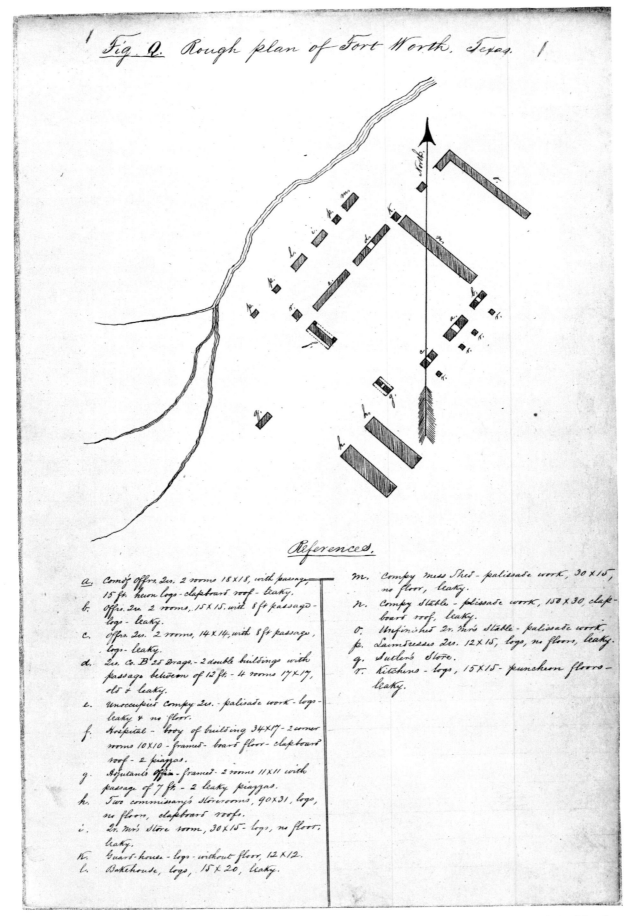

Fig. Q. Rough plan of Fort Worth. Texas.

Forth

References.

a. Com'y Offrs. 2v. 2 rooms 18×18, with passage, 15 ft. hewn logs- clapboard roof - leaky.
b. Offrs. 2v. 2 rooms, 15×15. with 8 ft passage - logs- leaky.
c. Offrs. 2v. 2 rooms, 14×14, with 8 ft passage, logs- leaky.
d. 2v. Co. B 2d Drags. - 2 double buildings with passage between of 12 ft. - 4 rooms 17×17, old & leaky.
e. Unoccupied Compy 2v. - palisade work - logs - leaky & no floor.
f. Hospital - body of building 34×17 - 2 corner rooms 10×10 - framed- board floor - clapboard roof - 2 piazzas.
g. Adjutant's Office - framed - 2 rooms 11×11 with passage of 7 ft. - 2 leaky piazzas.
h. Two commissary's Storerooms, 90×31, logs, no floor, clapboard roofs.
i. 2v. M's Store room, 30×15 - logs, no floor, leaky.
k. Guard-house - logs - without floor, 12×12.
l. Bakehouse, logs, 15×20, leaky.

m. Compy mess Shed - palissade work, 30×15, no floor, leaky.
n. Compy Stable - palissade work, 150×30, clap-board roof, leaky.
o. Unfinished 2v. M's Stable - palisade work.
p. Laundresses 2v. 12×15, logs, no floors, leaky.
q. Sutler's Store.
r. Kitchens - logs, 15×15 - puncheon floors - leaky.

Fig. 11. Plan of Fort Worth, Tarrant County (established 1849). (Photo from the National Archives)

Military Architecture

were whitewashed, and neatly kept, by taste and discipline."[12]

Another line of posts was developed in the southwestern section of the state to defend the Rio Grande frontier against Indians, as well as against Mexican bandits. In this isolated region, hot and dry in the summer, the physiography contrasted with that of the central part of the state so as to provide different materials. At locations that had been strategically selected for forts, officers and soldiers adapted to the environment in the same manner as they did in other regions. Using materials at hand or brought with them, they fabricated shelters, if only of a crude type, to shield from the sun and protect from the occasional rains.

After two years Fort McIntosh (established in 1849), near Laredo, consisted of several light frame buildings, weatherboarded and roofed with shingles, and several *jacal* shelters "made of mezquite poles placed perpendicularly in the ground."[13] However, several years later, it was reported that the men were quartered in tents.

While most of the inland forts for Indian defense had no actual works to defend against attack, Fort McIntosh, along with Fort Brown (established in 1846), near the mouth of the Rio Grande, originally was fortified with fieldworks. Designed to enable the garrisons to resist assaults by superior numbers armed with artillery, these fieldworks consisted of enclosures formed by throwing up thick earth parapets, with magazines built of masonry within. The defensive enclosure at Fort Brown in 1861 was comprised of six bastioned fronts, with a perimeter of 950 yards.[14] Fort McIntosh had an irregular trace with two half-bastions formed with sand, enclosing about an acre of ground.[15] Characteristic of fieldworks without masonry revetments, erosion played havoc with both these works; the rain washed down the parapets of Fort Brown, and the wind blew away those of Fort McIntosh.

As at other posts on the frontier, the buildings at the posts on the southwest cordon were indigenous. At Fort Duncan (established in 1849), where there was no timber except crooked mesquite, in addition to a building of adobe and several of stone, there were "six grass houses occupied by the companies, built entirely of willow poles and grass, no floors or windows."[16] Later, however, stone buildings with thatched roofs, financed with private funds, were built at Duncan. At Fort Ewell (established in 1852), the commissary, storehouse, blacksmith's shop, and two structures for company quarters were built of adobe made by the troops. At these and other posts, more permanence in the early buildings was common where security was critical. Thus, such structures as prisons and magazines were usually entirely of stone and brick, although they were often poorly built.

After the Rio Grande frontier was considered to be stable, permanent architecture could be projected for quarters, barracks, and other buildings. However, this work could not be commenced until titles to the sites for forts were obtained.[17] During negotiations for purchase, troops occupied temporary buildings.

In 1854 the need for convenient, yet portable, shelters motivated Quartermaster Parmenas T. Turnley, a graduate of the U.S. Military Academy, to develop a building specifically for use on the frontiers of Texas, Arizona, and New Mexico. When serving in Texas, he had noted the necessity for a type of shelter that would be better than canvas in timberless regions. As a result, the Turnley cottage was developed in two sizes: one, thirty by fifteen feet, for officers; the other, forty by eighteen, for troops. Similar in construction, both sizes consisted of sills, grooved on the top side,

[12] Frederick Law Olmsted, *Journey through Texas*, p. 286.
[13] U.S., Congress, House, *Report of Lieutenant Turnley*, H. Ex. Doc. 2, 32d Cong., 1st Sess., 1851, p. 281.
[14] See Allan C. Ashcraft, "Fort Brown, Texas, in 1861," *Texas Military History* 3, no. 4 (Winter 1963): 243.
[15] For a plan of Fort McIntosh, see J. K. F. Mansfield, "Colonel J. K. F. Mansfield's Report of the Inspection of the Department of Texas in 1856," ed. M. L. Crimmins, *Southwestern Historical Quarterly* 42, no. 3 (January 1939): 239.

[16] U.S., Congress, House, *Report of First Lieutenant J. B. Plummer*, H. Ex. Doc. 2, 32d Cong., 1st Sess., 1851, p. 279.
[17] When Texas was admitted to the Union, she retained all her public lands; hence all sites for forts had to be either leased or purchased. Experience had proven that it was a poor policy to undertake the erection of permanent buildings on lands that were rented.

and plates, grooved on the under side; boards, separated by grooved stanchions, stood vertically in the slots on the sill, forming the walls.[18] The roof was likewise prefabricated, and the whole was held together with bolts. According to Turnley, in four hours three men could set up the entire assembly of one small cottage, which could be hauled in an ordinary wagon. Although tents and *jacales* continued to be used, lightweight Turnley cottages appeared at several Texas posts, among them Fort Clark (established in 1852) and Fort Lancaster (established in 1852), the latter a short-occupied post.

At the permanent forts in the southwestern part of the state, after ownership was acquired, the temporary shelters were ultimately replaced with masonry. At Ringgold Barracks (established 1848 and later renamed Fort Ringgold), flimsy shelters, threatened by the winds, were replaced by substantial brick structures (beginning circa 1870). At Fort Clark, new buildings of limestone began rising in the 1870's (plate 10).

On the other hand, while the locations of the forts on the Rio Grande frontier were considered permanent, the north-south frontier was continually changing. At the time the sites for the first inland posts were selected, it was known that civilization would ultimately advance, forcing the military deeper into country then occupied by Indians. Indeed, only two years after the establishment of Fort Worth and the other posts in that chain, the secretary of war ordered a revision of the whole system of defense.[19] Following this order, the first line was eventually abandoned, and another cordon of posts that included Forts Belknap and McKavett was established between 1851 and 1852 in country that differed from that of the first line in climate, terrain, and geology. These new forts occupied the eastern edge of an arid region, where there was little wood for constructional purposes but a plentiful supply of limestone. Therefore, stone was

economical and naturally became the major building material.

As at other locations, while masonry buildings were rising around the parade ground, *jacales* temporarily housed troops and stores. At Fort Belknap (established 1851 by Lt. Col. William G. Belknap), walls of temporary shelters were of logs planted in the ground on end,[20] while first roofs were of canvas, succeeded by grass thatching.

At Fort McKavett (established in 1852), after temporary shelters were set up, work on masonry buildings was also commenced by the soldier-laborers. The stone used there was easily workable, but the soldier-mechanics had had little experience as masons. The lack of skill in workmanship became evident after the fort was abandoned in 1860. When reoccupied eight years later, "the post was found to be a mass of ruins—only one house being at all habitable."[21] In those that were rebuilt under the command of the famous Indian campaigner, Brig. Gen. Ranald S. Mackenzie, stone craftsmanship was better. Openings, always narrow, were generally spanned with either heavy stone lintels or flat arches. The points of greatest stress in the walls—corners and sides of openings—were often strengthened with quoins.

Although there were no regulations governing planning, and although cadets received no special instruction concerning arrangement,[22] most of the Indian forts were similar in layout. Officers in charge of the establishment of new posts usually developed plans after the layouts of existing posts with which they were familiar. Regardless of the terrain, the arrangement of the buildings was formal in plan and conformed to a hierarchical organization—recalling the disciplined plans of an ancient Roman military camp. The main buildings were positioned in an orderly pattern around a large square or oblong parade ground, often oriented with the axes close to the cardinal points. Officers' quarters occupied one side, with

[18] See Parmenas Taylor Turnley, *Reminiscences from Diary*, p. 128.
[19] U.S., Congress, House, *General Order No. 1*, H. Ex. Doc. 2, 32d Cong., 1st Sess., 1851, p. 117.

[20] Cartographic Branch, NA, RG 77, Drawer 148, Sheet 38½ (p).
[21] U.S., Surgeon General's Office, *Circular No. 4: A Report on Barracks and Hospitals with Descriptions of Military Posts*, 1870, p. 203.
[22] Ibid., p. xxv.

Fig. 12. Fort Davis, Jeff Davis County (established 1854, 1867). (Photo from the National Park Service, Fort Davis)

the commandant's house in the center, on the short axis. On the opposite side were the barracks, each of which was often surrounded with a broad veranda, sheltering the walls from the hot sun. The ends of the parade were either left open or occupied by various small buildings.

Characteristic of this formal organization was Fort Davis (established 1854), originally laid out under the command of Lt. Col. Washington Seawell, but later abandoned and subsequently reestablished in 1867 under the supervision of Lt. Col. Wesley Merrit (figs. 12 and 13). Extending along the west side of a monumental parade was officers' row. On the east side were aligned four T-shaped barracks, which at one time housed four regiments of Negro soldiers. The south end of the parade was open, but on the north

were a chapel, headquarters, and several miscellaneous buildings. Behind the officers' quarters was a hospital (1875), and behind the barracks were such service structures as stables, corrals, and storehouse—all in a typical arrangement.

The same discipline that was apparent in the plan of the posts also distinguished the buildings (plate 11). Except when asymmetrical plans were demanded by functional requirements, composition of façades was always axial—a reflection of the formality of military life and of the desire to have order in the wilderness. Thus, at Fort Davis, the most important buildings—those facing the parade—were all balanced forms with symmetrically placed openings.

Although several of the buildings of Fort Davis had walls of stone, as in other posts in the hot, arid south-

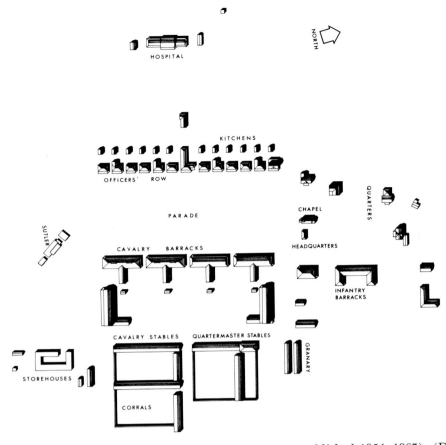

Fig. 13. Site plan of Fort Davis, Jeff Davis County (established 1854, 1867). (Drawing by author, from Historic Structures Report, Fort Davis)

western region of the state, adobe was the major building material (plate 12). As Spaniards and Mexicans had learned decades earlier, this material was economical and easy to manufacture. Moreover, thick walls of adobe blocks were good insulators against the heat and, with periodic maintenance, were durable.

At Fort Stockton (established 1858), northeast of Davis, where there were no trees for building, earth was also the primary material. By 1875 adobe walls on stone foundations enclosed three barracks and seven officers' quarters, the latter of which had walls, two feet thick, plastered and whitewashed on the inside. Farther east, Fort Lancaster (established 1855) also had buildings of adobe, part of which, like Stock-

ton, had shingle roofs and part of which were covered with thatch.

At the end of the fifties and the beginning of the sixties, many Texas forts had been abandoned. Changes in conditions of frontier defense resulted in the obsolescence of some posts; others were evacuated by U.S. troops at the beginning of the Civil War.[23]

After the war, the army, in reaction to numerous

[23] In 1859, for example, Major General Twiggs ordered the abandonment of Fort Brown, Fort McIntosh, Fort Mason, Fort McKavett, and Ringgold Barracks (see U.S., Congress, Senate, *Report of the Secretary of War*, S. Ex. Doc. 2, 36th Cong., 1st Sess., 1859, p. 359). Among the posts claimed by Confederates were Fort Chadbourne, Fort Clark, Fort Bliss, and Fort Davis.

Fig. 14. Barracks at Fort Concho, Tom Green County (established 1867). (Photo from the Texas State Library, Austin)

atrocities and depredations by the Indians, revived its program of defense. Many posts, such as Fort Davis and Fort McKavett, were reoccupied and rebuilt, some having been occupied by Confederates, again abandoned, and fallen to ruins. Others were newly located to increase the effectiveness of control along the north-south frontier. During the sixties, the conditions that determined the erection of forts along the new frontier were uniform, placing the posts in a contiguous geological and climatological region. Moreover, the buildings were designed by officers with common backgrounds and similar experiences, working under similar limitations. Therefore, the architectural forms possessed similar characteristics. All were straightforward designs with little embellishment. Their chief artistic merits were in their collectively restrained composition and in their organic harmony with their natural surroundings.

Among the new posts were Fort Richardson (established 1867) and Fort Concho (established 1867), intended to function in conjunction with previously established forts. The order of construction for these two was similar to that of the earlier forts. Upon arrival at the site of Fort Richardson, the cavalry immediately began setting up picket houses, which would shelter them while permanent stone buildings were under erection. One cavalryman-builder, H. H. McConnell—after lamenting that the spade appeared mightier than the sword—wrote that these were built

after "a trench of the proper size was dug, . . . four extra-sized posts were placed at the corners, then the remainder of the 'pickets' usually from four to six inches through, were . . . set in the ditch or trench, side by side, a 'plate' was spiked on the top, a roof, slightly inclined, was made by laying poles side by side, the interstices filled with twigs, and the whole covered thickly with dirt."[24] The interstices in the wall were then filled with chips and mud. After shelters for the entire command were completed, sandstone buildings began to rise, with civilian carpenters and masons performing the skilled work and the soldiers serving as laborers.

At Fort Concho, in order to build durably on the flat prairie—one of the healthiest locations in the state—craftsmen were recruited from Fredericksburg (fig. 14).[25] By 1870 "the buildings of the post were, in the order of their construction, a commissary and quartermaster storehouse, hospital, five officers' quarters, a magazine, and two barracks, all built of light-colored sandstone."[26] This was commonly the sequence in which post buildings were erected. When nearly completed, Concho was one of the most attractive and visually unified forts in the West, with barracks walls that were protected by dominant shelter-

[24] H. H. McConnell, *Five Years a Cavalryman*, pp. 53–54.
[25] Roger N. Conger, "Fort Concho," in *Frontier Forts of Texas*, ed. Harold B. Simpson, p. 92.
[26] *Circular No. 4*, 1870, p. 198.

ing hipped roofs, and with officers' quarters that were on a modest scale but dignified in design.

In the decades following the Civil War, the U.S. Army gave increasing attention to the influence of environment on the health and morale of the troops in their new territory. Surgeons and inspectors composed volumes of reports containing observations relative to the effect of climate and buildings on the physical condition of men at posts across the country. From these observations were developed recommendations concerning military architecture. Surgeons were concerned not only with orientation and the relationships between such buildings as hospitals, barracks, and sinks, but also with plans and the details of various building components, such as doors, windows, and ventilating devices. Ultimately, with the intent of eliminating architectural detriments to health, standard designs for hospitals and barracks were published by the Surgeon General's Office. Certainly no building had more effect on health than the barracks, and none made more impression on morale than the hospital—comfortable barracks and substantial hospitals attesting to the importance that the government placed on the welfare of the soldiers.

Significantly, the surgeon general did not overlook the problems that were inherent in standardization. Although the stock plans were evidently developed in Washington, it was wisely recognized that it was "manifestly impractical to plan a hospital . . . equally suited to the burning mesas of Arizona and to the bleak North Atlantic Coast."[27] Nonetheless, it was believed that a general plan could be established, with the details arranged according to circumstances by the officers in charge of construction. In recognition of variations in climate, it was specified that on all hospitals "south of latitude 38 degrees north, a veranda twelve (12) feet wide and one story high will be constructed around the whole hospital."[28]

At several forts in Texas, hospitals were built according to these plans, published in circulars. The

27 Ibid., p. xxii.
28 U.S., Surgeon General's Office, *Circular No. 4: Plan for a Post Hospital of Twenty-Four Beds*, April 27, 1867.

Fig. 15. Floor plans of the hospital at Fort Richardson, Jack County (circa 1870). (Drawings by author, from Surgeon General's Office, *Circular No. 4: Plan for a Post Hospital of Twenty-Four Beds*)

buildings for the sick at Fort Brown, Fort Concho, and Fort Richardson all conformed to the design specified by a publication issued in 1867,[29] although the veranda no longer completely surrounds the remains of the hospital at Richardson. These were on a pavilion plan —as distinguished from a block or corridor plan— where the wards were in isolated narrow pavilions with high ceilings (fig. 15).

Subsequent to the first publications, other circulars containing revised designs were issued. In modified form, the hospital at Fort McKavett was erected in conformance to *Circular No. 3*, issued from the Surgeon General's Office in 1870, and the hospital at Fort Clark followed the plans in *Circular No. 2*, issued in 1871.

Many ailments treated in these hospitals had resulted from overcrowding in quarters. In 1875, relative to these poor conditions across the nation, it was officially reported by John Billings, assistant surgeon,

29 Ibid.

"... it is no exaggeration to say that the service loses by death and discharge on account of overcrowded and badly-ventilated barracks and guardhouses, about 100 men every year."[30]

In Texas, regardless of the materials of construction—wood, adobe, or masonry—many of the early barracks were competently built but evidently congested and poorly ventilated. Although some, in addition to windows, had satisfactory ventilating devices in openings in gables or in ventilators at the ridge of the roofs, others had little provision for air circulation. Some soldiers' quarters, such as those at Ringgold Barracks, were criticized for being too wide for satisfactory air movement. Relative to these problems in the posts in Texas, the Surgeon General's Office critically reported: "The barracks proper evince some knowledge of the rules of building, but little of the principles of hygiene which should be applied in the construction of every habitation ... no thought is given ... to the proper space between barracks; ... nor to the proper height of ceiling; nor proper breadth of the barracks; nor to the cubic air-space and the superficial area per man."[31]

As in hospital design, authors of recommendations for barracks recognized that requirements should vary in different climatic regions. For barracks located in temperate climates, it was believed that each soldier should have at least six hundred cubic feet of air space, of which fifty or sixty feet should be surface area in his dormitory. These figures were increased to eight hundred cubic feet and seventy feet in area for posts below latitude thirty-six degrees—slightly below the northern boundary of the Texas Panhandle.[32]

The requirements for efficient natural ventilation and also for good natural light dictated plans for barracks with narrow dormitories and high ceilings.[33]

Recommended in the Surgeon General's Report of 1870 were twenty-four–foot–wide dormitories and twelve-foot-high ceilings. During the last three decades of the nineteenth century, Texas barracks were long narrow buildings, commonly two stories high, with numerous openings.[34]

The barracks and other structures along the Texas land frontier were usually not realized within a single year, but often required several decades, since new buildings were added as needed and as money, laborers, and mechanics were available for the work. When the Indians were finally subdued, the defensive function of the forts ceased and many were deactivated. Although the purpose naturally changed, others, such as Fort Bliss (established 1848) and Fort Clark, remained active in the twentieth century.

While the military was occupied with controlling the Indians and the Mexican bandits that ravaged the land frontiers, engineers were quietly contemplating the defense of the Texas maritime frontier—that long coastline extending from the Sabine River to the Rio Grande. This planning extended a large program for national defense on which, by the time that Texas joined the Union in 1845, the United States had been working for over a quarter of a century.

After careful study by military experts, multiple objectives had been developed for the national program: (1) key harbors along the Gulf of Mexico were to be defended against the advancement of hostile ships of war; (2) any potential enemy was to be deprived of positions where he might establish bases for direct attacks on important cities; and (3) enemy blockade of ports was to be thwarted. These objectives were to be accomplished by a system of permanent fortifications of brick and stone, erected at the navigation channels through which key bays could be entered. Designed by a board of engineers originally formed in 1816, they were to be located as far as possible from the city that they protected.

From the point of view of either defense or com-

[30] U.S., Surgeon General's Office, *Circular No. 8: A Report on the Hygiene of the United States Army with Descriptions of Military Posts*, p. xvii.

[31] Ibid., p. 182.

[32] Ibid., p. xi.

[33] This was the form of the regulation plan for barracks that was issued in 1873 (U.S., Quartermaster General's Office, Circular dated September 14, 1873).

[34] An interesting exception to the dormitory plan had been utilized several years earlier. At Fort Griffin (established 1867), the barracks consisted of four rows of small frame huts. Spaced about fifty yards apart, there were ten in each row. The dimensions of each hut were 13 by 8½ by 6 feet.

merce, the most important Texas harbor was Galveston Bay—comparable to Mobile Bay, Alabama, and Pensacola Bay, Florida. Although ships-of-war of the first class could not pass over the bar at the inlet, frigates *could* enter. Therefore, as early as 1846, batteries were recommended for the east point of Galveston Island, and towers mounting cannons were suggested for the shore in the rear of the city of Galveston. All these fortifications, according to the engineers' reports, would be economical, since materials could be readily manufactured near the sites where extensive clay banks for brick existed and banks of oyster shells were plentiful for the manufacture of lime.

Subsequently, Congress appropriated $80,000 toward defenses estimated to cost about $600,000. By 1859 plans had been prepared for a fort and land had been purchased as a site. Planned by a board of engineers, the fort was to be a formidable five-bastioned stronghold, built of brick and earth according to the latest theory on seacoast fortification.[35] Two years later, storehouses, cisterns, and quarters for the workers had been built, and materials collected for the defenses. However, the Civil War interrupted construction, and these works were never completed.

During the war between the states, the Confederacy attempted to continue the program for seacoast defense that had been begun by the United States. Along with other Gulf Coast cities, Galveston was extensively fortified with earthworks. A circumvallation was thrown up around the town on the south and east, the sides on which the town could be readily approached by the enemy. Outside this defense, a battery, two redoubts, and twelve forts, located on salient geographic features, strengthened the city. Then, to deny entrance to Union ships, the bay was obstructed.

After the war, because of the development of artillery with phenomenal destructive capacity, the earlier designs became obsolete. New plans were developed, and in 1880 earthen batteries of heavy guns were recommended for Pelican Spit, Galveston Island, and Bolivar Point,[36] the latter of which had been fortified many years earlier with an earthwork in quadrangular form.[37] These defenses were intended only to serve while a permanent system was being studied, but no appropriations were made.

Finally, by 1889 plans for a new system of permanent defenses had been completed for key cities along the Atlantic and Gulf of Mexico coasts. Harbors were to be protected by heavy artillery mounted on disappearing carriages and by systems of submarine mines placed in the channels. Rapid-firing guns of small calibre were to protect the mined areas. The batteries of cannons and gunners were to be shielded by thick concrete parapets, in front of which would be banked masses of sand, and the mines were to be operated from concrete casemates.

In 1896 work was underway on a mining casemate at Galveston Bay. Five years later, although violent tempests of 1897 and 1900 caused delays and necessitated reconstruction, Houston and Galveston were protected by Fort San Jacinto, Fort Travis, and Fort Crockett, all of which had batteries of heavy and rapid-firing guns.[38] Although weapons of attack continued to increase in power, these fortifications remained active into the twentieth century.

Thus, the army, in its defense of the military frontiers of Texas, responded to diverse exigencies—conditions that ranged from primitive warfare and local defense to scientific warfare and national defense, the nature of hostilities determining the forms of works for defense—or lack of them.

Military architecture was informed by geography

[35] See "Proposed Fortifications Bolivar Point," NA, RG 77, Drawer 91, Sheet 12. The design theory for the projected work was similar to that for Fort Gaines, Alabama, and Fort Clinch, Florida, both of which were constructed in the 1850's.

[36] U.S., Congress, House, *Report of the Chief of Engineers*, H. Ex. Doc. 1, 46th Cong., 3d Sess., 1880, II, 51.

[37] William Kennedy, *Texas: The Rise, Progress, and Prospects of the Republic of Texas*, p. 146.

[38] By 1901 the fortifications of Fort San Jacinto included a mining casemate, submarine-mining warehouse, and cable tanks. Mounted were eight 12-inch mortars, two 10-inch breech-loading rifles, two 4.7-inch rapid-fire guns, two 15-pounder and rapid-fire guns. At Fort Travis, there were two 8-inch breech-loading rifles and two 15-pounder rapid-fire guns. The armament of Fort Crockett was two 10-inch breech-loading rifles, two 15-pounder rapid-fire guns, and eight 12-inch mortars (U.S., Congress, House, *Report of the Chief of Engineers*, H. Ex. Doc. 2, 57th Cong., 1st Sess., 1901, p. 852).

and geology. Political and physical geography determined the locations for forts, while geology influenced the type of structures that could be built from the materials that were available for construction. With most of the materials of construction coming from the immediate area of any fort, military works, particularly along the land frontiers, were characteristically indigenous to the region in which they were built. There were no standard methods of building; techniques were adapted to the geology of the area, the expected service of the buildings, and the talents of the builders.

Having played its role in civilizing the wilderness, the military also had a spontaneous influence on the general development of communities in the entire state. For instance, the towns of Fort Worth, Fort Stockton, and Fort Davis all developed on or near the posts after which they were named and became county seats. San Angelo grew around Fort Concho, and Brackettville was laid out near Fort Clark.

Plate 10. Cavalry Barracks and Quartermaster Storehouse, Fort Clark, Kinney County (circa 1875)
Architect Unknown   Exterior View

Located near Brackettville, Fort Clark was established in 1852 as a link in the Rio Grande chain of defense. This cordon protected northern Mexico from the Rio Grande Indians residing in the United States—a stipulation of the Treaty of Guadalupe Hidalgo—and defended the El Paso–San Antonio road from the depredations of Mexicans and Indians.

The plan of Fort Clark was characteristic of posts along the land frontiers. Around a large parade were positioned officers' quarters and barracks. Behind these, various service buildings were located.

Like several other forts along the Rio Grande, Fort Clark was established on land that was leased; therefore, only temporary shelters were erected during

the early years. However, since the southern frontier was fixed by boundary, this ultimately became a permanent post. After the purchase of the land, construction on permanent stone buildings was begun. Among these was the Cavalry Barracks and Quartermaster Storehouse structure, distinguished by shingled dormers and the rough texture of limestone masonry. Windows were spanned by stone lintels, while openings for communication were spanned by carefully cut segmental arches.

With the purpose of the fort obviously changing over the years, it remained an active military base until 1946.

Plate 11. Officers' Row, Fort Davis, Jeff Davis County (1869–1882)
Wesley Merrit, Architect [?]   View Looking Southwest

Near Limpia Creek, in a canyon formed by metamorphic rocks, Fort Davis was first established in 1854 by Lt. Col. Washington Seawell. The location had been strategically selected to facilitate the protection of travelers traversing the El Paso–San Antonio road and to control the Comanche and Apache Indians. Abandoned during the Civil War, the post was reestablished in 1867 by Lt. Col. Wesley Merrit.

Erected under the supervision of Lieutenant Colonel Seawell, the first buildings had walls of pickets, roofs of thatching, and floors of earth or plank. However, before the fort was occupied by Confederates in 1861, several stone-walled shelters with thatched roofs had been erected.

After remaining deserted for five years, the post was reestablished, and an ambitious program of permanent stone construction was undertaken. Among

the buildings to be built wholly or partially of limestone from a nearby quarry were the officers' quarters on the west side of the parade. By 1870 four of these had been built of limestone, but the remainder were of adobe.

Although there was some variation of plans, basically each building along officers' row had a central hall with a room on each side. At the back of each were located a kitchen and other service structures.

Characteristic of the formality preferred by the military, all the buildings along the row on the parade side had Classical five-bay façades, comprised of a door and four windows. Each was fronted by a porch supported by six columns. Ornament was restrained, consisting of capitals and bases built up with moldings on the rectangular columns.

Plate 12. Officers' Quarters, Fort Davis (1885–1886)
View Looking Northwest

Lieutenant Colonel Merrit, in his reestablishment plans, had certainly visualized a post comprised of buildings of stone. However, building with masonry was slow and expensive. Consequently, to realize greater efficiency, adobe-block construction was adopted for most of the work.

Located north of the parade, away from the main formal line of quarters, this building was characteristic of the adobe technique employed at Fort Davis. The dried mud blocks were laid upon stone foundations. Supporting the blocks over the openings were wooden lintels,

bearing upon wooden jambs. When finished, the walls were plastered on both sides up to the plate line.

Although containing two stories, the plan was similar to the quarters along the parade: a central hall was flanked on either side by a large room. The single-story building at the back contained the kitchen.

Among the largest posts in the West, Fort Davis remained active until 1891. By that time, more than fifty buildings had been erected, including quarters for twelve companies. In 1963 the post became a national historic site.

Architecture of Enterprise

THE CIVIL WAR abruptly interrupted the nineteenth-century cultural era and period of development. Although Texas was not marred by the warfare that devastated other regions of the South, the growth of the state was seriously retarded. Immigration ceased; many houses and farms were abandoned. During the dark years of conflict, most available money was spent on the futile war effort; construction other than that for utility was curtailed.

Inevitably, the brief boom calling for public edifices that had occurred in the 1850's was ended by the opening of hostilities. During the war and afterward, during early Reconstruction years, very little new public building was done, while much existing work fell into disrepair. Perhaps the state of civic buildings epitomized the condition of architecture; in 1873 the miserable condition of Texas courthouses and jails prompted Governor Edmund J. Davis to suggest to the legislature that the state take charge of county buildings.

Near the end of Reconstruction, the economy on which pretentious architecture was dependent gained momentum. Although money was scarce immediately after the war, another wave of settlers seeking new opportunities commenced rolling into the state from other parts of the United States and from abroad. At the same time, industry, which had been given some impetus during the war,[1] began developing, as capital arrived in the state. With growing population and increasing exploitation of resources, a prosperous land was emerging to stimulate new building.

Summarily, the economy of Texas during the last decades of the nineteenth century was dissimilar to that of the Far West and only partially resembled parts of the Deep South. Unlike other sections of the South and West, there were no mineral bonanzas to lure those seeking an El Dorado. Although low-grade ore was processed near Jefferson and Rusk, there was no abundance of fuel for large iron smelters like those

[1] An act, passed in 1863 by the legislature, encouraged the erection of establishments for the production of iron, firearms, nitre, sulphur, and powder, and the processing of cotton, by awarding 320 acres of land for every $1,000 invested (see J. M. Morphis, *History of Texas from Its Discovery and Settlement*, p. 476).

of Birmingham, Alabama; although copper fields in Knox and King counties interested a few investors, there were no mines like those at Butte, Montana; although there was brief excitement around Brownwood and Fort Davis, there were no gold and silver lodes like those at Virginia City, Nevada, or Leadville, Colorado. "Black Gold" would not become a bonanza until the turn of the century.

Within the nineteenth century, the real prosperity of the Lone Star State derived, first, from cattle, cotton, and other agricultural products, such as rice and sugar cane; second, from industry. But the development of agriculture and industry required equipment to process and manufacture raw materials, and roads on which to move products. Buildings were required to house men and machines, and bridges were required to span wide rivers.

Among the first industries in the Republic and the antebellum state had been those that produced materials for the erection of buildings. By mid-century, in regions of East Texas where suitable clay was available, enterprising contractors had established numerous brickyards to fulfill needs for permanent building materials. Although on the primitive frontier most wooden materials were fabricated by hand—with whipsaws and axes—as early as 1834 one visitor reported that oak and yellow-pine lumber was being produced by a steam sawmill located at Harrisburg.[2] In 1837 a sawmill was also in operation south of San Augustine, and in 1850 Marshall was supplied with lumber from a steam-powered mill located north of town. As was often the case, the Harrisburg and Marshall steam engines also powered grist mills. Other mills were powered by animal-driven treads and water wheels.

In addition to mills and brickyards, cotton gins—the first of which evidently appeared in 1825[3]—became prominent on the agricultural scene of nineteenth-century Texas. The early gins were comprised of two separate structures, a gin house and a press. The former was a two-story frame work, housing on

Fig. 16. Anderson's Mill, south of Austin, Travis County. (Photo from T. U. Taylor Collection, Texas State Library, Austin)

the upper floor a Whitney gin stand, powered by horses, steam, or water. The lower level, which was open on three sides, contained machinery and storerooms.[4] Located near the ginned-cotton store, the press basically consisted of a framework containing a strongly braced wooden box, a block that fit into the box, and a large wooden screw twenty or more feet in height. Lint was compressed in the box by the block when the screw was turned down, and the bale was then tied with ropes. Turned by animal power, the mechanism was often sheltered by a roof that turned with the arms by which the screw was twisted. In the years prior to the Civil War, each planter commonly had a cotton gin, but, later, with the introduction of improved machinery and conveyor systems, ginning became a cooperative enterprise.

Structures housing the machinery for mills and gins, efficient in the use of building materials, were always strictly functional in form (fig. 16). The equipment and activities to be housed gave the enclosure

[2] *A Visit to Texas*, p. 74.
[3] George Louis Crocket, *Two Centuries in East Texas*, p. 93.

[4] Raymond E. White, "Cotton Ginning in Texas to 1861," *Southwestern Historical Quarterly* 61, no. 2 (October 1957): 260.

its shape. Characteristically, this honest expression produced interesting geometrical forms and massing, as in the cotton gin near Italy (plate 13).

As in other parts of the country, industrial structures, unless spectacular in magnitude, rated little esteem in Texas. Consequently, few records of their designs were made while they were active, and after they ceased to be productive they rapidly disappeared. It is indeed unfortunate that so few utility buildings and bridges from the nineteenth century have survived, and that those surviving examples are rapidly disappearing.

In the years following the Civil War—particularly the last two decades of the century—numerous bridges were erected across the rivers of the state, replacing the earlier ferries. Some were intended to carry pedestrians, equestrians, and wagons, but others were designed to support the huge "iron horses" and their trailing rolling stock. Although the first bridges were naturally of wood, later examples were commonly of iron, the components for which were prefabricated in eastern foundries and shipped to river-shore sites for assembly.

Like other utility works, bridges—lucid statements of technology—were spontaneous expressions of functionalism and were only occasionally decorated with unnecessary architectural details. Nevertheless, there was an inherent beauty in the logically conceived patterns of chords and diagonals of the trusses and in the voussoirs of arched structures. Although most bridges that were isolated in the country were designed without regard to the glorification of utility, others located near towns were sometimes decorated with interesting ornamental details. The philosophy of nineteenth-century bridge designers was summarized by Dennis Hart Mahan, an instructor at the U.S. Military Academy at West Point, where many who ultimately became civil engineers throughout the United States received their training:

The design and construction of a bridge should be governed by the same general principles as any other architectural composition. As the object of a bridge is to bear heavy loads, and to withstand the effects of one of the most destructive agents with which the engineer has to

Fig. 17. Waco suspension bridge, Waco, McLennan County (1868–1870). Thomas M. Griffith, engineer. (Photo by Gildersleeve; from the Texas State Historical Association, Austin)

contend, the general character of its architecture should be that of strength. It should not only be secure, but to the apprehension [*sic*] appear so. . . . it should conform to the features of the surrounding locality, being more ornate and carefully wrought in its minor details in a city, and near buildings of a sumptuous style, than in more obscure quarters.[5]

This point of view was beautifully embodied in the bridge across the Brazos (1868–1870) at Waco (plate 14; fig. 17). A suspension bridge supported by wire cables, this work was already dramatic by virtue of its structural form. Nonetheless, to further enhance the work, the brick piers that thrust skyward supporting the thin cables were decorated with stringcourses, recesses, and other features resembling Medieval crenellations. Later, numerous other wire-cable suspension bridges were built in the state, but none was as spectacular or as ornate as the one at Waco.[6]

Prior to 1900, within the towns to which these ear-

[5] D[ennis] H[art] Mahan, *An Elementary Course in Civil Engineering*, p. 209. This book was one of numerous texts that Mahan wrote on architecture and engineering.
[6] For example, by the end of the century Hunt County had at least eight suspension bridges.

ly bridges furnished communication, commercial architecture reflected the stages of town development. In the wilderness, services to the public were occasionally offered from temporary shelters, such as tents or canvas and crude frame works; but after towns had been platted, giving the promise of population, enterprising individuals were soon at work surrounding the public square with mercantile houses, hotels, banks, and livery stables. In the early stages of growth, these were modestly scaled, one story, wood framed, and covered by metal or shingle gable roofs. The composition of the front was always symmetrical, with double doors opening at the center, on either side of which was usually a window, often in a projecting bay for display (plate 15).

Universally, gable roofs were disguised by wooden false fronts—in the West, the symbols representing houses of business. These provided identity: in addition to signs that were painted on the fronts, distinction was achieved by form and details. Geometrically, false fronts sometimes incorporated a simple rectangular panel, sometimes a stepped feature, but occasionally round or angular forms (plate 16). While many of the false fronts were plain, embellished only with simple moldings, others were more elaborate, with interesting details. In an anonymous commercial building in the German community of Round Top, for example, spontaneous but pleasing proportions were enhanced by attenuated Classical details (plate 17). Like settlers' log cabins, these early structures belong to no particular time; with minor variations in details that may have occasionally reflected changing tastes in style, they were found in every town. Late in the century, in West Texas, false-fronted buildings of wood enclosed public squares at the same time sophisticated iron and masonry structures were rising in the older centers of population. Unfortunately, time has dealt harshly with those early commercial buildings. Most are now ashes or dust, with the few remaining to be found mostly in small, remotely located communities.

If a town's destiny were growth and prosperity, the early ephemeral commercial buildings were consistently replaced with more durable ones of native stone or locally manufactured brick. The early masonry structures usually reflected aspirations for some architectural distinction. Generally of one or two stories—although three occasionally appear—these were modest in scale, often dignified in composition, and commonly embellished with simple ornamental details. In an anonymous Chappell Hill commercial building (late nineteenth century), for instance, a conservative but positive desire for character was revealed by a decorative brick cornice that accents an otherwise straightforward and handsome design (plate 18). In another anonymous commercial building, in Belton (late nineteenth century), the pronounced arches and a simple coping relieved the austerity of massive stone walls (plate 19).

During the third quarter of the century, in the commercial centers of the state, masonry fronts, commonly three or more bays wide, had openings that were sometimes spanned with lintels but more often with arches, providing real as well as apparent strength. In any case, French doors closed the openings on the ground level. When round arches were used, fanlight windows filled the semicircular part of the opening—the tympanum (plate 20). In Jefferson, and later in other towns, rhythmic arcades marked the commercial district. On the ground floor of the Planters' Bank (circa 1860), for example, multiple round arches, fanlights, and French doors were characteristic features (plate 21). Typically, the smaller upper-story openings were spanned with segmental arches. Frequently, as in the Jefferson Jimplicute Building (circa 1860), these openings were furnished with decorative iron window hoods, which were sometimes structural. The openings were then closed with double-hung windows (plate 22).

Like the wooden, false-fronted buildings of the Texas frontier, two-story bricks, three or four bays wide, belong to no particular period, but to a stage of town development. In the towns that had developed permanence and wealth, they were popular throughout the latter part of the nineteenth century. Representative in the southern section of the state was the business building of Arnim and Lane (1886) in Flatonia (plate 23).

The plans for these commercial buildings were all similar and straightforward. Through the center of the first-floor space there was usually a row of columns —generally cast iron—supporting the second floor (plate 24). Since the space was long and narrow, counters and shelves were arranged parallel to the longitudinal walls to permit satisfactory circulation and to allow light to penetrate. At the back of the space was a stairway leading to the second floor or, less often, as in Arnim and Lane's, to balconies.

Although interiors were similar, more individuality was preferred on the exterior. In response to tastes for opulence of owners of commercial buildings, masons ingeniously developed abstract decorative details and patterns, which were integral with the construction of the walls. This trend was epitomized in Columbus by a brick commercial building (1875), which had remarkable richness of surface (plate 25).

As was apparent around the public squares of many towns, the variations on the masonry decorative theme were virtually limitless. Although building massing, because of uniform building lots and common floor heights, was generally similar, individual character was developed in the different parts of the façade. In D'Hanis, alternating one- and two-story buildings were distinguished by the variations in openings and patterns of ornamentation of the cornices (plate 26). Additional fine examples of variations on themes of similar proportions appeared in the commercial section of Goliad (plate 27).

A regional character was also noteworthy among the variations in commercial design throughout the state. Through the materials that were used in construction, buildings commonly reflected their locality. On the one hand, in East Texas and along the Gulf Coast, stone was scarce but clay was plentiful; thus, brick was the predominant building material for permanent works—as exemplified by the business blocks of Jefferson and Columbus. On the other hand, the Limestone Belt, extending in a northerly-southerly direction through the center of the state, provided an inexhaustible supply of stone that could be easily quarried. In Jacksboro, by the end of the century, light-brown limestone from local quarries visually

unified the Jack County Courthouse (1885–1886) and many of the commercial buildings surrounding the public square and related them to their region (plate 28). At Glen Rose, Santa Anna, Lampasas, Seymour, and other Central Texas towns in the limestone region, stone walls of county and commercial buildings also frequently reflected the geology of the locality. Although the buildings were similar in composition to their brick counterparts, detail was often rendered with originality and strength (plate 29). Moreover, the stonework on these commercial fronts, which were also usually arcaded, was often finely cut, although other walls were of rubble.

In other regions, architectural character was influenced by builders of various national origins—immigrants brought not only their own social habits but also their skills and architectural customs. Near the southern extremity of the state, a German, Heinrich Portscheller, left a strong imprint on Lower Rio Grande Valley architecture. By 1883, Portscheller had immigrated to Mexico and then to Roma–Los Saenz, Texas, after having served in the Prussian and Mexican armies.[7] A master builder, he planned buildings, manufactured brick for them, and either performed or directed the execution of the work. Using rubbed or cut bricks, he decorated his work with beautiful Classical profiles. Both the Knights of Columbus Hall (1884) and the Guerra Building (1885) of Roma exemplify the dignified regionalism inspired by this talented German artist and craftsman (plates 30, 31). Other examples of this style appearing along the Rio Grande were the post office in Rio Grande City and Saint Peter's Church in Laredo.

German immigrants also left their imprints on the character of architecture in other areas of the state. Traditionally excellent masons, they built with familiar techniques in locations where stone was available. While distinguished by a fine quality of workmanship, masonry walls commonly remained plain. But, to satisfy a general urge to versify, ornamentation

[7] Eugene George, Jr., Photo-Data Book, Tex-3136, Historic American Buildings Survey, Library of Congress, Washington, D.C.

was applied to the slight features, providing a lacy delicacy to many structures, as in the Dienger store in Boerne (plate 32). One of the foremost examples of the finesse of craftsmanship and decoration of which the German talent was capable was the White Elephant Saloon in Fredericksburg (plate 33).

Areas of Texas populated by Anglo-Americans reflected architectural trends of the East Coast cities of the United States. Building technology and artistic taste followed patterns of development apparent in the established cultural and commercial centers of the nation. However, distance and communication naturally created a time lag for changing fashions in Texas.

While wood and masonry business buildings were rising in many remote Texas towns, the urban centers of the United States were employing iron. Throughout the East and Midwest, in the decades between 1850 and 1880, iron had become a popular material for new commercial blocks. The structural advantages of cast and wrought iron had been proven earlier in mill buildings and in military work; compared to wood and stone, iron was, of course, very strong. Iron beams were capable of wide spans, and iron columns of a relatively small cross-sectional area could support heavy loads. Moreover, obviously incombustible, iron construction was at first believed to be fireproof. However, this assumption ultimately proved fallacious; although iron was incombustible, intense heat drastically deformed structural members, causing collapse of walls and floors.

The visual appeal of cast iron, which made it popular from an aesthetic point of view, lay in its plasticity. It could be cast into an infinite variety of ornamental forms, satisfying growing tastes for opulence. Entire fronts for commercial buildings could easily be prefabricated with profuse details. Since these decorative components were mass-produced in standard forms, they were economical and could be shipped to various parts of the country.

Eastern manufacturers found the growing Lone Star State to be a good market for iron products. The appeal of the material to Texans was apparent in the advertisements of the foundries. In 1858 a builder's foundry advertised in the *Texas Almanac*:

IRON FRONTS AND BUILDING WORK
in all its varieties, furnished at the
shortest notice . . .
Iron Fronts of any design, . . .
Caps and Bases for Pilasters and Columns,
Brackets for Cornices
Enriched, Mouldings and Ornaments. . . .[8]

Later, an iron works from Philadelphia advertised in the *Galveston Daily News*:

Ornamental iron works in
The largest assortment to be found
in the United States, all of which are
executed with the express view of
pleasing the taste, while they combine
all the requisites of beauty and
substantial construction.[9]

Although there were eventually numerous foundries in Texas that produced building components,[10] many iron fronts were imported. In 1866 the façade for J. W. Jockusch's new four-story building at the corner of the Strand and Center Street in Galveston was shipped from Boston.[11] Others came from Baltimore and Saint Louis, and by 1879 a rising three- or four-story building with an iron front was not an unusual sight in Galveston and Houston.

In Texas the early use of cast iron was dependent upon developments in transportation. Galveston and Houston, connected to eastern foundries by the sea route, led the state in iron construction. The inland cities, however, had to await efficient transportation

8 *Texas Almanac*, 1858.
9 *Galveston Daily News*, August 24, 1870, p. 1.
10 Within the state, the Lee Foundry in Galveston and the Phoenix Iron Works in Houston were manufacturers. As early as 1869, the Lee Foundry produced the front for a building at the corner of Tremont and Market streets in Galveston (*Galveston Daily News*, August 21, 1869, p. 3). The foundry in Houston advertised iron fronts in James Burke, Jr., *Burke's Texas Almanac and Immigrants' Handbook*. Later, in Fort Worth, the Vulcan Foundry and Iron Works produced what was claimed to be the "HEAVIEST IRON FRONT ever made south or west of St. Louis" (*Fort Worth Daily Democrat-Advocate*, March 16, 1882, p. 4).
11 According to S. O. Young, *A Thumb-Nail History of the City of Houston, Texas*, p. 50, the first iron front in the state was on a four-story building in Houston, erected by J. R. Morris around 1859.

from the manufacturing centers. Because of weight and shipping costs, iron construction in such cities as Fort Worth and Dallas was not practical until the railroads arrived.

By the seventies and eighties, the cast-iron front was regarded as a symbol of progress. Newspapers of the period were filled with announcements of new iron-fronted buildings, most of which were acclaimed for ornateness and beauty, as well as the community improvement that they represented. A Fort Worth reporter, when lauding the rapid progress of the "Queen City," relative to competitor Dallas, wrote, ". . . the railroad had been in Dallas *two years* before it could boast of the first iron front."[12] By 1890 the streets of Dallas, Fort Worth, and Houston were lined with ironwork, with details derived, usually, from Classical architecture of past ages.

Available by order from catalogs, iron building components were produced in many forms, some of which were inspired by tastes for elegance, others by functionalism. Although cast iron, as a material, had unique expressive qualities, popular taste preferred forms imitative of ancient stone architectural details. However, when functionalism prevailed, it was cast into simple, logical forms. On the ground floors of commercial buildings, the need for large plate-glass windows to allow light to penetrate interiors and to provide for the display of goods required minimal structural obstruction. In deference to these requirements, columns were thin, with simple lines. In the stories above, however, where there was less need for transparency, building owners demanded details that would delight the eye. This required opulence was fulfilled by ornamental columns, capitals, bases, bosses, brackets, and finials, arranged in horizontal compositions, derived from the Renaissance architecture of Europe. Many of these details were standardized and, if the building was more than two stories, all the levels above the ground floor generally received a uniform treatment. Then the building was boldly capped by a projecting terminal feature, usually manufactured from galvanized sheet iron.

Galvanized iron, adaptable for molding into various

complexities of detail, was ideal for cornices of commercial buildings. Light metal components, with details patterned after the monumental cornices of the Renaissance, created impressions of massiveness and beauty. Terminating not only iron fronts, but also those of wood and stone, these crowning metal works were generally symmetrical in composition. In the center was a vertical projection into which was often stamped the name of the owner of the building and often the date of construction (plate 34). Only on buildings at street intersections, where the identifying feature was placed on the corner, was there often deviation from this practice (plate 35).

The technique of fabricating ornamental work from galvanized sheet iron was thoroughly exploited during the years when cast iron was ascending in popularity. For nonstructural work, components manufactured from thin metal sheets were economical to produce, light to transport, and easy to install. It was found that the entire facing for buildings could be easily manufactured from thin sheet metal (plate 36).

Manufacturers discovered that sheet iron had virtually limitless possibilities in appeal to the taste and thrift of builders. Stamped panels with patterns imitative of brick or rough stonework often appeared on frame commercial buildings facing public squares in rural communities, if the owner could not or would not afford masonry. Other times, stamped panels with a variety of geometrical designs were used (plate 37). In addition, stamped panels, both plain and with elaborate decorative patterns, were manufactured for finishing interior walls and ceilings. In 1869 the *Galveston Daily News* announced that these had been lately invented, and that they were "fitted for every kind of decoration in color, . . . combining with lightness and durability, artistic and ornamental effect, at a comparatively small cost."[13]

Texas Germans also found iron to be suitable for their tastes. Galvanized-iron cornices were commonly employed to decorate wood and stone structures (plate 38). But cast and galvanized iron was also employed

[12] *Fort Worth Daily Democrat*, October 1, 1876, p. 4.

[13] *Galveston Daily News*, February 21, 1869, p. 4.

for entire store fronts in immigrant communities (plate 39). For the most part, iron in its various forms was used for façades in manners similar to applications for buildings in other parts of the state.

While the designs of iron cornices and fronts that were used in German communities certainly revealed the assimilation of Anglo-American technique, the enclosures around balconies and porches revealed more of the quality of decorative character that was so admired by the Germans (plate 40). Rather than casting iron into forms imitative of heavy stone ornament, they imparted into the material—some of which they themselves manufactured—a delicacy that was much in the spirit of the style of the wooden ornamentation that appeared on their houses and commercial buildings.

Although used on new commercial blocks in small communities throughout the state until around 1900, the fashion of building entire fronts with sheet and cast iron—never universally accepted—declined in the cities near the end of the century. The standardization of mass production could not completely satisfy the demand for individuality and opulence that prosperous times had initiated. Moreover, the fireproofing of structural metal required that it be protected from heat and flames with brick, stone, terra cotta, and other such material—a prevailing practice in high-rise buildings by the 1890's—thus, spontaneously producing outward designs in masonry. If this had not been sufficient reason to cause a decline in popularity, changing architectural fashions would certainly have contributed to making iron unfashionable as a material selected to fulfill aesthetic needs.

If decisions regarding the decorative use of iron depended upon trends and taste—as well as economy—the strength of the material assured structural applications. Since thin iron columns allowed large expanses of glass, behind which merchants could arrange their displays of goods to entice prospective buyers, builders frequently employed thin cast-iron columns on ground floors of commercial buildings. This practice developed and continued throughout the latter part of the century, despite the impression of weakness or lack of apparent support created by col-

umns with small cross-sectional area under ponderous masonry fronts, designed as if they were to bear on a heavy base. Indeed, the structural use of cast iron in storefront design continued in both the cities and the rural areas of the state, regardless of the architectural style of the upper stories. This approach to storefront design was, of course, quite consistent with that of other parts of the country.

Texas builders, then, followed eastern cities in modes of building—just as the eastern cities looked to Europe. Local success or progress was evaluated by comparison of Texas buildings with those in the established cultural centers of other states. Exemplifying this judgment, for instance, in 1869, about a large jewelry store under construction in Galveston, it was written, ". . . in completeness of finish and style of architecture, [it] will probably be unsurpassed by any in New Orleans."[14] These same values were later expressed by others, among them a Weatherford reporter, who wrote that the stone and brick buildings around the square "would be an ornament to New York City."[15]

The fulfillment of demands for sophistication to compare with buildings in eastern cities brought various historical architectural styles into the state. Among these was the Italianate style, popular at mid-century in the cultural centers and evidently spread by various catalogs and publications, such as *City Architecture*, one of the stated objectives of which was "to assist the development of taste for ornamental building."[16] The designs that were illustrated were adaptations of the street architecture of the Italian cities of Rome, Florence, and Venice. Quite in the spirit of these illustrations, numerous commercial buildings appeared in Texas with Florentine or Venetian arches, brackets, heavy cornices, and pilasters with Classical orders. By the 1860's Galveston had three- and four-story buildings in this mode along the famous Strand and along Tremont Street, and during the

14 Ibid., July 9, 1869, p. 3.
15 *Fort Worth Daily Gazette*, April 25, 1884, p. 3.
16 M. Field, *City Architecture: Designs for Dwelling Houses, Stores, Hotels, etc.*, preface.

1870's and 1880's this fashionable style spread to other business centers of the state.

Among other popular fashions was the Second Empire style, which had been imported to the East from the France of Napoleon III and was used as early as 1862 in commercial work in New York City.[17] Throughout the populated areas of the Lone Star State, mansard roofs—the dominant hallmark of the mode—were familiar sights to travelers seeking overnight accommodations. Since this style was adaptable to buildings on various scales, mansarded roofs crowned both the hotels with domestic character in small communities—typified decades earlier by the antebellum Greek Revival hostelries—and the large commercial establishments in cities. Built with walls of grey limestone, the El Paso Hotel in Fort Worth (1877, burned 1891) had three stories in the Second Empire mode, a style, according to a contemporary, that was "popular and elegant."[18] A mansard roof with dormers—also features of the Second Empire style—likewise covered the three-story Southern Hotel (circa 1879) in Llano (plate 41). Although the popularity of the fashion had declined in Texas, as late as 1885 a mansard roof appeared on the new Ellis Hotel, a large four-story edifice in Fort Worth.

Near the end of the century, other stylistic forms were also seen in hotels and other commercial work. Among these, the spindles and gingerbread of the Eastlake style—named after the prominent English tastemaker—which characterized so many residences in the 1880's and 1890's appeared on the adobe-walled Annie Riggs Hotel (1900–1902) in the southwestern town of Fort Stockton (plate 42).

Yet other styles and romantic mixtures of details appeared in the commercial work of the thriving cities of the state, such as Houston and Fort Worth (plate 43). Epitomizing the expression of the Romantic was the Joseph H. Brown Wholesale Grocery in Fort Worth (1885–1886), designed by Eckel and Mann, architects from Saint Louis—a large sandstone building decorated with a potpourri of details, such as tur-

[17] Winston Weisman, "Commercial Palaces of New York: 1845–1875," *Art Bulletin* 36, no. 4 (December 1954): 296.
[18] *Fort Worth Daily Democrat*, March 25, 1877, p. 4.

Fig. 18. Perspective of the Bankers' and Merchants' National Bank, Dallas, Dallas County (circa 1890). (*Frank Leslie's Illustrated*, September 27, 1890, p. 4; photo from the Library of Congress)

rets, couchant lions, and Corinthian columns. The T. H. Scanlan Building in Houston (1885) was in the style of the street architecture of Paris.

Significant among the other styles was the Romanesque Revival, with its multiple ranges of round arches (fig. 18). In many Texas towns, arcades, stacked one above the other, characterized commercial buildings of various magnitudes (plate 44). However, out of context with the heavy arches of the Romanesque, thin iron supports and lintels were typically employed on the ground floor for openness. Of course, the most unified designs resulted when the arches were used throughout (plate 45).

Bankers were among the builders seeking prominence and distinction of architectural character. Although there was consistency of style between banks and other commercial buildings, a different quality resulted from different aesthetic and functional requirements. Banks were usually more substantial in appearance, as if to symbolize permanence and security. Since there was little need for openness for display on the ground floor, less glass was required, allowing more freedom in developing heavy bases of masonry that were consistent in design with the upper stories.

Seeking to assert their architectural image, bankers preferred prominent locations on street corners, where buildings would be readily accessible from two avenues. Corner entrances were developed in response to this location and were often emphasized with turrets overhead. In addition to forming a visual transition between two street façades, this situation called attention to the corner access (plate 46).

As with other commercial establishments, Texas banks generally reflected the popularity of the historic styles but often revealed a robust regional quality through the use of native materials. Although the First National Bank of Stephenville (1889) was characterized by Classical details that might have been found in any of the other states, the use of local building stone produced a vernacular aspect. In the Bank of Fredericksburg—decorated by popular cupola, finials, and balcony—the use of native materials also produced a provincial character (plate 47).

However, it is evident that provincialism was not a conscious goal of builders. Rather, they were eager to indicate cultural advancement through sophistication of design. Texans were justly proud of the materials that they quarried and manufactured, but they preferred to use them in a manner that was consistent with developments in the commercial centers of the country. Thus, in many banks in the state, regional overtones gave way to the use of materials to erect structures that would have been at home in eastern and midwestern cities. For example, the N. R. Royall Bank in Palestine (1899) was a fine brick work in Romanesque Revival—the style popularized by a great Boston architect, Henry Hobson Richardson (plate 48). Round arches, but under a mansard roof, also, characterized the Bay City Bank (1900–1901) in Bay City, another edifice with refined details and materials (plate 49).

Akin to the buildings erected solely for business were the opera houses, built either by individuals or by associations. As symbols of cultural progress, theaters were generally highly esteemed by communities—indeed, virtually every well-established town boasted an opera house. While local talent often performed, towns that were connected with the East by ship or rail frequently enjoyed talented actors, the minstrels, and the pomp and pageantry that accompanied them.

In small communities, the opera house was multifunctional. It was generally a two-story structure, with the auditorium on the upper level and two or more commercial spaces for rental on the lower, similar to Crow's Opera House (circa 1890) in Stephenville (plate 50). A more elaborate arrangement of this scheme occurred in the Fort Worth Opera House (1881). J. J. Kane, architect, planned spaces for seven stores on the first floor, with an auditorium and a hall for the Knights of Pythias on the second.

As with other structures in the commercial district, the style of opera houses reflected popular trends and occasionally the endemic influence. However, their character often derived from styles that appear to have been selected to fulfill associations with drama and romance. Expressive of this idea were the picturesque features of the Grand Opera House (1891) of Uvalde (plate 51).

Thus, in the years following the Civil War, in these opera houses and other architecture of enterprise were seen the expressions of strong demands for architectural distinction. Despite the fact that the industrial structures were straightforward and functional in form, the desire for character was manifested in trends that conformed to those found in the commercial centers of other parts of the country. Nevertheless, there were significant regional expressions, originating as a result of foreign immigration and of the spontaneous use of native materials. Regardless of sources of influence, while these comparatively modest examples were rising in communities scattered across the state—most of which had an agrarian economy—architecture demonstrative of considerable material and cultural attainment was rising in the growing commercial and financial centers of the Lone Star State.

Plate 13. Cotton Gin, near Italy, Ellis County (late 1800's)
Architect Unknown   View of Storage Unit, Wagon Runway, and Ginnery

During the latter half of the nineteenth century, numerous mechanical improvements were made in the process of ginning that had been developed by Eli Whitney in 1792. After the Civil War large mechanically powered gins, located in towns, replaced the small animal-powered plantation gins.[1] At the same time efficient methods of compressing and storing cotton were developed. To eliminate manual labor, belts were developed to move seed cotton from wagon to gin. By 1884 a mechanical pneumatic system of conveyance was developed by R. S. Munger, a Texan. With this system, cotton was conveyed to storage and to gins by air suction developed with fans.

[1] See Raymond E. White, "The Texas Cotton Ginning Industry, 1860–1900," *Texana* 5, no. 4 (Winter 1967): 346.

Typical of nineteenth-century industrial works, the forms for buildings housing cotton and machinery were developed to efficiently contain the required functions within. In this cotton gin near Italy cotton was conveyed from the wagon runway in the center either to the octagonal storage unit on the left or to the gin on the right. If it was to be stored, the cotton was conveyed to the cupola, then to separate storage bins below. Since each bin was filled through a conduit that rotated in the cupola, a radial arrangement of partitions was used, requiring the octagonal enclosure.

The buildings containing the equipment for processing cotton were commonly two stories, with the gin stands and condensers above and the power machinery below. A linear arrangement of machinery in batteries required the long, narrow building.

Plate 14. Waco Suspension Bridge, Waco, McLennan County (1868–1870)
Thomas M. Griffith, Engineer   View from the West Bank of the Brazos River

In the fall of 1866, the state legislature granted to the Waco Bridge Company—an organization of Waco businessmen—a twenty-five–year charter for the construction of a bridge across the Brazos River, and in 1868 stocks were sold to raise the initial funds to finance the project.[1] Later that year, after negotiations by John T. Flint, president of the bridge company, Thomas M. Griffith arrived to design the bridge. A suspension structural concept was selected because of strength and economy. The structural efficiency of cables in tension reduced the amount of required material. This was an important consideration not only for savings in the initial cost, but also for transportation, since the material was shipped from New York to Galveston by ship, thence to Millican by rail, and finally by wagon from Millican to Waco, the latter a distance of over one hundred miles.[2]

The structure spanned 475 feet. A roadbed of yellow pine was carried on trusses supported by fourteen wire-rope cables, each one and a half inches in diameter, manufactured by John A. Roebling and Son, Trenton, New Jersey, engineers of the famous Brooklyn Bridge

(1869–1883). Although Griffith had originally specified cut stone for the towers supporting these cables, brick was used because of economy. Remodelings have removed picturesque Medieval decorative features resembling crenellations. In addition, decorative recesses in the surface have been filled, and the masonry has been covered with stucco.

Maximum toll rates for crossing over the bridge were set by the charter. "For each wagon, cart, carriage or other vehicle drawn by more than two horses or other animals, not more than twenty cents per wheel and five cents for each animal by which the same is drawn; and when the same is drawn by two animals or less, ten cents per wheel and five cents for each animal; for each animal and rider, ten cents; for each loose horse, mule jack or jennet, five cents; for each loose animal of the cattle kind, five cents; for each foot passenger, five cents; for each sheep, hog or goat, three cents; and from all citizens of McLennan County, one-half of the above rates."[3]

In 1889, in response to pressures from the citizens requesting a free bridge, the McLennan County Commissioners purchased the bridge for $75,000. It was then immediately sold to the city of Waco for $1.00, after which it became toll free.

[1] Roger Norman Conger, *Highlights of Waco History*, p. 52.
[2] Roger Norman Conger, "The Waco Suspension Bridge," *Texana* 1, no. 3 (Summer 1963): 193.

[3] Cited in ibid., pp. 195–196.

Plate 15. Anonymous Commercial Building, New Ulm, Austin County (late 1800's)
Architect Unknown   View

Although evidently built late in the century, this building is a fine example of the type of false front that appeared in the early development of every postbellum frontier community in Texas. A hallmark of the western frontier, the stepped front was trimmed at the edges with simple moldings. As with many wooden-framed commercial buildings, the sides were covered with vertical boards and battens, an economical finish; the front was covered with milled siding, more expensive, but more attractive. The composition of the placement of the openings was typically symmetrical, although a single bay window and the simple rectangular opening were unusual. While the building cannot be classified according to any specific historical style, the rectangular transom comprised of numerous panes recalls Greek Revival windows.

Plate 16. Anonymous Commercial Buildings, New Ulm, Austin County (late 1800's)
Architects Unknown   View

Since the front of a commercial building was the primary advertisement for the business within, variations
of form, although often subtle, were common along the
street. As in this composition, each front had distinction,
yet the repetition of geometry and materials as well as a
continuous porch unified several buildings along a row.

Although they vary in design, each of these buildings

was a common type. The dominant front on the right has
the usual symmetrical arrangement of double entry
doors and bay windows. To the left, the structure of secondary dominance also has symmetrical composition but
simple openings. The smaller units between, however, because of their confined size, are asymmetrical in design.

Plate 17. Anonymous Commercial Building, Round Top, Fayette County (late 1800's)
Architect Unknown   View

Interesting details, along with satisfactory proportions, make this simple false-fronted building distinctive. Although the details are quite simple, a Classical point of view is suggested by boards and moldings that were used to build up parts representing pilasters, capitals, cornice, and pediment. The composition of the front is typical. Bay windows, paneled below the openings, flank the access. Unfortunately, original doors, windows, and porch are now missing.

Plate 18. Anonymous Commercial Building, Chappell Hill, Washington County (late 1800's)
Architect Unknown   View

The one-story masonry commercial buildings that replaced the first wooden, false-fronted buildings in most
frontier towns were probably similar to this structure; a
large rectangular front with openings containing French
doors was characteristic. Although the use of French
doors provided good ventilation in the hot summer
months, their use was evidently also in deference to the
need for light—the latter is suggested by the fact that
openings spanned by lintels or arches and containing

French doors were also common in the northern states.

Craftsmen were often remarkably adept at creating ornamental details. Cornices were enhanced by corbeled
brickwork, the visual strength of which unified the façade. Above the cornice was a panel, which at one time
probably contained the identity of the business or owner.
The canopy, apparently a twentieth-century addition,
ruins an otherwise attractive front.

Plate 19. Anonymous Commercial Building, Belton, Bell County (late 1800's)
Architect Unknown   View from Southwest

Thick walls of stone enclosed this commercial building. Openings were spanned by round arches with keystones and voussoirs that were carefully cut to produce structural strength. Because of expense—and perhaps also because of a shortage of skilled stone dressers—the walls were laid up with rough stones and irregular joints. Interestingly, the desire for finesse became apparent, possibly at a later date, when the front of the building was stuccoed and marked with linear impressions to represent the joints of cut-stone work.

Plate 20. Anonymous Commercial Building, 107 Austin Street, Jefferson, Marion County (circa 1860)
Architect Unknown   Detail of Arcade

Located near the heart of the early commercial district, this building demonstrates a typical use of French doors and fanlights in nineteenth-century business structures. Two stories high, the building has a three-bay front, with round-arched openings on the ground level and segmental-arched windows on the second story. The ornamental fanlight muntins are cast iron. As on most French doors of the period, each leaf was double paneled at the bottom and glazed above.

Plate 21. Planters' Bank, Austin and Walnut Streets, Jefferson, Marion County (circa 1860)
Architect Unknown   View from North

Located near the turning basin of Big Cypress Bayou and erected by John Speake, a promoter, realtor, and contractor, this was a fine example of commercial architecture built in small but growing towns during the 1860's, 1870's, and 1880's. It had the usual ground-floor arcade, with openings containing French doors and fanlight transoms. Except for a row of columns through the center of the building, the ground floor was entirely open. The second floor was at first used for storage but later divided into offices.

During the early years the building was occupied by merchants Samuel Sterne and Isaac Pinsky. In 1868 the building housed a private bank and forwarding house, and then in 1889 it contained the National Bank of Jefferson. At present the building is unoccupied. The structure on the right is the Red River warehouse (circa 1860), architect unknown.

Plate 22. Jefferson Jimplicute Building, 112 Vale Street, Jefferson, Marion County (circa 1860)
Architect Unknown   View from West

Although remodeling has altered the left bay, all the openings on the ground level were spanned by lintels and originally filled with French doors. As was common in two-story commercial buildings, segmental arches spanned the openings on the second floor.

While there are indications that they may have appeared on other buildings, the ornamental wrought-iron balcony enclosures and supports appear today in Jefferson only on this building and the Planters' Bank. These recall the ornamental iron work so characteristic of buildings in New Orleans and were probably shipped by steamboat to Jefferson from the Crescent City. In neither building were they functional.

At the top center of the front appears a boss in the form of a star. Many nineteenth-century buildings have required stabilization with rods attached to the floor or roof structural members running the length of the building. The boss anchored the rod and retained the front.

Plate 23. Arnim and Lane Building, Flatonia, Fayette County (1886)
Architect Unknown   Exterior View

This was a fine example of the brick commercial architecture of the latter part of the nineteenth century. Noteworthy were the use of pilasters and the relief of the arches, producing contrasting shadow patterns to relieve the austerity of flat surface. As with many buildings from this period, detail was restrained, yet distinctive.

Plate 24. Arnim and Lane Building, Flatonia
Interior View of Store Looking toward the Entry

This fine nineteenth-century mercantile still retains its original character on the interior. The materials were characteristic. The ceiling was finished with wooden boards with grooved edges, although the use of stamped metal was also common at this time in other buildings. Walls were plastered and floors were pine. Supported by rods attached to the overhead framing, the mezzanine was enhanced at the edges with panels and fine wooden moldings, revealing the pride of craftsmen in their work. The cast-iron columns through the center were enhanced with ornamental capitals and bases.

Plate 25. E. M. Ehrenwerth Building, 1120 Milam Street, Columbus, Colorado County (1875)
Architect Unknown   View

The trend toward opulence in commercial buildings during the late seventies is well expressed in this façade, distinctively built of brick. Contributing to the richness of detail was the brick corbeling near the cornice and below the semicircular window hoods. The designer intended to create the impression of rusticated stonework by forming blocks and joints with patterns of brickwork. The pilasters on both floors and the voussoirs on the first floor were then given a smooth coat of stucco to complete the representation of stone.

Parts of the details are now missing. Originally, the semicircular panels at the parapet were trimmed with brick. It is also evident that there was a balcony, to which the two center second-story openings provided access.

Plate 26. Commercial Row, D'Hanis, Medina County (late 1800's)
Architects Unknown   View

The builders of these blocks developed subtle distinctions between structures by slight variations of ornamental details and openings, although less pretentious than much nineteenth-century commercial work. In each front, detail was varied in pattern and complexity. In the two-story buildings at the left the openings were spanned with lintels; in the center, segmental arches of polychromatic brick spanned the openings; and on the right, round arches with molded archivolts and pronounced imposts were employed. On the one-story buildings on the far right, both belonging to the same owner, contrasting features call attention to the name.

Plate 27. Commercial Row, Goliad, Goliad County (late 1800's)
Architects Unknown   View from East

To develop character for these buildings, variety of detail and the plasticity of brick were exploited. In the bank on the left, vertical proportions, flanking towers, and prominent archivolts created romantic impressions of Medieval architecture. On other parts of this front, interest was developed in ornamental panels of brick and openings spanned with stilted arches. Although time and paint have deteriorated the original design, it is evident that additional interest emanated from the color and texture of the brick and stone. Although not so flamboyant, the two buildings on the right were also enriched with brick decoration. Corbeling, finials, pronounced arches, and contrasting patterns provided distinction. Yet, in all, a subtle unity results from uniform building width and similar floor levels.

Plate 28. First National Bank (1897) and Edward Eastburn Building (1898), Public Square, Jacksboro, Jack County
Architects Unknown   East Elevations

In communities located on the Limestone Belt, stone was frequently used in the erection of business buildings. It was readily quarried and could easily be cut to form attractive details. In the First National Bank, coursed ashlar, wide voussoirs, and an ornamental cornice produced a strong, if rather coarse, architectural statement—unfortunately, the contemporary remodeling does not favor the original design.

Greater finesse is apparent in the adjacent building. Bearing the first owner's name, a segmental pediment crowned a projecting feature, which stressed the entrance. Other refinement was apparent in smooth cut molding, consoles, and columns, all of which were emphasized by contrast with the rough texture of the stonework of the walls.

Plate 30. Knights of Columbus Hall, Roma–Los Saenz, Starr County (1884)
Architect Unknown   View

Dignity of composition and handsome proportions created a handsome work. Relief from the austerity of plain rectangular form is provided by pilasters adjacent to each opening, subtly modeled with brick. At points of access, these pilasters have capitals and bases, and over all openings appears a complete entablature—architrave, frieze, and cornice. The dentil courses on the roof cornice and cornices over the openings complement the Classical motif.

Plate 29. First National Bank, Barnard and Elm Streets, Glen Rose, Somervell County (1896)
Architect Unknown   View

Noteworthy for its robust native-stone details, this structure was erected by A. P. Humphreys. At first it housed a saloon on the ground floor. On the second floor was a hall, which served for lodge meetings and other public functions. In 1902 the First National Bank moved into the building and still occupies it.

Plate 31. Guerra Building, Main Plaza and Hidalgo Street, Roma–Los Saenz, Starr County (circa 1885) Heinrich Portscheller, Architect [?]   View

Like the Knights of Columbus Hall, the Guerra Building was a dignified composition. The formality of the regular rhythm of the second-story openings and the horizontal lines of the roof cornice unified the irregularity of the openings on the ground floor. Classical details, such as the roof cornice, were built with molded bricks, a technique of construction that was introduced into this region by Heinrich Portscheller.[1] The wrought-iron balcony was, of course, a somewhat delicate addition to an otherwise masculine statement.

[1] Historic American Buildings Survey, Tex 3129, Sheet 1.

Plate 32. Dienger Store Building, Boerne, Kendall County (1884)
Joseph Dienger, Builder   View

This building attests to the German tradition of fine craftsmanship in construction. Revealing the skill of German masons was the excellent workmanship in the walls, which, except for projecting lintels, had little relief. The quatrefoil decorative features, also common on many residences, contributed to the distinctive character.

Square columns, with capitals formed with wooden moldings, and jigsawn brackets were characteristic of much German architecture in Texas. The detail provided interest not only in profile but also in the play of light and shadows on the walls.

Plate 33. White Elephant Saloon, 242 East Main Street, Fredericksburg, Gillespie County (1888)
Architect Unknown   View from West

This interesting building, identified by the prominently framed sculpture, was marked by handsomely cut masonry, French doors, and elegant wrought-iron work. Although the building is now vacant, at one time the interior was certainly as attractive as the façade if, like other nineteenth-century saloons, it was enhanced by large plate-glass mirrors and a long bar with carved details and brass trim.

"White Elephant Saloons" appeared in several towns and cities of the state in addition to this German community, among them Denison, Waco, Fort Worth, and San Antonio. Acclaimed as "places of resort for gentlemen," all featured long mahogany or cherry wood bars, decorated with elaborately carved ornamental details, above which hung numerous mirrors.

Plate 34. C. E. Dilley Building, Palestine, Anderson County (1882)
Architect Unknown   View

On the front of this fine example of nineteenth-century commercial design, multiple materials were employed to obtain visual richness. Ground-floor columns were cast iron, window and door frames were wood, the cornice was sheet metal, and the second-floor façade was polychromatic stone and brick. Stone decoration accented the composition. The Lone Star, appearing here over the center second-story windows, was a common ornamental motif in nineteenth-century public buildings. Unfortunately, in several places, the crisp lines of precisely cut detail have yielded to deterioration from decades of exposure.

Plate 35. Masonic Hall, Calvert, Robertson County (late 1800's)
Architect Unknown   Overall View

Throughout the West during the latter part of the century, secret societies often erected business buildings and leased the commercial space on the ground floor, while retaining the upper story for the ceremonial hall and adjunct rooms. With this scheme, they had a revenue-producing space to pay for the hall. Corner lots were preferred, since convenient access to the hall could then be had from the side of the building.

Lodges followed the trends of other builders of commercial buildings. The ground-story façade was constructed with cast iron and glass, while the upper section was finished with stylish sheet metal, formed to imitate elaborate carved stone construction. This was distinct, yet economical in cost and easy to erect.

Plate 36. Baskin Building, First and Houston Streets, Cameron, Milam County (1891)
Architect Unknown   Overall View

Although erected near the end of the century, this building was also characteristic of many metal-fronted business houses appearing in the seventies and eighties. It had a typical three-part composition, consisting of the ground-story façade, middle section, and termination, or cornice. Supporting the second-floor front, thin cast-iron columns—bearing the foundry mark of "Mesker & Bro., St. Louis, Mo."—allowed the installation of large plate-glass display windows. Above this section the intent was to provide visual interest with elaborate details, which were fabricated from sheets of zinc.

While the building gives the appearance of only two stories, the first floor, which once housed a furniture dealer, had a balcony and mezzanine, creating, in fact, three stories. For several decades the top story housed telephone offices at the front and a funeral parlor at the back.

Plate 37. Commercial Row, Rochelle, McCulloch County (late 1800's)
Architects Unknown   View

Since ornamental work of galvanized iron was light, it was easy to transport to any section of the country. Consequently, prefabricated stamped sheets appeared on small commercial buildings in many remotely located communities. In these examples, under the sheet-metal cornice and finials, doors and plate-glass windows were framed with wood. The side walls of the buildings were set up with stone, obtained from a local source. However, on the front, where more refinement was desired, brick was used to trim the walls.

Plate 38. August Faltin Building, Comfort, Kendall County (1879)
Alfred Giles, Architect   View

A splendid stone-fronted building, this structure was marked by stilted arches with pronounced keystones over the openings. The light decorative detail, so loved by Germans, was provided on the porch by wooden balusters, moldings, and scrollwork. This porch was then capped by a sheet-metal cornice with prominent consoles.

The architect, Alfred Giles of San Antonio, designed numerous business houses in the southern region of the state and in northern Mexico. Included among these was the Soledad block on Alamo Plaza in his home town, where his office was at one time located.

Plate 40. Schultze Building, 115 Goliad Street, San Antonio, Bexar County (1891)
Architect Unknown   View from Southeast

Herman Schultze, a native of Berlin, Germany, came to Texas in the 1840's, and in 1864 he established a hardware business. In addition to this enterprise, he manufactured metal building components and installed metal roofing. Near the end of the century Schultze erected this handsome new building using local products. The cast-iron columns were founded at the Alamo Iron Works. Schultze, himself, produced the galvanized iron cornice and finials and the delicate wrought-iron ornament for the porch, which also extends along the side and back.

Plate 39. Felix Reinbach Building, 227 East Main, Fredericksburg, Gillespie County (1904)
Architect Unknown   View from Southeast

While built shortly after 1900, this building was characteristic of much nineteenth-century commercial architecture in the German communities of Texas. The straight-forward form of the thin columns on the first story was largely determined by structural function, although slight decoration appeared on the faces. Decorative galvanized-iron work was used to face the second-floor front and the cornice. As was common in German business buildings, the second floor of this structure contained living quarters.

Plate 41. Southern Hotel, Llano, Llano County (circa 1879)
Architect Unknown   View from Southeast

Many early visitors arriving in Llano by stagecoach were accommodated in this hostelry. Located on a corner diagonal from the courthouse, it was built by J. K. Finlay and John Goodman in the fashionable Second Empire style. Unfortunately, elaborate scrollwork on the columns and below the railings of the porch and balcony has been removed, detracting from the nineteenth-century elegance of the structure.

Plate 42. Annie Riggs Hotel, 301 South Main Street, Fort Stockton, Pecos County (1900–1902)
Architect Unknown   View of Entry

Built on a residential scale characteristic of many hotels in small towns, this hostelry had walls of adobe, a material indigenous to the region. The broad veranda sheltered the walls from the hot sun and provided a shady space where guests could congregate. At the turn of the century, applications of shingles in ornamental patterns similar to those decorating the far gable were also common in residential buildings throughout the state.

The first hotel in Fort Stockton, it was operated by Annie Riggs from 1902 until her death in the 1920's. At the back is an open courtyard, accessible from many of the rooms. In 1955 the heirs of Annie Riggs donated the structure to the Fort Stockton Historical Society, and it is now the Annie Riggs Memorial Museum.

96

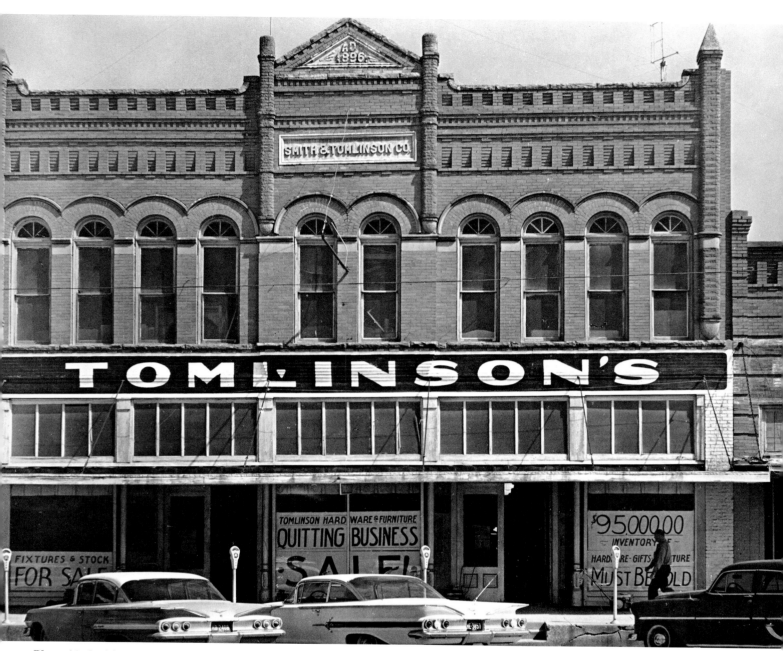

Plate 44. Smith and Tomlinson Company Building, East Elm Street, Hillsboro, Hill County (1896)
Architect Unknown   View from South

In round-arched style, this building was characterized by dignified composition and attractive details. For the upper part, brick was employed to create subtle ornamental patterns and textures. Used for imposts, coping, pinnacles, and window sills, stone accented the color and texture of the façade. On the pinnacles, rough-textured brick provided other interest. Although massive in appearance, the entire second-floor masonry façade was supported by light iron columns.

Plate 43. Anonymous Commercial Building, Main and Congress Streets, Houston, Harris County (1883)
Architect Unknown   View

Although remodeling has extensively altered the ground floor, this Victorian building yet retains much of its nineteenth-century picturesqueness. The ornamental front was built with brick and iron but has been stuccoed. As was characteristic of many commercial blocks located on corner lots, the turret, capped by a metal cone, provided a focal point and a visual transition between the two sides of the building. Pilasters with recessed panels, stringcourses, and other decorative features provided additional interest. Enhanced with small panes of stained glass, the window transoms were other noteworthy details.

Plate 45. C. Eckhardt and Sons Building, Yorktown, DeWitt County (circa 1895)
Architect Unknown   View

This was a fine example of the Romanesque Revival style. Brick was used to turn the arches and to form decorative panels, while stone was employed for window sills and to terminate the rectangular pinnacles—both functional applications. Unlike that of many commercial buildings, the support of the façade satisfied the eye, since the structural elements were clearly visible.

Plate 46. First National Bank, South Belknap and West College Streets, Stephenville, Erath County (1889)
Architect Unknown   View from Southeast

Typical of many Texas banks, this structure was located on a corner site, across from the public square. Contrasts in color, texture, and pattern make it a particularly remarkable work. Smooth blue marble columns and the carved pediment formed rich counterpoint with the rough native-stone walls, light gold in color. Further highlighting the work were random rough ashlar jointing of the walls and regular coursing of the parapet, all characteristic of the Romanesque Revival. Forming an interesting contrast over the corner access, the turret was decorated with garlands and a bull's-eye window.

Plate 47. Bank of Fredericksburg, 120 East Main Street, Fredericksburg, Gillespie County (1897–1898)
Alfred Giles, Architect   View from West

A Romantic work, this delightful building was note-worthy for its tower and decoration. Light-gold limestone was accented with pink granite trim. Carved pinnacles and the beautiful organic ornamentation merged with the contrasting textures of the wall. In the delicate wrought-iron work on the balcony was the same plastic geometry found in the stone carvings.

Plate 48. N. R. Royall Bank, Palestine, Anderson County (1899)
Architect Unknown   View

Characterized by fine details, this was a good example of late-nineteenth-century bank design. Smooth brickwork was accented with rough stone. Adding interest to the details were recessed panels in the pilasters and the corbeling that supported these. Garlands mounted to the surface added a luxuriant mark.

101

Plate 49. Bay City Bank (Rugeley Building), Avenue F and Seventh Street, Bay City, Matagorda County (1900–1901) Jul Leffland, Architect   View from Southeast

Built when Bay City was only six years old, this structure occupies a site across from the public square, formerly the location of the Town Company offices.[1] Only three years after it had been organized in 1898, the Bay City Bank Company moved into its new building. The mansard roofs and precise brickwork produced a sophisticated character, appropriate for the function housed within. The structure was erected by Robert Allert of Cuero.

[1] Junann Stieghorst, *Bay City and Matagorda County: A History*, p. 36.

Plate 50. Crow's Opera House, West Washington and North Belknap Streets, Stephenville, Erath County (circa 1890)
Architect Unknown   View from Southwest

With stores on the ground floor and an auditorium on the second, this opera house was typical of many in small towns across the state. Built of off-white stone, the detail was strong and robust. The vertical termination of the mass was made with a cut-stone cornice and structural consoles, rather than with the usual galvanized-iron work. Accenting the openings were alternating rough and smooth voussoirs. Although a rather precarious-appearing element, the pinnacle softened the corner.

Plate 51. Grand Opera House, East North and Getty Streets, Uvalde, Uvalde County (1891)
B. F. Trister, Jr., Architect   Overall View

Located on the public square and designed by a San Antonio architect, this building revealed much of the fantasy associated with houses of entertainment. Decorating the brick building were several dramatic figures. In the gable was a mask; on the mast atop the turret appeared the likenesses of a dragon and a snake. On the interior the romance was continued in an ornately designed auditorium.

Architecture of Affluence

AFTER THE CIVIL WAR, the acquisition of the wealth necessary for large and pretentious buildings in Texas hinged on the development of transportation. At mid-century, ships from Galveston and riverboats from Jefferson had conveyed agricultural products out of the state, but this commerce propitiated only the fringe areas. Those regions that were without water transportation awaited the railroads.

To promote the laying of rails, in 1854 the General Law for the Encouragement of the Railroads was passed, awarding grants of land as bounty to every railroad company that built no less than twenty-five miles of track. By 1860 the Buffalo Bayou, Brazos, and Colorado Railway Company had completed sixty-eight miles of track through Richmond to Eagle Lake, and the Houston, Tap, and Brazoria Railroad had advanced a comparable distance from Houston to Columbia; however, it was not until after the war between the states that a railroad boom actually occurred.

The impact of the railroads on the destiny of Texas communities was phenomenal. On the one hand, Jefferson, once an important and colorful center at the head of steamboat traffic between East Texas and New Orleans, declined rapidly when bypassed after promoters neglected to woo magnate Jay Gould with land for his Texas and Pacific Railway. On the other hand, Fort Worth and Dallas—both of which, although mere villages, had donated money and right of ways to entice the railway companies to build to them—became thriving commercial centers. In the four years following the arrival of the Texas and Pacific in 1876, the "Fort" increased in population from an estimated 2,000 to over 6,000; in the next five years, during which time the Gulf, Colorado, and Santa Fe and the Fort Worth and Denver City arrived, the population more than tripled. In 1868 the population of Dallas was estimated at 2,000; in 1880 it was officially over 10,000, and a decade later it was 55,000. Houston, already assured of becoming a major trade center, grew in similar leaps and by 1890 had approximately 40,000 people.

Such growth and prosperity were not created by arbitrary or accidental extensions of the railroads. Westward, beyond the established communities, the route of the Texas and Pacific across the state was located after consideration of commercial potential, in response to recommendations of topographical engineers. The plan was to run the tracks through country where agricultural and mineral resources would favor the growth of communities, thereby assuring profits to the magnates of the rails through commerce. In addition, as a fringe benefit, the railroads then realized substantial profits through the sale of real estate in new towns located at temporary railheads.

Laid out by railroad engineers, these "terminal towns" were communal products of a stage-by-stage system of expansion across the prairies. Among them were Ballinger (1886), a Gulf, Colorado, and Santa Fe Railway Company town, and Midland (1883), Odessa (1881), and Abilene (1881), all Texas and Pacific towns. Abilene was characteristic of the development of a railroad town. In less than a week after the first lots were sold at auction, according to a reporter, "the prairie was dotted with houses, half a dozen dry goods stores, as many groceries, . . . and fifteen or twenty saloons, those great fore-runners of American civilization. Three hundred people had become citizens, and the prairie had become the town of Abilene."[1] In only two weeks the population was purported to be fifteen hundred. Although not all terminal towns survived, many, like Abilene, eventually became thriving cities.

In addition to this influence on material growth, the railroads naturally had a considerable impact on the culture. Now talent and culture from the East would come directly into the state. The prosperity stimulated by the railroads made possible construction of houses of entertainment and employment of talented artists whereby Texans were able to enjoy the humor of the minstrel show, the excitement of the circus, the drama of the theater, and the glamour of the grand opera. Magazines, newspapers, and recently published books exposed residents to all the popular fashions of out-of-state cultural centers. Then, too, mass-produced art objects and building ornaments were imported to

[1] *Fort Worth Daily Democrat*, March 27, 1881, p. 1.

satisfy the artistic taste of the period. In exchange, the products of the soil rode the rails out of the state, accompanied by calls for more capital to further develop resources. Just as the settler and the mechanic had been key figures in the early settlement and growth of the state, the capitalist was most certainly the dominant character during the latter decades of the century. It was he who financed large factories and pretentious new commercial buildings.

During the last quarter of the century, to solicit capital, to promote commerce, and to encourage civic building, boards of trade were organized in most of the progressive towns of the state. As early as 1874, Houston had a board of trade and cotton exchange; Weatherford formed a board of trade in 1881, Abilene in 1884, Fort Worth in 1888, and Bonham in 1889. In advancing their communities, these organizations promoted investment in growing cities.

The eighties and nineties were boom years in the Lone Star State. As resources were exploited and new industries established, immigration rapidly increased the population of the towns. Trade centers outgrew their squares and new multistory commercial buildings rose around them and along the main avenues leading to this public space.

But just as these were years of growth, they were also inevitably years of change. In established towns and cities, expansion was accompanied by numerous public ameliorations. Dusty or muddy streets and squares were constantly being improved. At first, in towns along the coast, they were paved with shells; inland, with gravel. Later, some public thoroughfares were lined with blocks of mesquite, pine, or bois d'arc wood; others were macadamized, but brick ultimately became standard. Other street improvements consisted of installation of artificial lighting and, beginning in the 1880's, replacement of rotten, broken, and uneven wooden sidewalks with concrete.

During the last two decades of the century, the residents of Texas cities marveled at other improvements brought about by the wonders of technology. Waterworks and ice plants appeared in most towns, but other important changes were made possible by electricity. In the late seventies and the early eighties telephone systems were installed in growing towns and cities. By the latter part of the decade, buildings were still plumbed for gas lighting, but many were also wired for electricity and most of these were soon converted. In 1889, Fort Worth boasted the first electrical street railway in the Southwest, and, shortly thereafter, mules were in little demand to pull streetcars in any city.

Equally significant was the development of community pride in public beauty, both for the enjoyment of the residents and for attraction to outsiders. This trait was manifested in many county seats where courthouses were surrounded with ornamental iron fences and were landscaped with trees, walks, and grass. Some squares were enhanced with delightful bandstands (plate 52). In Dallas the spirit for beautification was promoted by city ordinance. Any person who planted a shade tree by a public sidewalk and maintained it for two years received the reward of one dollar. In another demonstration of public spirit, according to one reporter, in the spring of 1890 the concern for civic beauty in Fort Worth resulted in the planting of over thirty thousand trees.[2]

Representations of the considered importance of beauty in the townscape were common in the newspapers published throughout the state. Typical of these expressions, in the *Galveston Daily News* it was written: "A city must make itself attractive as well as useful. It may have everything for sale which any actual, probable, or possible customer can demand; but it must display its wares in fine buildings and in an attractive manner. It may have 'the best that markets afford,' but it must serve them [the customers] in splendid restaurants and magnificent hotels."[3] Newspaper articles acclaiming new public structures as "ornaments to the city" or "credits to any city" revealed the importance attached to architectural expression. While buildings, regardless of the scale of construction, were considered "welcome additions," pretentious new edifices were commonly hailed as "the finest of their kind" or as "having no equal" in the city or state. Public sentiment seemed to encourage the production of fine buildings.

During this period, architectural merit was judged on the basis of character. Although buildings were sometimes acclaimed for their commodiousness and comforts, distinction created by elegant finishes and "fashionable" appearances brought the most encomiums. The requisite eminence demanded expression in the styles deemed as "modern" by the taste of the times. One reporter epitomized this point of view when he wrote: "No one of the elements that go to make up the prosperity of a city is more indicative of its substantial growth than its building improvements. And it is not so much the number of buildings that are erected as the style and costliness of the same."[4]

It was, of course, the demand for large and elegant buildings that provided the impetus for the encouragement of architecture as a profession. Rather than serving in the capacity of a master builder—as he had done in antebellum times—the architect became a professional, providing the services of design, of preparation of contract drawings and writing specifications, and of supervision.

However, in Texas, as in other states, the professional qualifications of those who called themselves architects were quite varied. Although there were some with academic backgrounds, few had received formal training to prepare for practice. Many were immigrants, and most of them learned through apprenticeship with other architects or through practical experience with construction. They then increased their abilities through association with other professionals and, as today, through studying or emulating buildings published in books or periodicals. Despite the lack of formal education, many were talented and produced competent levels of artistic work.

For example, James Riely Gordon (1864–1937), a native of Winchester, Virginia, had no formal education in architecture. At age eighteen, he began his career by study and an apprenticeship with W. C. Dodson. In 1883 he journeyed to Washington, D.C.,

---

[2] *Fort Worth Daily Gazette*, June 12, 1890, p. 6.
[3] *Galveston Daily News*, October 12, 1869, p. 2.

[4] Ibid., October 3, 1875, p. 1.

and worked under the supervising architect of the Treasury. In 1887 he opened his office in San Antonio.[5] Two other architects, the brothers F. E. Ruffini and Oscar Ruffini, were born in Cleveland, Ohio, of immigrant parents—their father had immigrated from Florence, Italy, and their mother from Dresden, Germany. While a young man, F. E. moved to Austin to establish a practice and was later joined by his brother. Oscar later moved to San Angelo, "because of his health." F. E. died in 1885, but Oscar lived until 1957.[6] Another architect, Alfred Giles, was born in England. Following some academic training in construction and a period of apprenticeship in London, he immigrated to the United States in 1873. After settling in San Antonio he worked for a contractor, John H. Kampmann, for three years and then established his own firm. During the last two decades of the nineteenth century, Giles was among the most active architects in the state.[7] Born in 1849, Nicholas J. Clayton was brought to the United States from Ireland at the age of two. After serving in the navy in the mid-1860's, he studied architecture and structural engineering with W. H. Baldwin of Memphis. He moved to Galveston late in 1872 and shortly thereafter opened an office to practice architecture. During the latter part of the nineteenth century he was highly regarded not only as an excellent designer but also as a talented structural engineer.[8]

But in the nineteenth century, ethical standards were virtually nonexistent. Unlike today's professional, an architect could solicit work through advertisement and, without fear of reprimand, could use almost any legal means to compete with rivals for commissions. The need for uniform practices during the 1880's made professionals keenly aware of the necessity for organization, especially in the cities. In 1889 in Fort Worth the Board of Architects was formed, "to unite in common fellowship all professional architects in Fort Worth and vicinity and by united effort and cooperation to formulate, adopt and practice uniform business methods and modes of practice and to obtain a more artistic, practical and scientific knowledge of architecture and all its branches."[9]

Previously, in 1885, the Texas Association of Architects had been organized and was working to improve the integrity of the profession. At the annual meeting in Houston in 1888, following the recommendations of the president, J. J. Kane, a committee was appointed to persuade the state legislature to secure passage of an act to regulate the practice of architecture. In the interest of assuring the competence of those who practiced, the committee proposed that architects be licensed through examination. However, despite repeated petitioning, the procedure of licensing through written test was not adopted until mid–twentieth century, and even then the regulation was legally only a title law.

If early Texas architects were concerned over ethical standards of practice, they were also involved with the new technology of the period. During the first three-quarters of the century, buildings on modest scales were commonly erected without services of architects. For the interior, plans were straightforward, requiring little imagination to develop conventional arrangements; for the exterior, masons or iron foundries supplied the ornamental details that embellished the façade. But, during the last quarter of the century in the commercial centers, the opulent taste of the times and the magnitude of construction created a demand for professionals with both artistic and scientific talents. When they advertised, some architects appealed to the public through their abilities with "large or difficult construction."

This era of technology also created opportunities for the architectural specialist. In areas of manufacturing that involved complex mechanical equipment, practitioners with experience in industrial building were sought. For instance, before the Texas Brewing Company in Fort Worth undertook its plant, officials

[5] See *American Architect* 150 (April 1937): 143; *Houston Daily Post*, December 2, 1891, p. 4.

[6] Elise Ruffini to James Day, August 29, 1961, Texas State Library, Austin.

[7] Mary Carolyn Hollers Jutson, *Alfred Giles: An English Architect in Texas and Mexico*, pp. 1–2.

[8] Howard Barnstone, *The Galveston That Was*, p. 89.

[9] *Fort Worth Daily Gazette*, February 12, 1889, p. 8.

Fig. 19. Capitol Hotel, Houston, Harris County (1882). (Advertisement, *Houston Daily Post*, March 2, 1884, p. 1; photo from the Texas State Library, Austin)

Fig. 20. Perspective of the Cotton Exchange, Houston, Harris County (1884). Eugene T. Heiner, architect. (*Houston Daily Post*, May 4, 1884, p. 1; photo from the Texas State Library, Austin)

journeyed to Chicago to hire the firm of Griesser and Martizen, which specialized in breweries. In this and other manufactories, functionalism determined the form of the building, but in works wherein there were definite desires to create favorable public images, towers and other structural forms were embellished with various ornamental details. Epitomizing this industrial design was the Pearl Brewery (1890), also designed by August Martizen (plate 53).

In the closing years of the nineteenth century, the wealth created by the breweries and other industries naturally influenced the character of architecture. This was true not only in terms of magnitude, but also in terms of opulence. During this Romantic era, merchants imperiously commissioned ostentatious buildings that expressed their prowess in business ventures. Just as they wanted residences that reflected their social status through size and luxuriance, they also demanded business blocks that were expressions of commercial success through opulence. Moreover, they disliked insipidity and demanded buildings with distinction, particularly since illustrations of buildings often appeared with advertisements in newspapers, thus presenting an identifying image to the public (fig. 19).

Although aspirations for architectural distinction were commonly expressed by the ornamental details and composition of small Texas buildings, earlier in the East the trend toward the demonstration of affluence had been well established. Attitudes concerning pretentious expression of attainment were manifest with the rise of the commercial society. Associating their success with that of the wealthy Italian merchants of the Renaissance, businessmen considered the character of the Italian street architecture to be appropriate for their desires. With the exuberance of its Classical details, the Italian mode (called the *palazzi*)[10] that they imitated provided the grandeur so loved by people during the latter part of the nineteenth century. It was both lavish in detail of decoration and noble in composition of form.

It was, of course, in the trading centers of the state that the architecture of affluence reached its most elaborate expression. In the Gulf Coast cities of Gal-

[10] See Winston Weisman, "Commercial Palaces of New York: 1845–1875," *Art Bulletin* 36, no. 4 (December 1954): 285–302.

veston and Houston and the inland cities of Fort Worth, Dallas, and San Antonio, thriving enterprises produced large and luxuriant commercial buildings. During the late 1870's and 1880's in cities near the coast, brick and metal were employed to create the lavish-appearing commercial buildings that businessmen demanded and that the public admired (fig. 20). Details, often freely composed, were chiefly borrowed from the Renaissance architecture of Italy and France. To convey an aristocratic appearance, appropriate for the prestige of the prosperous businessmen who built them, decoration was profuse. Characteristic of Galveston affluence was the First National Bank (1878), a brick edifice decorated with Renaissance details cast in iron and capped with a brick parapet and sheet-metal cornice (plate 54).

Further contributing to the opulence of this street architecture were deep arches and ornamentation with strong relief of surface. Compositions of these elements were surmounted by heavy cornices, projecting boldly outward to terminate oblique perspectives from sidewalk level. The distinctive character of the Kauffman and Runge Building (1881–1882) was due to deep recesses of openings, along with multiple moldings that, except for cut-stone trim, were all formed with Philadelphia pressed brick (plate 55). In the H. M. Trueheart Building (1881–1882) the architect Nicholas J. Clayton creatively used brick, carved stone, and iron in order to produce a lavish appearance with complex configurations of recesses and a bold cornice (plate 56).

Although designing basically for brick construction, architects along the Gulf occasionally emulated stone by patterns in wall surfaces that gave the impression of large-scaled masonry units. The Moore, Stratton, and Company Building (1882) and the Greenleve, Block, and Company Building (1881–1882) of Galveston possessed exterior walls of brick, but, in both, the scale of stone construction was conveyed by the articulation of the surface (plates 57, 58).

There was virtually no end to the variety of design that was possible in patterns of surface, in form of ornamental details, and in configuration and rhythm of openings. In addition to form and pattern, materials with contrasting hues could be combined to variegate the work. Furthermore, even such precious materials as marble and stained glass could be included as accents to impress the viewer. However, although the rage for profusion in expression could easily result in a statement wherein it appeared that lavishness dominated aesthetics, a talented designer, such as Nicholas J. Clayton, could produce splendid and unified compositions. In Baroque form, he combined iron, glass, polychromatic brick, and marble to create an astonishing design for the Galveston News Building (1883–1884; plate 59).

In some buildings, romantic symbolism attracted the interest of the viewers. The Galveston Cotton Exchange (1877–1878) was elaborately decorated with carved representations of the cotton leaf, flower, and boll. In addition, according to a contemporary description, "over the entrances at each side are two shields, upon which are carved, respectively, a bull's and bear's head—a jocose indication of the buyers and sellers."[11]

Although Renaissance-detailed commercial buildings were the most common in the Lone Star State, other styles of antiquity also appeared in the works of the affluent. The Evans block (1889) in Fort Worth was described as "Venetian Romanesque." In San Antonio, George W. Brackenridge captivated attention when he designed his San Antonio National Bank (1885–1886) in the Islamic style (plate 60). In addition, near the turn of the century many architects did not hesitate to combine details from different historic periods for the same building. However, in the cultural centers of the state—with the national rise of the authority of the renowned French school, the École des Beaux-Arts—the stylistic vocabulary was then often restricted to Classical forms with more boldness of effect and, perhaps, greater repose than had characterized much earlier work (plate 61).

In many of the pretentious commercial works in Texas, the intent of some of these elaborate designs

---

[11] *Frank Leslie's Illustrated Newspaper*, April 19, 1879, p. 109.

was clearly indicated by the appellation "palace." The Evans block in Fort Worth was acclaimed as the "handsomest dry goods *palace* in the South."[12]

The palatial image was also characteristic of the large commercial hotels of the state. During the last two decades of the century, many new hostelries appeared, but in some cases, as in the Menger Hotel in San Antonio, old buildings were merely enlarged to accommodate increasing trade (plate 62). In either instance, since the concept of design was similar to that producing elaborately detailed business blocks, the same styles appeared in both. Although the mansard roofs of the Second Empire style crowned many new or remodeled hotels in the late seventies and early eighties, thereafter until the end of the century the Renaissance Revival provided many with an imposing appearance. When the Menger Hotel was expanded, the remodeling was in lavish Renaissance rather than in the simplified Greek of the original building (plate 63). Another fine example of the Renaissance Revival style was the five-story Capitol Hotel in Houston (1882)—located on the site of the first capitol of Texas (fig. 19).

However, in the Romantic period extending over the last quarter of the century, styles other than the Renaissance were also fashionable for hotels. In the Driskill Hotel in Austin (1885–1886) the Romanesque Revival, with its picturesqueness of many offsets, pinnacles, and balconies, provided the magnificence so admired (plate 64).

The Driskill exemplified the point of view that prevailed regarding character and comfort. There, as in other large hostelries in the state, multiple entries, spacious lobbies, and grand stairways were all featured to celebrate the visit of distinguished guests (plate 65). Often the scenes of important social events, the lobbies and ballrooms were decorated to form elegant backdrops for the lace-and-crinoline dress of the period. Adding to the palatial image, guest rooms were designed to be commodious: most hotels (new or remodeled during the last two decades of the century) boasted about their gas or electric lights, run-ning water, steam heat, and marble-top furniture. Ornately designed elevators often furnished conveyance to these rooms.

No less elegant were the grand opera houses, designed exclusively for the performing arts, the interiors of which were conceived as grandiose spaces, decorated in Baroque style, reflecting the pomp of the events. In the status-conscious society of Texas, plans were evolved that segregated audiences, providing the most prominent seats in the house for the "fashionable set." Just as the small theaters were simple in plan, the auditoriums of the large houses were segregated according to levels of society. The dress circle, often approached up a grand stair, was the show section into which the flamboyant were accustomed to making their late entries. The seating in the parquette, on the main floor, was often approached through secondary entrances on either side of the grand stair. Finally, a gallery or balcony was provided for the demimonde and boys; not uncommonly, entrances into this section were on a street around the corner from the grand entry.

On the exterior the style of these houses of entertainment often reflected the drama of the interior. In the Millett Opera House (1878) in Austin grandiose entrances and details, borrowed from historical Classical architecture, represented the dramatic function (plate 66). Other opera houses were more picturesque and romantic, as if to portray the fantasy of the *Arabian Nights*. For instance, Gordon and Laub's designs for the Corpus Christi Opera House (1890) called for a fantastic building in Moorish style with a huge gilded dome and one-hundred-foot-high minarets, also surmounted by domes.[13]

At the time these palatial hotels and opera houses—usually three or four stories high—were rising, the skylines of Dallas and Fort Worth were beginning to reflect advancements in commerce through high-rise buildings. Above the horizon extended five- to eight-story buildings, utilizing techniques of framing structural skeletons with iron similar to those employed in the 1880's in Chicago—home of the skyscraper—

[12] *Fort Worth Daily Gazette*, May 16, 1889, p. 8.

[13] Ibid., December 4, 1890, p. 6.

Fig. 21. Perspective of the Hurley Office Building, Fort Worth, Tarrant County (1889–1890). Armstrong and Messer, architects. (*Fort Worth Daily Gazette*, September 25, 1890, p. 3; photo from the Texas State Library, Austin)

Fig. 23. Perspective of the Board of Trade Building, Fort Worth, Tarrant County (1888). A. J. Armstrong, architect. (*Fort Worth Daily Gazette*, June 5, 1888, p. 5; photo from the Texas State Library, Austin)

Fig. 22. Perspective of the Binz Office Building, Houston, Harris County (1894). Lorehn and Friz, architects. (*American Architect and Building News* 46 [1894]: pl. 986; photo from the Library of Congress)

and utilizing for vertical communication the elevator, which had been invented in New York City in the 1850's. The elevator and metal framing made spaces on the upper floors desirable as rentals; the former provided ease of access, and the latter allowed for the use of large glass areas for light and ventilation, as well as for rapid construction and flexibility. In addition, near the end of the century some architects on the midwestern prairie were beginning to notice that metal-skeleton buildings withstood tornadoes better than other forms of structure.

Although high-rise buildings involved modern technology, architects provided character for the exterior of these—which were fireproofed with terra cotta, brick, or stone—by using styles from the past that had been intended for masonry and that were currently fashionable. Consequently, the Italian Renaissance Revival continued its popularity. For example, the Hurley Office Building in Fort Worth (1889–1890) was an eight-story achievement—117 feet high—designed by the firm of Armstrong and Messer in Renaissance Revival style, the exterior being sheathed with Millsap sandstone, trimmed in marble (fig. 21). The North Texas National Bank (1888) in Dallas, designed by J. B. Legg Architectural Company of Saint Louis, was six stories with both round and segmental arches, but with "all modern appliances necessary to make it a first-class office building."[14] The six-story Binz Building (1894) of Houston was also in the fashionable Italian Renaissance mode (fig. 22).

Many of these large commercial works of the Gay Nineties and before were financed by imported capital—not only from the United States but also from Europe—and were used to promote more investment. As enticements to attract outside capital to invest in more new buildings and new industries, boards of trade frequently called attention to their fine commercial blocks. As status symbols, their substantial construction and sophisticated style, according to optimistic promoters, demonstrated the security of Texas cities as sound places for outlay of money. Evidencing this attitude, the Board of Trade Building in Fort Worth (1888), a magnificent five-story edifice finished with polychromatic stone in Renaissance Revival style, was proclaimed by one reporter to be "a monument to encourage capital to locate in Fort Worth" (fig. 23).[15]

Although many of these commercial works provided fringe benefits by evidencing progress, others were planned with the sole objective of promoting the state. In a romantic age that used architecture as a refuge, state pride (dedicated to attract men and money) motivated the construction of pretentious exhibition buildings. To rival the Corn Palace of Sioux City, the Cotton Palace of New Orleans, and the Ice Palace of Saint Paul, Texans conceived the Texas Spring Palace (1889) in Fort Worth (fig. 24). This fascinating structure, designed by the firm of Armstrong and Messer and described as being in "composite" architectural style, was decorated with products of the soil—including, for example, a covering of wheat on

[14] *Dallas Morning News*, June 24, 1888, p. 16.
[15] *Fort Worth Daily Gazette*, March 22, 1888, p. 8.

Fig. 24. Texas Spring Palace, Fort Worth, Tarrant County (1889). Armstrong and Messer, architects. (Photo from the Fort Worth Public Library, Fort Worth)

the exterior of the main dome—and designed to house exhibits of products and resources of the state. The Spring Palace was destroyed by fire the year following its construction, but new energy was directed to the Texas Pavilion at the World's Columbian Exposition in Chicago (1893), which offered an opportunity for Texans to display their resources to the world, on the four-hundredth anniversary of Columbus's discovery of America.

On a site near the north entry to Jackson Park—location for the exposition—a large structure, 60 by 384 feet, to include exhibits and assembly rooms, was erected according to the plans of Gordon and Laub of San Antonio. The building was constructed of staff (plaster of Paris and hemp), in a style reminiscent of the Spanish Renaissance. Reflecting the architectural character of the Alamo, made famous by Texas valor and patriotism, this mode was considered appropriate for conveying the image of the state to visitors. This was among the first pretentious works in the nineteenth century to be inspired by the Spanish architectural heritage.

Perhaps Gordon and Laub established a trend. Even the Cotton Palace—built in Waco in 1894, consumed by fire, and rebuilt the following year—was also in Spanish Renaissance style (fig. 25). As with other exposition and exhibition buildings, this edifice, lo-

Fig. 25. Perspective of the Cotton Palace, Waco, McLennan County (1894). (*Fort Worth Daily Gazette*, June 23, 1894, p. 2; photo from the Texas State Library, Austin)

Fig. 26. Perspective of the Beach Hotel, Galveston, Galveston County (1883). Nicholas J. Clayton, architect. (*Frank Leslie's Illustrated*, May 31, 1890, p. 365; photo from the Library of Congress)

cated in Padgitt Park, was intended to attract people to the state. Although obviously an overstatement, one reporter expressed the optimistic hopes for this building when he wrote romantically that the palace would have a statewide impact in its "grandeur, in its scope, its object lessons, educational, artistic, industrial, mechanical, agricultural, scientific and commercial features: in its immigration-bringing, advertising feature, capital-inducing, public spirit begetting tendencies."[16]

Also among the architectural attractions of the state were structures for therapy and pleasure. In Texas, as in the nation, these were ultimately a consequence of efficiency in mass production and of expanding commerce, both of which increased the amount of time available for leisure and provided opportunities for luxury and pleasure to the bourgeois—the middle class enjoyed many of the luxuries formerly belonging only to the aristocracy. In response, entrepreneurs demanded an architecture suitable for housing pleasurable activities. Billiard parlors and roller-skating rinks were opened; clubs, chautauquas, pavilions, natatoriums, and resort hotels were designed.

During the eighties and nineties, luxurious natatoriums rose throughout the West. In Texas these featured an assortment of baths—including Russian, Turkish, Roman—and large swimming pools, all supplied with mineral waters that were acclaimed for their therapeutic value in curing all kinds of ailments.

On the interiors regal appearances were created with marble, tile, and jardinieres, while on the outside various historic styles gave character. Of these recreational structures, however, the only vestiges remaining are old photographs.

Resort hotels were also prominent in the eighties and nineties. In style, these were quite different from the impressive commercial hotels. Although large, the resort hostelries were picturesque and intimately scaled, with numerous balconies and verandas. Structured wholly or largely out of wood, the design exploited the decorative potential of the materials by utilizing patterns of woodwork, shingles, and gingerbread. In residential styles, the English Queen Anne and the American Colonial, Stick, and Shingle modes furnished the vocabulary for design.[17]

Several fine resorts rose along these lines in the state. The Beach Hotel in Galveston (1883), designed by Nicholas J. Clayton, was an ornate and colorful

---

[16] Ibid., February 26, 1894, p. 5.

[17] For a discussion of the development of these styles, see Vincent J. Scully, Jr., *The Shingle Style: Architectural Theory and Design from Richardson to the Origins of Wright*; and idem, "Romantic Rationalism and the Expression of Structure in Wood: Downing, Wheeler, Gardner, and the 'Stick Style,' 1840–1876," *Art Bulletin* 35, no. 2 (June 1953): 121–142.

Fig. 27. Perspective of the Arlington Heights Hotel, Fort Worth, Tarrant County (1892, burned 1894). Messer, Sanguinet, and Messer, architects. (*Fort Worth Daily Gazette*, November 12, 1894, p. 2; photo from the Texas State Library, Austin)

three-story pile with multiple balconies, constructed entirely from wood (fig. 26).[18] The Arlington Heights Hotel near Fort Worth (1892), envisioned by the firm of Messer, Sanguinet, and Messer—"for the great middle classes, the salt of the earth"[19]—was in the "old Colonial style of architecture" (fig. 27). A large four-story building, it was finished on the exterior with Bennett pressed brick, Pecos sandstone, weatherboards, and shingles and was provided with numerous gables, towers, and dormers. However, both the Beach and the Arlington succumbed to flames before the turn of the century.

Although on a smaller scale, a unique example of the picturesqueness that characterized many of these hotels appeared in the Hexagon House in Mineral Wells (1897).[20] Designed and supervised by David G. Galbraith, this building was three stories high and, on a floor plan comprised of seven contiguous hexagons, was an interesting experiment with geometry.

In the nineteenth century, pretentious resort and exhibition architecture, of course, would not have been possible without the railroads. In addition to providing the necessary communication and freightage, they

energetically shared in the promotion of the state. Through advertisement of opportunities for both business and pleasure, they enticed people to vacation and to immigrate. By attracting tourists and new residents, the railway companies naturally profited immediately from transporting them, and ultimately from providing services in conveying products to and from the state.

The railroads also contributed to the architectural scene in Texas with buildings that were commensurate with their development. In crossing the prairies, since the first concern of each company was to lay tracks and establish its railroad as a competitor, only small wooden-framed depots and section houses for the maintenance of employees appeared (plate 67).

But, as commerce increased, new buildings became more pretentious, larger, and more permanent, reflecting the prosperity of the railroad. Service facilities, such as water towers, round houses, freight houses, and engine houses, rose at the same time with new passenger stations. In small but progressive towns, the depots—which also generally reflected the size of the community—were commonly of frame construction (plate 68) and occasionally of brick. In form, they were long, narrow structures, parallel to the tracks, containing passenger facilities at one end and freight storage at the other. In style, they generally reflected the taste of the period through the decorative use of wooden brackets and through the geometrical articulation of the wall surfaces.

But in the new passenger stations of the railway hubs of the state, the affluence of the railroads was expressed in architectural sophistication (plates 69, 70). Cities were always eager for the railway companies to erect pretentious new depots, since these gave visitors auspicious first impressions of the community. On the exterior a Baroque character generally favorably impressed travelers, and on the interior the decoration served as fitting introduction, or termination, to the elegance that would delight those who rode in ornately furnished "palaces on wheels." However, it was after the turn of the century before the golden era of railroading produced many of the opulent new depots, office buildings, and employee facilities.

[18] Barnstone, *Galveston That Was*, pp. 126–132.
[19] *Fort Worth Daily Gazette*, February 14, 1892, p. 5.
[20] For illustrations of this structure, see Clay Lancaster, *Architectural Follies in America*, pp. 146–149.

Thus, during the nineteenth century, the architecture of enterprise in prosperous areas of the state was characterized by affluence and pretentiousness. Through elaborate decoration and fashionable styles these qualities reflected the success of the enterprise that financed them. But the romance, optimism, and prosperity that produced such lavish work for enterprise also found outlet in other areas of construction, indirectly contributing to the erection of beautiful churches and stately governmental buildings.

Plate 52. Victoria Bandstand, DeLeon Plaza, Victoria, Victoria County (1899)
Architect Unknown   View

Built at the request of Wagner's Band,[1] this structure was designed to delight those who congregated during summer evenings on the square for concerts. Popular on wooden buildings at the end of the century, gingerbread designs were delightfully exploited. Scrollwork enhanced the fascia of the roof and the turned spindle columns. Other scrollwork decorated these columns and crowned the roof.

[1] Roy Grimes (ed.), *300 Years in Victoria County*, p. 479.

117

Plate 54. First National Bank, 2127 Strand, Galveston, Galveston County (1878)
J. M. Brown, Architect [?]   View from Northwest

The First National Bank in Galveston was organized in 1865. Over a decade later it built this edifice along the Strand, on the site of a building that had been destroyed by fire. The design is attributed to J. M. Brown, who also evidently supervised construction.[1]

This was a fine example of the opulence of Renaissance-inspired architecture. A lavish design was created with brick, metal, and glass, projecting an image for the prosperity and permanence of the banking institution.

[1] Howard Barnstone, *The Galveston That Was*, p. 110.

Plate 53. Pearl Brewery, San Antonio, Bexar County (1890)
August Martizen, Architect   View of the Brewhouse

During the latter part of the century, many capitalists invested in breweries. Among these, in 1886, the Pearl Brewing Company was organized, and shortly thereafter Martizen, a specialist, was hired to design the plant.

Functionally, breweries were multibuilding complexes, usually consisting of an office wing, a bottling house, storage, and a brewhouse. The brewhouse was a multistory building, with equipment arranged for vertical processing. Proceeding from the top floor down, on different levels were malt storage; a malt weigher; a malt mill and screening reel; a mash tub, copper grant, and varmasher; a copper brew kettle; a copper hop jack; and a cooler and beer pumps.

To present a favorable public image, brewery structures were enhanced with various ornamental details. In these brick buildings round arches, stringcourses, pilasters, and the tower all provided decorative interest not often found in other industrial buildings.

119

Plate 55. Kauffman and Runge Building, 222 Twenty-second Street, Galveston, Galveston County (1881–1882)
Nicholas J. Clayton, Architect [?]   Detail of Arches

The firm of Kauffman and Runge was established in the 1840's by Julius Kauffman, a German immigrant from Bremen. He was one of the first Galveston merchants who imported merchandise from foreign countries. By 1880 a thriving business necessitated a large new building from which to operate the wholesale business dealing in fancy groceries, liquors, woodenware, and other products.

The architect's design called for red brick as the basic material with white stone as an accent. In addition, brick, plastically formed with molding profiles, relieved the austerity of surface and softened the corners of first- and second-floor openings. Cut stone was then employed for keystones, imposts, and stringcourses. An elaborate cornice that originally surmounted the building has been removed.

Plate 56. H. M. Trueheart and Company Building, 212 Twenty-second Street, Galveston, Galveston County (1881–1882)
Nicholas J. Clayton, Architect   View

"For the better security of their accumulations of title deeds, and other valuable papers and data relating to lands, titles and estate," H. M. Trueheart and Company, real estate and general tax agents and stock brokers, commissioned Nicholas J. Clayton of Galveston to design a new fireproof building. The success of the organization was apparent in the elaborate and interesting design of the façade of the company's office building—in which it occupied the first floor.

With Italian Renaissance architecture as a point of departure, Clayton created lavish surface decoration with the polychromatic use of masonry. Pressed bricks of different molds and patterns were used to create a variety of abstract geometrical patterns. Light-colored stone, carved into ornamental pilaster capitals and bases, provided contrast, while the dominant cornice unified the composition. Of additional interest were the ornamental designs in the French doors, one set of which opened to a stair, the other to the first-floor offices.

Plate 57. Moore, Stratton, and Company Building, 2120–2128 Strand, Galveston, Galveston County (1882)
Architect Unknown   View from Southwest

In Renaissance Revival style, this structure was erected by cotton factors and wholesale grocers. Although the walls were of brick, the surface was finished with stucco in patterns and forms to represent stone construction. Unfortunately, a large cornice has been removed, leaving an incomplete composition.

Plate 58. Greenleve, Block, and Company Building, 2314 Strand, Galveston, Galveston County (1881–1882)
Nicholas J. Clayton, Architect   View from Southeast

Built by a wholesale dry-goods firm organized in 1865, this was another noteworthy example of the commercial opulence that was so in demand from successful merchants. The front of the building was supported by elegant columns with elaborate detail cast by the Lee Iron Works of Galveston. These columns supported a front comprised of Philadelphia pressed brick and cut stone. The strong relief of the masonry created strong shadow patterns, vividly emphasizing the details. Originally four stories high, with an overall measure of seventy-five feet—approximately equivalent to most seven-story structures of today—the scale of the building approached the colossal. Originally, it had elaborate cornices, but storm damage caused their removal. The two end sections of the ground-floor street façades have also lost most of their character and beauty through remodeling.

Plate 59. Galveston News Building, 2108–2116 Mechanic Street, Galveston, Galveston County (1883–1884)
Nicholas J. Clayton, Architect
View

Acclaimed at the time of its completion as a monument to enterprise, this work attracted state-wide attention and was one of the finest nineteenth-century commercial buildings in Texas. Philadelphia brick and iron were used throughout. The front was of iron, pressed red and yellow brick, with ornamental features of white and pink marble.

The ground floor contained the counting room, presses, and engine room. On the second floor were the editorial rooms, and on the top level were the composing rooms. With elevators and running water, the "latest improvements" were provided. The building was built over large cisterns with a capacity of 170,000 gallons.

Plate 60. San Antonio National Bank, 213 West Commerce Street, San Antonio, Bexar County (1885–1886)
George W. Brackenridge, Architect   View

George W. Brackenridge, to whom the design of this building is attributed, was not an architect by profession but a prominent businessman in San Antonio. He was also the owner of this bank, which he established in 1866, and is believed to have been the contractor.

In architectural style, Brackenridge, who had studied engineering at Harvard University,[1] was inspired by ancient Islamic architecture. Horseshoe arches appear on both of the stories, and the large arched opening on the ground floor was enhanced by an arabesque panel. Other noteworthy features included the corbel tables and the tower, the latter reminiscent of a minaret.

The materials of construction were durable and beautiful throughout. The bank, with its attached structure for carriages and horses, had walls of rough limestone in random ashlar pattern. On the interior, marble tile was used for the floors, and the walls were frescoed. The building still functions as a bank and has been altered little.

[1] Lillie May Hagner, *Alluring San Antonio*, p. 31.

Plate 61. Hutchings, Sealy, and Company Building, 2326 Strand, Galveston, Galveston County (1895–1897)
Nicholas J. Clayton, Architect   View from Southwest

During the last half of the nineteenth century, George Ball, John Hutchings, and John Sealy were all prominent among the builders of Galveston. As early as 1854, the banking firm of Ball, Hutchings, and Company was established. The company subsequently occupied a building on the Strand, next to which John Sealy erected a new structure in 1870. After operating in various buildings in Galveston, the banking firm determined to erect this edifice, with Classical stateliness and exuberance. At the same time, the name of the firm was changed.

The building was noteworthy for its durability. In 1895 it was reported in the *Galveston Daily News* that the structure would be fireproof "with all modern conveniences."[1] The footings and walls were designed to support an additional five stories, if they had been needed.

[1] *Galveston Daily News*, September 1, 1895, p. 2.

Plate 62. Menger Hotel, Alamo Plaza, San Antonio, Bexar County (1859, remodeled 1909 and other years)
John Fries, Architect of 1859 Work; Alfred Giles, Architect of 1909 Addition   View of Main Façade

When the Menger Hotel opened in 1859 near the Alamo, it was a two-story building with Greek Revival details. Although remodeled many times, the entablature over the second-story windows, the round arches of the projecting pavilion, and the rustication of the ground-story façade have been retained. Originally, the second-floor windows had shutters. Additions have increased the height and width of the original building. On the east, an enclosed patio opens onto a delightful landscaped courtyard.

Plate 63. Menger Hotel, San Antonio
View of Rotunda

The rotunda was a focal point in the hotel, requiring richness of décor. Here, Classical ornamental iron work enriched a space that was often further enhanced by the seasonal colors of profusions of flowers. Distinguished guests who passed through this rotunda include John J. Pershing, William Howard Taft, and Warren G. Harding.

Plate 64. Driskill Hotel, 117 East 7 Street, Austin, Travis County (1885–1886)
J. N. Preston and Son, Architects   View from Southwest

On the evening of July 4, 1885, illuminated by electric lights, the Burnet granite cornerstone of the Driskill was set into place. The stone had been presented by the mayor, on behalf of the citizens of Austin, to the builder of the hotel, J. W. Driskill, as a token of their appreciation of the enterprise.

With walls of brick trimmed with limestone, the hotel was an elaborate design with three grand entrances, the northeastern one of which was designated as the ladies' entry. Balconies and porches contributed to the picturesqueness of the Romanesque building. Carved-stone details of the longhorn, the Lone Star, and busts of Driskill and his sons added accents of local interest.

Claimed as the finest in the South upon completion, the palatial edifice was not operated by Driskill but was leased. The year following the opening, it was briefly closed, apparently due to lack of volume of business, but it was soon reopened.

Plate 66. Millett Opera House, 111 East 9 Street, Austin, Travis County (1878)
F. E. Ruffini, Architect   View

During the last two decades of the century, the Millett Opera House was one of the social centers of Austin. In addition to providing a setting for operas, its elegant interior, which seated eleven hundred, was the backdrop for inaugurations, for political conventions, and for commencement exercises of the University of Texas. In the early eighties, after the antebellum capitol was razed by flames, the House of Representatives met there, pending the erection of a temporary state building.

Although extensively altered, much of the original character can still be seen. Decorative features on the façade, all borrowed from the ancient Greeks, included antefixes, paterae, and the lyre in the tympanum of the triangular pediment. Other early features can also be seen in the heavy cornice and pilasters.

At the turn of the century, after ceasing to function as an opera house, it was completely changed. In 1901 a third floor was added, the balcony was replaced with a floor, and the ground level was transformed into a roller-skating rink.[1] In 1911 the Knights of Columbus purchased the property, after which the façade was remodeled with the addition of the colonnade and porch. In 1965 the merit of the structure was recognized by designation as a Texas Landmark.

[1] M. Lynn McDonald, "Millett Opera House," *Texas Architect* 20, no. 6 (June 1970): 17.

Plate 65. Driskill Hotel, Austin
View of Lobby

Entered under what was once claimed as the largest arch in the state, the Driskill was one of the social and political centers of Texas. Early in its history, several governors, including Lawrence Sullivan Ross, had inaugural balls there. Among other activities were the commencement balls of students from the University of Texas.

Before the doors were closed in 1969—after remaining open an additional period to accommodate state legislators—the hotel housed many politicians. In recent years, it served as the White House Press Corps headquarters when President Lyndon B. Johnson visited his LBJ Ranch.

The Driskill was threatened by demolition after it was closed in 1969. However, a corporation was formed to save the structure. Through the sale of ten-dollar-a-share stock to individuals interested in preservation, its restoration was financed, and today its hotel rooms and splendid dining rooms are once again open.

Plate 67. Missouri Pacific Railroad Station, Kyle, Hays County (late 1800's)
Architect Unknown   Overall View

Early railroad stations were generally diminutive wooden-framed structures. Although the stations were similar in size and material throughout the state, subtle individuality among them resulted in variations of details and patterns of finish. In many, walls were decoratively articulated into panels with patterns of thin boards; in others ornamental shingle patterns were distinguishing characteristics. This example was characterized by triangular-form window hoods, board-and-battened walls, and prominent roof brackets.

Plate 68. Burlington Railway Depot, Bowie, Montague County (late 1800's)
Architect Unknown   View

In scale, nineteenth-century depots were commensurate with the prosperity of the railway company that built them and the importance of the town they served. Throughout the West, regardless of size, these were generally one story and were universally long, narrow buildings, situated parallel with the tracks. At one end was passenger ticketing, at the other freight nandling.

A dominant hip roof with broad overhangs protected passengers here. As was usual, dormers accented the roof form, while the short tower formed a landmark. The bay window provided the operator a view of the tracks.

132

133

Plate 69. Fort Worth Union Station, Fort Worth, Tarrant County (1899)
Architect Unknown   View

In 1895, Fort Worth railway companies determined to erect a new passenger depot to replace an old structure, which had "long been an eyesore and a reflection upon the progress and enterprise of the city."[1] However, the project encountered numerous obstacles. First, the railways could not legally cooperate with each other on the construction of a union depot until the legislature amended laws restricting corporations from taking stock in other corporations or in private enterprises. Then, disputes among the railway companies over location and approaches further retarded progress. Finally, the obstacles were removed and work was begun on a new station to handle rail traffic listed in 1895 as forty-five passenger-train arrivals and departures per day.

[1] *Fort Worth Gazette*, August 4, 1895, p. 6.

Plate 70. Fort Worth Union Station, Fort Worth
View of Lobby

With its ornate appearance, the Fort Worth passenger depot typified the opulent depots that were produced by railroad prosperity. On the exterior, Renaissance richness was created by deep polychromatic contrast of materials in the walls and arches. On the interior, wall and ceiling decoration contributed to the richness of appearance. A massive portico with Ionic columns and Chinese railing, which once formed a transition between the exterior and this lobby, has been removed.

Institutional Edifices

THE GROWING POPULATION AND PROSPERITY that had produced the ostentatious commercial work of the latter part of the nineteenth century also made possible pretentious institutional buildings. While there were frequent criticisms directed toward the lack of stately edifices dedicated to the Deity by those who were at one time or another concerned about the moral condition of the state, established churches expanded, and many new organizations were formed. However, it was not until near the end of the century that the prevailing censure of ecclesiastical architecture changed noticeably to plaudit.

To a significant extent, the patterns for the erection of religious edifices reflected the ethnic history of the settlement of each region. In areas where the population included many of Latin descent, Catholicism was strong; in regions populated by German immigrants, the Catholic and Lutheran faiths were prominent, the latter reflecting the homeland through the native tongue; in sections settled predominantly by Anglo-Americans, the Episcopalian, Methodist, Baptist, and Presbyterian beliefs were vigorous. Thus, there resulted a regionalism of religious prevalence—a certain pattern being reflected by the number and magnitude of church buildings belonging to each denomination.

Throughout the United States, during the latter part of the nineteenth century, the outward character of the churches of all denominations was subject to the Romantic influences of the times, but distinctions between the various sects were strongly reflected by the inward forms of their architecture. The interiors were commensurate with the nature of the ritual of the worshippers. Plans for Christian edifices were functionally informed by the required relationships between clergy and laity, by the sacraments, and by the emphasis placed upon the furnishings necessary for the service. The design of interiors was then developed to enhance the mystery of the Catholic service, to the same degree that it was developed to stress the directness of the Protestant service. In Catholic churches lofty naves, side aisles, subdued light, reverberatory acoustics, and directed views all contributed to the emotional impact; in Protestant churches unobstructed sight lines in the auditoriums, clear acoustics, and physical comfort were a part of the backdrop for the spiritual experience of churchgoers.

The outward character of churches was developed from both objective and aesthetic considerations. Forms typically expressed the configuration of the plans, while the style of the decorative elements was generally developed in response to motivations to express ecclesiastical function. A religious edifice, it was firmly believed, should clearly declare its sacred purpose, as well as reflect the dignity of its builders. There should be no difficulty in distinguishing the church from other buildings. To communicate this identity and to convey the dedication of the parish or congregation, builders looked to the great ages of religion and sentimentally sought refuge in association with the styles of architecture that these had produced—styles that provided symbols and ornaments representing the spiritual meaning that was so essential. To most Christians, inspired by the ages of great European cathedrals, the Gothic Revival style romantically appealed because of its relationship with the architectural magnificence that originated from profound devotion to God. J. Coleman Hart, a church architect, expressed this point of view when he wrote, "It would be an error to urge the introduction of Gothic Church Architecture upon any other basis, than that of its symbolical meaning."[1] This same attitude prompted others to conclude that the Greek Revival style, which had characterized many antebellum Texas churches, was, by historical association, pagan.[2]

In the Gothic Revival, introduced into America on the strength of European precedent (chiefly English)[3] and becoming fashionable nationally in the decades after 1830, Texans sensed the same emotional qualities that were appreciated by others across the whole country. It symbolized and expressed dedication to Christianity.

Although there was a significant Spanish Colonial Catholic architectural heritage in the southern sections of the state, Spanish-inspired forms never became popular in the nineteenth century. For one thing, strong traditions and associations were brought to Texas by immigrants from other parts of the United States. Then, as an aftermath of the years of conflict, a patriotic dislike for things associated with despotic Mexico perhaps further negated any inclination to identify with Spanish or Mexican architecture. All this assured the popularity of revived Medieval styles in Texas.

The Gothic inspiration in the Catholic churches and cathedrals of the state appeared in various European derivations. Recalling French ecclesiastical work of Medieval times was the San Fernando Cathedral (1868–1873), San Antonio (plate 71). Built over an eighteenth-century Spanish Baroque church, this Catholic edifice had twin towers and triple portals, all appropriate for receiving processionals. In Fort Worth, in a style described as "modern English Gothic,"[4] was Saint Patrick's Catholic Church (1888), built out of stone, with handsome spires 250 feet high. More picturesque in composition, Saint Mary's Cathedral in Austin (1873–1884) was another example inspired by English work (plate 72). The German origins of its builders seemed to be reflected in the appearance of Saint Joseph's Catholic Church (1868–1871) in San Antonio (plate 73). Although it is not so clear in nationalistic character, yet another fine example of the Gothic was the San Agustin Church in Laredo (1872–1877), a large edifice with a single tower and rather heavy details (plate 74).

While various forms of the Gothic were generally the sources of inspiration for most large religious edifices, other styles occasionally proved acceptable. While some critics argued that the elements that had been derived from ancient Greece and Rome were pagan, proponents of Classical styles pointed out that these were no more anti-Christian than some pagan religious rites that had been incorporated by Christians. Moreover, one of the most beautiful monuments in the world, the magnificent Saint Peter's Cathedral in Rome, was Classic Renaissance in style.

For the Church of the Annunciation (1869–1871, 1884) in Houston, architect Nicholas J. Clayton drew freely on the Italian Renaissance that he used for many other building types (plate 75). On the exterior, round arches with heavy archivolts spanned the openings of the nave, while round arches supported by engaged Corinthian columns were salient features of the tower. On the interior, Corinthian columns and coffered vaulting complemented the Classical theme

---

[1] J. Coleman Hart, *Designs for Parish Churches*, pp. 18–19.
[2] See "Methodist Church Architecture," *National Magazine, Devoted to Literature, Art and Religion* 8 (February–March 1856): 223.
[3] Nikolaus Pevsner, *An Outline of European Architecture*, p. 290.

[4] *Fort Worth Daily Gazette*, June 27, 1888, p. 8.

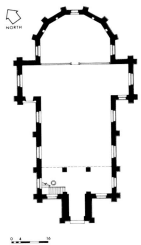

Fig. 28. Floor plan of Saint Mary's Catholic Church, Fredericksburg, Gillespie County (1861–1863). (Drawing by author, from Historic American Buildings Survey)

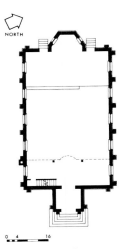

Fig. 29. Floor plan of the Gethsemane Lutheran Church, Austin, Travis County (1883). (Drawing by author, from Historic American Buildings Survey)

(plate 76). However, although the style of Annunciation was Classical, the plan was Medieval.

The configurations of plans for Catholic churches were developed and maintained in accordance with long-standing traditions established with respect to the requirement for the administration of the sacraments. They were either on the basilican plan—a rectangular form—or the cruciform—an axial cross-shaped configuration. In either case, the perspective of the nave, the central aisle, and openings in the walls created a strong visual movement from the entrance toward the sanctuary, where the altar was the focal point as the holiest place.

Fulfilling these objectives for their new Saint Mary's Church (1861–1863) in Fredericksburg, German Catholics employed the cruciform plan (fig. 28). This was also in a Gothic mode, recalling the homeland (plate 77).

The various forms of Gothic Revival proved to be very adaptable to the fulfillment of the urges of all nationalities to build with distinction. Although it was undoubtedly most impressive when most ornate, decoration could easily be restrained or modified while yet retaining the character of the style with basilican or cruciform plan and with simple pointed-arched openings and steeply pitched roofs. Saint Stan-

islaus Catholic Church in Bandera (1876), built by a group of Polish origin, was a simplified version of the style, characterized by lancets and a broad spire (plate 78). In the Praha Catholic Church (1891), built in a Czech community, although the composition was awkward, stone buttresses and lancets conveyed the impressions of the Gothic (plate 79). In the remarkable interior of this second example, the Gothic theme was carried out in the wooden ceiling and supports (plate 80).

Similar in form and scale to these Catholic edifices were the Lutheran churches of both the Germans and the Swedes. Although Lutherans differed from Catholics in their basic belief in the priesthood of the individual, the sacraments retained primary importance in the ritual of both. As did the Catholics, the Lutherans expressed the dogma of their religion with richly decorated chancels, stressed as focal points by formal interior balance (fig. 29). Within the chancel, there was a hierarchy of composition, the altar serving as the dominant form and the baptismal font and pulpit receiving secondary emphasis.

In churches reflecting the stress of ritual through focus upon the altar, a central tower, complementing the axial form, appropriately introduced the main entrance to the nave (plate 81). However, the Lutherans, like some other denominations, occasionally moved this dominant feature to the corner, thereby forming a more picturesque composition. This often occurred when the church was located at the corner of a street intersection, where there was a need for entrances into the tower from each street.

Although naturally concerned with economy and geology, the builders of churches of all denominations were also mindful of their selections of materials. Stone was preferred by most parishes, since it conveyed the concept of durability and honesty associated with the group that occupied the church and, at the same time, was picturesque and warm. If stone could not be had, brick was preferred, but, if this was also not available, the honest use of wood was sanctioned.

Like the Lutherans, the Episcopalians built distinctively. Although theirs was the official religion of the English colonies, brought to America by Captain John Smith in 1607, it was not established in Texas until the 1840's; and as late as 1859 there were only twelve of their churches in the entire state.[5] However, in postbellum years a great increase occurred in membership, and many new churches were built. As with most other denominations, the earliest Episcopal churches were wood framed, but even the smallest works were not without charm. When wood was used, style-conscious builders innovated details that had been developed for masonry in the architecture of antiquity. Thus, lancet openings and buttresses both formed from wood, as well as board-and-batten wall finishes with the lines stressing the perpendicular, appeared on many small churches in "rural Gothic" style (plate 82).

While other denominations also used Medieval English and Episcopalians did use other styles, to a significant extent their churches of the Lone Star State that were built from stone reflected the inspira-

tion of the architecture of the birthplace of the Anglican faith. Therefore, buildings inspired by the various phases of English Gothic were fairly common. In small churches, where detail was restrained, the style was Early English. Although many of these edifices seem to have been directly inspired by English paradigms, occasionally the influence was indirect, as in the Episcopal Church in Jefferson (1868–1870), which, according to legend, was modeled by E. G. Benners after a church in Virginia.

Several fine examples of the revived Early English Gothic were found in communities across the state, of which Saint Mary's Episcopal Church in Lampasas (1884) and Saint John's Episcopal Church (1892) in Brownwood were representative (plates 83, 84). Using native stone, both were distinguished by offset towers with crenellations and steeply pitched roof forms.

Although rare within the state, another phase of the English Gothic appeared in San Antonio. Saint Mark's Episcopal Church (1859–1875), the design of which is attributed to the "Dean of Episcopal architects," Richard Upjohn, was a fine expression of the English Perpendicular (plate 85).

From the point of view of association, these Medieval styles outwardly represented the spirit of inward ideas. Because of the focus upon the Eucharist (the liturgy of the Episcopal church in its separation retained the sacraments of the Catholic church), there was a close relationship between the Catholic and Episcopal rituals; therefore, the architectural emphases of the plans were similar. For example, in deference to the ritual, as exemplified by the interior of Saint Mark's, the focal point was the sanctuary—the "holy of holies" (plate 86). Secondary emphasis was then placed upon the chancel, with the choir, pulpit, and lectern all occupying traditional places in the composition.

Even though the character of the exteriors of Episcopal churches was subject to different stylistic expressions, there occurred little deviation from the traditional interior composition (plates 87, 88). In Saint James Episcopal Church of LaGrange (1885), the interior was formally composed, but the exterior, designed in an American version of the English Queen

[5] *Texas Almanac* (1859), p. 138. In 1840 in Matagorda, a church was assembled that had been constructed in New York and shipped in sections (see DuBose Murphy, "Early Days of the Protestant Episcopal Church in Texas," *Southwestern Historical Quarterly* 34, no. 4 [April 1931]: 296). Another church building, a Gothic-styled work, was opened in Galveston in 1842. In 1847 a church was completed in Houston, and in 1848 one was commenced in Nacogdoches.

Anne style, was picturesque and irregular. Similar in picturesque charm, but less pretentious, was the Saint Stephen's Episcopal Church (1896) in Fort Stockton (plate 89).

But while many Episcopal churches were distinguished by the antiquated English modes, others revealed varied sources of inspiration. As in many other architectural types of the last decades, several influences often evolved in the same edifice, particularly in large structures where there were opportunities to develop profuse decoration. A remarkable example of this was the Eaton Memorial Chapel of the Trinity Episcopal Church in Galveston (1878–1879; plate 90). According to one reporter—who certainly based his information on an interview with the architect, Nicholas J. Clayton—the style was "an adaptation of modern French gothic, based on the practice of such masters as Viollet la Duc [sic] and Spiers, Waterhouse, Seddon, Barry and the Younger Pugin of England"[6]—or, simply, Victorian Gothic.

The architecture of the other Protestant sects likewise reflected the nature of their religion. Just as the builders of Catholic, Lutheran, and Episcopal edifices brought to Texas traditions based on a heritage of ritual and on their knowledge of elaborate and beautiful churches and cathedrals in Europe, so other faiths, such as the Congregational, Methodist, Presbyterian, and Baptist, brought points of view based on different interpretations of the Scriptures and different traditions. The interiors of their churches reflected the nature of their devotions, with functional emphasis placed on the elements that were appropriate for their service. Since the church was considered to be eminently a "place where the word of God, the living word, is expounded and enforced by the living voices,"[7] the pulpit, rather than an altar, was the focal point. In the basilican plan, often adopted because many argued that the transepts of the cruciform plan were inappropriate, a large pulpit for preaching was commonly centered on the axis of the audience room. Then, the symbol of the great atonement, the table of

the Lord's Supper, was visually stressed by its location in front of the pulpit, on a lower level.

The interior spaces for the audiences likewise revealed the nature of the service. Without chancels and without processionals, there was little need for long central aisles; hence, many designers advocated placing seats in the center rather than allowing for a wide aisle. Access to the pews was provided from the sides. With less stress on ritual and less emphasis on formal composition of the interior, more attention was given to comfort and convenience. Seating plans were developed relative to good acoustics and good sight lines to the pulpit. Nonetheless, axial interior arrangements still prevailed in some churches.

A matter of some contention among architects, clergy, and laity was the appropriate character for the exterior of Protestant churches. For example, the Congregational church—New England church of the Pilgrims and Puritans—had developed out of protest against the lengthy ritual of the Church of England and domination by the priesthood. At first, the architectural consequences of this reaction were the elimination of decoration and symbols from the meetinghouses, thus expressing the rigid Puritan doctrine by simplicity of architectural form. Although the seventeenth-century meetinghouses were plain—similar to the dwellings of the Puritans—by the end of the nineteenth century the decoration of Congregational churches was sanctioned so that the religious edifice might not appear tawdry in the midst of surrounding buildings. As advocated by a convention of ministers, the adornment of the church "should correspond in style to the better class of dwellings possessed by those who are to occupy the church."[8] Indeed, to dwell in luxury and worship in poverty seemed paradoxical.

To assist congregations and builders, numerous books on church architecture were published.[9] Writ-

[6] *Galveston Daily News*, July 6, 1879, p. 4.
[7] Convention of Ministers and Delegates of the Congregational Churches in the United States, *A Book of Plans for Churches and Parsonages*, p. 6.

[8] Ibid., p. 11.
[9] For example, F. J. Jobson, *Chapel and School Architecture, as Appropriate to the Buildings of Nonconformists*; and Richard Upjohn, *Upjohn's Rural Architecture*. Richard Upjohn, an Episcopalian, published his book specifically for "those parishes who were too poor to afford even the most modest architect's fee or too distant to permit personal attention" (Everard M. Upjohn, *Richard Upjohn, Architect and Churchman*, p. 90). Convention of Ministers, *A Book of Plans*, contained designs by Richard Up-

ten by clergymen or architects, these contained plans and elevations of religious edifices, often prepared by talented designers. Most authors intended that their designs should generally serve only as guides to promote economy, good planning, and good taste, and therefore they recommended that architects be commissioned to prepare more complete designs and specifications. As if they understood the intent of these publications, when architects or contractors followed the demands of building committees in adhering to published designs, they invariably innovated on the details and dimensions.

Even if time has obscured their influences, it is apparent that some of these books reached Texas. Quite possibly inspired by some such designs was the First Presbyterian Church (1873) in Jefferson (plate 91). Although there was considerable modification of ornamental features, the two-story form with Classical proportions, recalling some of the early New England churches, was similar to a design in *Chapel and Church Architecture*.[10] The First Presbyterian Church in Waco (1872) was also similar to this published paradigm. The central tower with a high spire was characteristic of this design and of this period (plate 92).

Since the nonconformist religions had no direct association with the Catholic Medieval period, the Gothic Revival style was less meaningful to their parishioners and certainly had less impact on their churches. For Presbyterians and others, any architectural mode was generally considered acceptable, although some authorities advocated that several styles should not be mixed in the same building. Notwithstanding, many churches of the eighties and nineties did exhibit mixtures of details. Paradoxically, in the First Presbyterian Church in Bonham (1884–1885) pointed and round-arched forms, shingles and weatherboards, pinnacles and brackets suggested a variety of sources (plate 93). The wood-structured First Presbyterian Church in Mexia (late nineteenth century) had

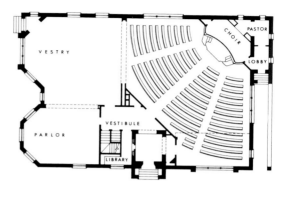

Fig. 30. Floor plan of the First Presbyterian Church, Fort Worth, Tarrant County (1889–1890). (Drawing by author, from the *Fort Worth Daily Gazette*, August 31, 1890, p. 11)

pointed Gothic, as well as horseshoe arches, the latter recalling Islamic details (plate 94).

Slightly more unified if not more consistent was the First Presbyterian Church (1891) in Paris (plate 95). In this edifice the Classical character of the Renaissance prevailed on the interior, where functionalism determined the form (plate 96), as well as on the exterior.

The emphasis on good acoustics, sight lines, and flexibility, along with the single focus on the pulpit and communion table, occasioned the development of the Akron plan in Akron, Ohio. Originated by George Washington Kramer, the elevated platform for preaching was placed in the corner or center of the audience room, with the seating in circular pattern focusing upon the preacher.[11] This plan became very popular in Texas.

A fine example of this scheme was the First Presbyterian Church (1889–1890) in Fort Worth (fig. 30). A large polychromatic edifice of Granbury limestone in combination with Pecos stone, the church was de-

___

john, Andrew Jackson Downing, James Renwick, and Gervaise Wheeler, all prominent architects.

[10] George Bowler, *Chapel and Church Architecture, with Designs for Parsonages*, design no. 4.

[11] According to Kramer's obituary, the plan was developed upon the suggestion of Lewis A. Miller, father-in-law of Thomas A. Edison. The time of its development was between 1879 and 1885. Although Kramer, who designed over 2,200 churches, evidently had had no academic training in architecture, he designed numerous religious edifices in the East (*New York Times*, October 21, 1938, p. 23).

signed "to provide everything necessary to comfort and convenience, and . . . to avoid all features which in other buildings have been found to interfere with perfect enjoyment." These attributes, it was claimed, were the advantages of the quarter-turn and semicircular seating of the Akron plan. As was characteristic of this plan, the interior circular geometry was not outwardly reflected by any curved forms on the exterior. Instead, irregular masses, numerous gables, and asymmetrically placed towers were featured.

The Akron plan was also used in Texas by the Methodist church. Methodists likewise believed that the church design should reflect the object of the worship; hence, the pulpit for preaching the Gospel—the central idea of the church—was the focal point of the auditorium. Seating concentric to this point was then consistent with their objective. In the Methodist Episcopal Church in Fort Worth (1887), a brick edifice trimmed with stone in Gothic Revival, the auditorium was sixty by ninety feet, with seating on a circular plan upon a sloping floor, as in a theater. With a forty-foot-high ceiling and numerous ventilators, the building was also praised for its excellent air circulation.

Near the end of the century, while Methodists frequently erected pretentious places of worship in large cities, they often excluded any embellishment from rural churches. Originally, the teachings of the church had been taken to remote areas by circuit riders, who attempted to integrate religion and everyday activities. Methodists had become accustomed to practicing their religion with little aid in the way of architecture and with minimum ritualistic requirements. A barrel sometimes served as a pulpit, and often benches were logs or boxes placed under the shelter of an oak tree. The earliest meetinghouses were small and without tower or steeple. Late in the century, even in large churches, a plain tower, along with a few lancets, still comprised the chief ecclesiastical features. Epitomizing this was the Channing Methodist Church (1898), located in the Panhandle (plate 97). Usually these towers were offset, as in the Salado Methodist Church (circa 1890), a wooden structure (plate 98).

Since the Methodists' association with the great ages of Christian architecture of antiquity was indi-

Fig. 31. Plan and perspective of the First Baptist Church, Fort Worth, Tarrant County (1888). Bullard and Bullard, architects. (*Fort Worth Daily Gazette*, April 8, 1888, p. 8; photo from the Texas State Library, Austin)

rect, founded in eighteenth-century England, they consequently were not as style conscious as some other denominations. However, they generally believed that the house of worship ought to reflect the wealth of the parishioners. Although any architectural style was permissible, as long as the edifice proclaimed its ecclesiastical nature, Gothic Revival details were found on many of their churches throughout the state (plate 99).

The Baptist church was among the denominations that considered architectural adornment of comparatively little importance. Throughout the state, numerous small buildings were erected with little or no decoration on exteriors or interiors, often as a consequence of limited means of their builders, other times perhaps as a fulfillment of ascetic taste.

Baptist interiors indicated the nature of their religious faith. Since its emphasis was on the Bible, the pulpit, with the open Book, was the focal point from which the preacher related everyday problems to the

Fig. 32. Design for the Alamo Baptist Church, San Antonio, Bexar County (circa 1891). J. Riely Gordon, architect. (*Inland Architect and News Record* 18, no. 2 [September 1891]: pl. 2; photo from the Library of Congress)

Fig. 33. Perspective of Saint Paul's Methodist Episcopal Church, Fort Worth, Tarrant County (1892). (*Fort Worth Daily Gazette*, March 21, 1893, p. 20; photo from the Texas State Library, Austin)

life of Christ. In front of the pulpit was the table of the Lord's Supper, and behind was usually the choir, both located on the axis of the auditorium. Therefore, for the Baptists, plans which provided a major emphasis upon the pulpit, with the secondary emphasis upon adjunct features, were also appropriate.

The First Baptist Church in Fort Worth (1888), designed by the firm of Bullard and Bullard, was a noteworthy example of the embodiment of Baptist religious dogma in architecture (fig. 31). A square auditorium contained concentric seating that focused upon the rostrum. On the main level, folding doors permitted the auditorium and a large Sunday-school room to be utilized as one unit, to accommodate an overflow audience. In the basement folding doors allowed the organization of a large space for Sunday school, prayer meetings, and social purposes. Although the smaller churches were commonly unpretentious, this church, a large edifice of Granbury limestone, was truly a picturesque work with turrets, pointed arches, and tall spire, described as "modern English Gothic."[12]

While the Baptist belief differed considerably from the Catholic faith that had produced the Gothic, that same style was to be found in some Baptist churches. However, it was perhaps more meaningful to Baptists as a fulfillment of demands for architectural distinction than as an association with Medieval religious fervor. Certainly, this reason for its use was evident in the First Baptist Church in Carrizo Springs (1888–1891; plate 100).

More than the Catholic, the Lutheran, and the Episcopal churches, where the Gothic prevailed, the styles of the large buildings of the nonconformist denominations evidenced changes in architectural fashions across the nation. Thus, many edifices of Baptists, Methodists, and Christians erected during the nineties were in the popular and imposing round-arched Romanesque Revival style. Outstanding examples of this were the Alamo Baptist Church in San Antonio (circa 1891; fig. 32)[13] by J. Riely Gordon—an architect who did some of his finest work in this style—and Saint Paul's Methodist Episcopal Church in Fort Worth (1892; fig. 33).

[12] *Fort Worth Daily Gazette*, June 17, 1888, p. 8.

[13] See *Inland Architect and News Record* 17, no. 2 (September 1891).

143

The Christian church—the only one of the Protestant denominations that originated in America—adopted patterns similar to those of the Baptists, to which denomination they were close. Churches, if small, were plain, but, if large, they generally featured the opulence of various styles, reflecting the wealth of the members.

Minority religions in Texas produced interesting although not numerous buildings. Enjoying the religious freedom of the state, some, such as the immigrant Moravians (Wesley Brethren), built simply but incorporated into their architecture a symbolism that was certainly nostalgic of their homeland, Bohemia (plates 101, 102).

Nineteenth-century synagogues were not numerous in Texas. While oriental character might have appeared historically appropriate for those that were built, as an identifying image of the Jewish faith, the temples conformed to no one particular style. Jefferson's synagogue was Greek; Galveston's Congregation B'nai Israel Synagogue (1870) was Gothic with Moorish details.

Associated with many of the religious edifices of Texas was the requirement for parochial educational buildings, which contributed substantially to the architectural scene during the closing decades of the nineteenth century. Academies that had been founded before the Civil War were either maintained and expanded or relocated. In addition, after Reconstruction many new church-supported and privately financed academies and colleges were established for the education of both males and females in art, music, language, and literature.

Everywhere in the state the architectural trend for these was toward a general consistency in style with other similar building types. In undeveloped areas a straightforward design was characteristic, while in other regions the sophistication of historic architectural modes indicated cultural development and economic affluence. Commonly, the affiliation of parochial schools with the church was suggested by variations of the Gothic, associated with Christianity.

A conservative version of this style was exemplified by several buildings of the Ursuline Academy in San Antonio. Although the first buildings housing educa-

Fig. 34. Main Building, University of Texas, Austin, Travis County (1883–1899; razed 1934). Drawing by F. E. Ruffini, architect. (Photo from Texas State Library, Austin)

tional activities were unpretentious in form and style —similar to much other early architecture in the Alamo City—additions were larger and more elaborate (plate 103). In the latter examples simple Gothic Revival details suggested building functions with ecclesiastical purpose (plate 104).

With progress and affluence, more elaborate examples of the decorative Gothic were developed. The desire to express the esteem of both the church and the public for their educational institutions created an avid appreciation of the flamboyant. The bravura of the Medieval elements well denoted the subjective importance attached to buildings dedicated to the advancement of culture. Following an interview with architect F. E. Ruffini, one reporter emotionally expressed the intent of the "very imposing" appearance of the main building at the University of Texas (1883–1899), a Victorian Gothic structure, when he wrote, "The effect of the entire building, when it is completed, will be at once grand, and will compose a fitting monument to remind coming posterity of the high estimate placed upon education by the founders of our great state"[14] (fig. 34). The opulent Victorian Gothic, expressive of the prestige of the institution, was also employed at Sam Houston Normal Institute (State College) at Huntsville in the Main Building,

14 *Houston Daily Post*, September 16, 1883, p. 1.

Fig. 36. Main Hall, Texas A&M College, College Station, Brazos County (1871–1874, burned 1912). Jacob Larmour, architect. (Photo from the Texas State Library, Austin)

Fig. 35. Ursuline Convent, Galveston, Galveston County (1891–1894, razed 1962). Nicholas J. Clayton, architect. (Photo from the Texas State Historical Association, Austin)

the cornerstone for which was laid in 1888 (plate 105).

Probably no architect in Texas did more, through example, to popularize the Victorian Gothic than the prolific Nicholas J. Clayton of Galveston. One of his most elaborate expressions of this Medieval-inspired mode was the Ursuline Convent in Galveston (1891–1894, razed 1962), a delightful Venetian Gothic edifice (fig. 35). (In the picturesque, Clayton also created the Palestine Masonic Temple [1878, razed 1962], a red brick structure trimmed with iron.)

Yet another remarkable example in which this mode appropriately conveyed the image of the school was Saint Edward's University (1885, 1903), located near Austin (plate 106). As was common wherever possible among educational institutions, the main building occupied a commanding eminence, which further contributed to its imposing appearance and to the pomp of its image.

Although the various forms of the Gothic could easily be associated by the public with ecclesiastical purpose, other styles were also employed on church-supported institutions. The mansard roofs of the Second Empire, a secular mode that at one time or another was popular for virtually every kind of building except churches, also characterized many educational structures of the seventies, eighties, and nineties. For the Saint Ignatius Academy (1889) in Fort Worth this mansardic mode was selected (plate 107). A more pretentious expression of this fashion had been created in the Trinity University building (Westminster Bible College; 1871) at Tehuacana (plate 108).

When this mode was used, the mansard roofs covering the main mass were usually dominated by a rather pretentious tower, as in the Main Building at Baylor University (1886; plate 109). Projecting boldly forward and upward, with the main accesses in their base, towers were capped with ornamental crestings and often contained clocks, many of which have been removed in the twentieth century. Also among the many secular educational institutions of the Second Empire style was Main Hall (1871–1874) at Texas A&M College (University), a four-story brick edifice with twin mansard-roofed towers (fig. 36).[15]

[15] Homer S. Thrall, *The People's Illustrated Almanac, Texas Hand-book and Immigrant's Guide, for 1880*, p. 77.

With the decline in popularity of the mansard roof, other styles became fashionable in educational buildings, such as the picturesque Romanesque. At Southwestern College (University) in Georgetown, a Methodist school, "Old Main" (1898–1900), with its towers and pinnacles, was a picturesque example of this fashion (plate 110). Among the most handsome works in the state in the Romanesque was the University of Texas School of Medicine (1889–1890) at Galveston (plates 111, 112).

In the small Texas college of the nineteenth century, the diverse functional needs of the institution were all housed in a single edifice until the enrollment expanded beyond the designed capacity. Students of Texas Wesleyan College in Fort Worth (1885), planned by Sanguinet and Dawson, entered the doors of a round-arched-styled pressed-brick building of three stories. On the ground floor were the president's offices, classrooms, and a chapel; on the second were the library and dormitories for both sexes, separated by a reception room; on the third were an art room and an observatory.[16]

In cities and towns throughout the state, character and form similar to those of the academies and colleges were also found in the elementary and secondary schools, springing up in large numbers from the late 1880's until the turn of the century. Usually of substantial masonry to endure for many decades, these were rigid and balanced in composition and form, suggestive of the sternly disciplined academic programs. Multistoried, with large classrooms and halls, they customarily had large, formally composed cupolas or towers.

As with the academies and colleges, the sophistication of architectural design revealed the public's esteem in its city's educational program, and the visual expression of the school was considered as a cultural image. The Cleburne Public School (1883), designed by A. N. Dawson, was described as a "substantial 'emblem' to speak volumes for the intelligent and enlightened citizens."[17] When Galveston chose formal

Fig. 37. Ball High School, Galveston, Galveston County (1884). (Photo from the Texas State Historical Association, Austin)

Renaissance Revival for Ball High School (1884), the public was also making a strong statement relative to its pride in its program of secondary education (fig. 37).[18] However, few of these formally designed structures remain today.

Perhaps not so highly regarded as those for culture and religion were other public institutional structures, such as hospitals, sanatoriums, infirmaries, and mental hospitals. In the nineteenth century, however, structures for medical care were not without significance. Although some were makeshift affairs, others owned by the churches, the public, or the railroads were formally planned and durably constructed. In character, the permanent works generally conformed to the architectural trends of the period, commonly Second Empire or Romanesque, although they were not usually as ornate as other building types. Saint Mary's Infirmary in Galveston (1875), one of the early "substantial" medical buildings in the state, was mansard roofed (plate 113). Saint Paul's Sanitarium in Dallas (1896), a masonry structure decorated with Pecos sandstone, was three stories and Romanesque.

Thus, historical evidence reveals that institutional edifices of Texas were expressions of both culture and purpose. Conforming to national trends in architec-

---

[16] *Fort Worth Daily Gazette*, October 13, 1885, p. 8.
[17] *Houston Daily Post*, October 16, 1883, p. 6.

[18] See Ralph Julian, "A Recent Journey through the West," *Harper's Weekly*, November 9, 1895, p. 1064.

tural fashion, they reflected the cultural values, as well as the wealth, of those who erected them; in their exterior and interior composition and form they reflected the nature of the activities they housed. With style, there was an awareness of picturesquely expressing function, as well as "modernity." Through this character, they revealed the delight of the various organizations and communities in their religious, educational, and medical institutions. Nevertheless, the most pretentious and elaborate buildings were the civic edifices erected collectively by the people.

Plate 71. San Fernando Cathedral, 115 Main Avenue, San Antonio, Bexar County (1734–1873)
Francis Giraud and Others, Architects   View from Southeast

Construction on the parochial church of the Villa de San Fernando was commenced in 1734, but it was not until 1738 that the cornerstone was laid and 1749 that it was dedicated under the invocation Nuestra Señora de la Candelaria y Guadalupe. Facing east, this early work was built of stone on a cruciform plan, similar to the mission church of San Antonio de Valero. Vaults spanned the arms of this cross, while a dome (which collapsed several times) spanned the crossing on a pendentives. With little decoration, the architectural character was that of strength and severity.

In 1868 the cornerstone for the present large structure was cemented into place. Designed by Francis Giraud, the new church was literally built over the old one, with part of the eighteenth-century walls of the apse and transept being incorporated. The church was consecrated a cathedral the year following completion.

Although considered complete in 1873, the building had only the north tower. The south appendage was added in the twentieth century. However, two projected high spires were never completed. Also in the twentieth century, a chancery was added to the Spanish section.

With its lancet openings, twin towers, and triple portals, this is a beautiful example of the Gothic Revival. Of native stone, the buttresses of the nave and towers visually strengthen the work and emphasize the heavenward urge, while the quatrefoils, pinnacles, and moldings elaborate on the Christian theme.

148

Plate 72. Saint Mary's Cathedral, East 10 and Brazos Streets, Austin, Travis County (1873–1884)
Nicholas J. Clayton, Architect   View

In 1852 the walls of Saint Patrick's Church rose at the corner of Brazos and Ash streets on land that had been purchased by Father J. M. Odin,[1] shortly after Austin had been platted. Right after the Civil War, a tower was added and the name of this edifice was changed to Saint Mary's.

Determination to worship within a structure expressive of profound dedication to God resulted in the commencement of work on this beautiful edifice. In Early English Gothic style, it was distinguished by a dominant tower with octagonal spires and by a magnificent rose window. Bold hood moldings, trefoils and quatrefoils,

tooth moldings, and diamond-pane glass were less dominant elements amplifying the Medieval theme.

Changes in the architecture of Saint Mary's, built of Austin stone, occurred with time. In 1922 the roof of Pennsylvania blue slate was replaced with clay tile. Stained-glass windows symbolizing the saints and apostles of the Catholic faith were installed after the church was completed. The tower was completed near the turn of the century.

[1] Mary Starr Barkley, *History of Travis County and Austin, 1839–1899*, p. 280.

Plate 73. Saint Joseph's Catholic Church, 221 East Commerce Street, San Antonio, Bexar County (1868–1871)
G. Freisleben and Others, Architects
View

German immigrants of the Catholic faith arriving in San Antonio before mid-century joined the old parish of San Fernando Church. In the 1850's, a desire to have a "national church," where the tongue of the fatherland was spoken, prompted the Germans to establish their own church. In 1868 the cornerstone, one side of which bore the inscription "Sieh die Wohnung Gottes bei den Menschen" (Behold the dwelling of God among men), was set into place, and three years later the church edifice, sans steeple and glass windows, was blessed.

Many artists contributed to the design and construction of the Gothic Revival edifice. In 1868 architect Freisleben, who planned the building, resigned and was replaced by Theodore Giraud.[1] Father Henry Pefferkorn, during his tenure as third pastor of Saint Joseph's (from 1878 to 1896), designed the main and side altars, painted the *Assumption of the Blessed Virgin* and the *Ascension of Jesus* for the side altars, and may have painted the stations of the cross. In 1897 James Wahrenberger designed the steeple, which was constructed the following year. Designed by European artists and imported from the Emil Frei Art Glass works of Munich,[2] stained-glass windows were installed in 1902. The frescoing of the ceiling and interior walls was done in 1901 by F. Stockert and A. Kern.

[1] Ray Neumann, *A Centennial History of St. Joseph's Church and Parish, 1868–1968*, p. 8.
[2] Ibid., p. 34.

Plate 74. San Agustin Catholic Church, 214 San Agustin Avenue, Laredo, Webb County (1872–1877)
Pierre Yves Keralum, Architect   View from Southwest

Although documentary evidence is lacking, the first church of San Agustín de Laredo was apparently com-

150

pleted by 1764.[1] This was a structure with walls of brick and stone. With some alterations, it served for approximately a century, until this nineteenth-century edifice was erected.

Located across from San Agustin Plaza, this church has been remodeled numerous times. Consequently, some changes in the exterior appearance may have resulted.

It was a cathedral until 1911, when the seat of the diocese was moved to Corpus Christi.

[1] Sister Natalie Walsh, "The Founding of Laredo and St. Augustine Church," M.A. thesis, p. 107.

Plate 76. Church of the Annunciation, Houston
View of Nave

The interior was elegant and dignified. Rhythmic movement toward the altar—the focal point of the entire edifice—was created by the columns and arches. As was common in Catholic churches, the apse containing the altar was semicircular in plan, was physically separated from the nave, and was covered with a dome roof. Entry to the nave under the vaulted access increased the drama of the space.

Clayton also designed numerous churches for his home town, Galveston. Among these were Saint Patrick's Cathedral (1872–1878), a fine Gothic Revival edifice on a cruciform plan, and Grace Episcopal Church (1894–1895), a white limestone work also Gothic in style.

Plate 75. Church of the Annunciation, Crawford Street and Texas Avenue, Houston, Harris County (1869–1871, 1884)
Architect of Original Church Unknown; Nicholas J. Clayton, Architect of Remodeled Church   View from North

Slightly over a decade following its completion, the original building showed dangerous signs of deterioration. Wide cracks had opened in the walls from ground to cornice, the towers at the front were leaning away from the building, and numerous leaks had appeared in the roof. Subsequently, Clayton was commissioned to renovate the edifice, remodeling it in Renaissance Revival style. Buttresses were added to the existing walls, a new roof was constructed, and at the front a graceful 175-foot-high tower and spire were added between the old towers. At the base of this addition a new entrance was created. The limestone structure was then stuccoed and trimmed with brown marble.

Plate 78. Saint Stanislaus Catholic Church, 703 Cypress Street, Bandera, Bandera County (1876)
Architect Unknown   View

Erected by a congregation that had been organized by sixteen Polish families, this church was a rugged work. Although details of native stone were coarse, offsets of the tower and the profile of the entrance features nonetheless reflected the builders' sensitivity to refinement. The different quality of the masonry, in both the wall and the pointed arches, on the uppermost section of the tower indicates a later addition.

Plate 77. Saint Mary's Catholic Church, South Orange and West San Antonio Streets, Fredericksburg, Gillespie County (1861–1863)
Architect Unknown   View from Southwest

Saint Mary's Church was built on land purchased in 1848, only two years after Fredericksburg had been laid out. While the church temporarily occupied a log building, some eighteen feet wide and forty-six feet long, German Catholics commenced work on a new permanent stone edifice. Under the direction of Father Peter Baunach, a Benedictine priest, most of the labor was done by members of the parish.

Recalling the German Gothic of the homeland, the structure was dominated by a tall tower, terminated at the sky by masonry vaulting. Clocks were mounted on the southeast and northeast faces of the steeple.

On the interior the walls were finished with plaster, and the ceiling with tongued-and-grooved boards. Six-pointed stars, located above the nave, chancel, and crossing of the arms of the plan, formed interesting features of the ceiling. The aisles were paved with soapstone flagging, but the floor under the pews was covered with sand. At the back of the nave formerly was a balcony, under which was the baptistry.

This building was used until 1906, when a new church was completed nearby on the northwest. Subsequently, with remodeling and the addition of a second floor in the nave, it became a church school, but it was ultimately entirely abandoned. The wooden spandrels were added to the windows when the second floor was installed.

155

Plate 80. Praha Catholic Church, Praha
View of Nave

Although evidently without actual structural significance, the intent of the interior was to represent Medieval stone vaulting with wood. On the tongued-and-grooved ceiling boards were painted decorative impressions of the ribs of vaults, as well as various religious symbols. In addition to the jeweled cross, the symbols included the blazing star, representative of the omnipresence of the Deity; the all-seeing eye, symbolic of the innermost acumens of the heart; the chalice and the paten, representative of Holy Communion; and the orb-and-cross chalice, which stands for power and justice in Christianity.

Plate 79. Praha Catholic Church, Praha, Fayette County (1891)
Architect Unknown   View

An additional example of the use of the Gothic by European immigrants, this edifice was built in a Bohemian settlement near Flatonia. The first Catholic church built by the community—which included among its early residents M. Novak, F. Branitzky, and Jos. Vyvjala—was a wooden-framed work set up in 1868. Only seven years later it was replaced, and, finally, these permanent stone walls rose. Although the tower lacks visual structural clarity, since it appears to bear on the roof, the design successfully conveys the ecclesiastical function.

Plate 81. Gethsemane Lutheran Church, West 16 Street and North Congress Avenue, Austin, Travis County (1883)
August Swenson, Architect   View

Although Swedish immigration to Texas had begun in 1838, it was not until 1868 that the first Swedish Lutheran services were held in Austin.[1] Shortly afterward, the congregation occupied a small building at the corner of Ninth and Guadalupe streets. In 1883, they moved into this new edifice, which had been designed by Swenson, a cabinet maker. Located near the Capitol, it was built by S. A. Carlson.

Much of the material was salvaged. Both stone and brick came from the old Capitol, which had been destroyed by fire in 1881. In 1934 doors from "Old Main" at the University of Texas, which had been razed, were installed on the front.

In 1965 the state purchased the structure, intending to maintain it as a museum. However, the building is presently used by the Texas State Historical Survey Committee for offices and meetings.

[1] Texas State Historical Survey Committee files, Austin.

Plate 82. Christ Episcopal Church, Ayish Street, between Main and Market Streets, San Augustine, San Augustine County (1869–1870)
The Reverend R. R. Richardson, Architect   View

Several years after the conclusion of the Civil War, San Augustine Episcopalians commenced work on a charming new church to replace a mid-century building that, after only a decade of use, collapsed because of faulty construction.[1] Land had been donated by George F. Crocket, and lumber for the frame structure was contributed by Col. S. W. Blount. As was often the case, the tower was omitted from the original construction but was later added (1891).

Several renovations have been made to keep the structure sound. Among these, shortly before the turn of the century, the roof was replaced, and, soon after, the foundations were repaired.

[1] George Louis Crocket, *Two Centuries in East Texas*, p. 290.

159

Plate 83. Saint Mary's Episcopal Church, 503 South Chestnut Street, Lampasas, Lampasas County (1884) W. T. Campbell, Architect [?]   View

   With walls of native stone, this building was reportedly patterned after a church in Rugby, England, by W. T. Campbell, an Englishman.[1] Particularly noteworthy were the crenellations and rose window. Although the craftsmanship of the masonry is rough, the overall quality of the church impresses one with its permanence and strength.

[1] Texas State Historical Survey Committee files, Austin.

Plate 84. Saint John's Episcopal Church, Depot and Main Streets, Brownwood, Brown County (1892)
Lovell and Hood, Architects and Builders   View from Northwest

In charming Gothic Revival style, this edifice was characteristic of the beauty of Episcopal churches throughout the West. On the exterior warm brown hues were created with native stone; on the interior the brilliant purple and yellow hues of stained glass and the exposed wood structural members contributed to the eloquence of the building. The beauty and variety of the cut and pitch-faced masonry are also noteworthy in this view.

Plate 85. Saint Mark's Episcopal Church, 307 East Pecan Street, San Antonio, Bexar County (1859–1875)
Richard Upjohn, Architect   View from Southwest

From the very beginning, labor on Saint Mark's was beset by many delays. Work first commenced in 1853 but was shortly thereafter abandoned. Six years later construction was resumed, and near the end of the year the cornerstone was laid. Under the supervision of the Reverend Lucius H. Jones, work continued slowly until the beginning of the Civil War—when most civil construction was suspended—leaving the thick limestone walls only partially raised. Not until 1873 were the sounds of mechanics' tools again heard, but on Easter 1875 the nave finally received worshippers.

The window tracery, hood moldings, and bold projecting buttresses were characteristic of the English Perpendicular style. The Reverend Walter Raleigh Richardson, who moved to San Antonio in 1868 and whose remains are entombed under the chancel, designed the stained-glass windows, as well as the frescoing on the ceiling on the interior.

An addition on the west was built in 1936.

Plate 86. Saint Mark's Episcopal Church, San Antonio
View of Nave and Apse

The plan of Saint Mark's was basilican, with narthex, nave, side aisles, chancel, and apse. The columns, from which spring the wooden arches, created a strong forward rhythm to the sacred areas. Characteristic of Episcopal churches, the latter were physically and visually well defined. The apse, in the form of a half-decagon, was enframed by the apse arch. Within the sanctuary, the altar was stressed by high position.

The interior was enhanced by beautiful decorative features, which were emphasized by contrasting white plaster. The pulpit was mahogany, and the doors were oak with carved details. Apse and floor steps were decorated with inlaid patterns of hardwood. The quatrefoil motif was employed frequently in the ornamental patterns.

163

Plate 87. Saint James Episcopal Church, Monroe and Colorado Streets, LaGrange, Fayette County (1885)
Richard M. Upjohn, Architect   View from Northwest

Designed by the son of the older Upjohn, who was widely known for his Episcopal churches, the decoration of this edifice, built by a parish formed in 1855, conformed to the taste of the period. The Queen Anne, based on a revival in England and made popular abroad by Richard Norman Shaw, was a style of half-timber work, brick, hung tile, and stucco. After the influence reached America in the 1870's, the fabric was often entirely transformed into wood, with walls covered with shingles. Surfaces were commonly articulated with boards as if to simulate half-timbering. In recent years, this construction has been labeled the "Shingle Style" by art historian Vincent Scully, Jr. Although this mode had a most pro-

found impact on residential work, it also appeared in other building types, as attested by this church.

In this wooden-framed building, shingles covered most of the walls and the steeply pitched roof, the vastness of which was relieved by eyebrows. The tower was then decorated with boards in geometrical patterns. Tudor spindles, also characteristic of the style, supported the porch roofs.

The church is also noteworthy for the manner in which the design responded to the climate. Louvered and screened openings, which were closed by removable solid panels on the interior, flanked the pews, allowing for air circulation in hot weather.

164

Plate 88. Saint James Episcopal Church, LaGrange
View Looking toward Chancel

The interiors of nineteenth-century Episcopal churches were typically characterized by warmth and by structural truth, attributes well expressed in this view. Structural columns and trusses were featured, creating interesting patterns and expressing the clarity of the structure. Wooden decorative details and furnishings were stained to maintain the natural beauty of the material. The charm of this interior was greatly enhanced with brilliant color from the leaded stained-glass windows.

Plate 89. Saint Stephen's Episcopal Church, East Second Street and Spring Drive, Fort Stockton, Pecos County (1896)
Architect Unknown   View

Various ornamental features identify this picturesque building with its era. Channeled siding, etched glass, and decorative patterns of shingles were characteristic of much late-nineteenth-century wooden-framed archi-tecture. However, the lack of a dominant long axis was unusual in an Episcopal church.

In 1958 the building was moved from its original site to the present location.

Plate 90. Eaton Memorial Chapel, Trinity Episcopal Church, 710 Twenty-second Street, Galveston, Galveston County (1878–1879)
Clayton and Lynch, Architects   View from Southwest

Built as a memorial to the Reverend Benjamin Eaton, first rector of Trinity Episcopal Church, Galveston, this edifice was designed to contain schoolrooms, a library, and a chapel for a parochial school. The plan was rectangular—forty-five by eighty-five feet—and symmetrical, with transepts projecting slightly from each long side.

Massive buttresses, large pinnacles, thick stringcourses, and window hoods created a statement of strength and conviction. Other notable features on the exterior included the portal, with its fine moldings and tracery. In the transepts were rose windows with quatrefoil tracery and stained glass. Ornamental crosses and crestings, originally important in the silhouette against the sky, have been removed.

The chapel interior was finished with native pine and cypress, stained to imitate ash, oak, and walnut. The paneled ceiling was decorated with foliated forms.

Plate 91. First Presbyterian Church, 600 East Jefferson Street, Jefferson, Marion County (1873)
John Ligon, Architect
View from South

While the window and door openings, filled with diamond patterns, suggested pointed features associated with the Gothic Revival, the design also owes much to the Renaissance. On the exterior both the roof slope and the round-arched openings were Classical. On the interior heavy wooden cornices with dentils of Classical design surmounted the windows.

The brick-and-metal ornamentation is also noteworthy. A heavy stringcourse marks the level of the main floor, which was approached by ascending an exterior stairway made of iron and an interior one made of wood. A heavy cornice terminated the walls, and each pilaster was capped with a sheet-metal finial.

Since the congregation is now small, the auditorium is no longer used.

Plate 92. First Presbyterian Church, Jefferson
Detail of Spire

Spires were considered to be essential elements for Christian temples by virtually all nineteenth-century writers on ecclesiastical architecture. Without them, towers appeared stunted and unfinished. Moreover, they stressed verticality, symbolic of the heavenward urge.

Although they occasionally appeared, clocks were not common on church towers. Indeed, there was, in fact, no timepiece here; rather, representations of the face and hands of a clock were simply painted on sheet metal. Perpetually set hands were an ever-present reminder that the service began punctually at eleven o'clock.

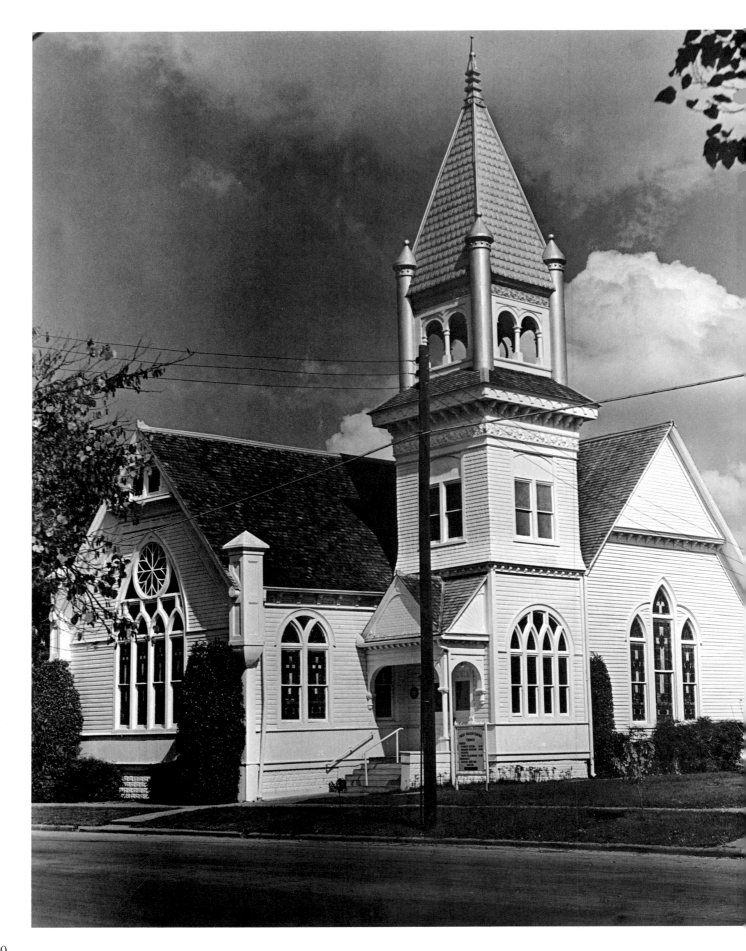

Plate 94. First Presbyterian Church, Mexia, Limestone County (late 1800's)
Architect Unknown   View

A large example of wood-frame construction, this edifice is noteworthy for the variety of form and scale of its details. Large wall areas of weatherboards contrasted sharply with the delicate scale of the stained glass. The lancet form was a salient feature of the large windows, while flat lintels spanned the smaller openings. Other variety occurred at the upper section of the tower, where openings were bell-shaped. Additional features of interest were the scrollwork and the surface treatment of the tower walls.

Plate 93. First Presbyterian Church, Main and Ninth Streets, Bonham, Fannin County (1884–1885)
Architect Unknown   View from Southwest

Like several other nonconformist organizations, Presbyterians emphasized the development of commodious interiors. After this building had been planned, but not yet begun, one reporter wrote that the progressive Presbyterians of Bonham "will depart from orthodox church architecture in so far as goes to make comfortable the physical man while the spiritual man is being built up."[1]

Erected by a congregation that had been organized in 1872, according to the medallion plate of the Texas State Historical Survey Committee, it is the only church in the area with a belfry and spire.

[1] *Fort Worth Daily Gazette*, January 24, 1884, p. 5.

Plate 95. First Presbyterian Church, 410 West Kaufman Street, Paris, Lamar County (1891)
L. B. Volk and Son, Architects   View from Southeast

The ceremonies celebrating construction of this church included the laying of two cornerstones. The main stone, a red sandstone block laid with Masonic ceremony, commemorated the dates of organization (1871) and construction. Designated as the children's cornerstone, the other block was laid by the Children's Society of the Church and was inscribed "For the Glory of God the Children built the wall; the Children, God's Cornerstone."[1] This commemorated the contributions of the youngsters in the congregation, who raised enough money to pay for the construction of one of the walls of the building. During the ceremonies, over $1,200 additional was raised to be applied to the cost of construction.

Built by contractor W. R. Eubanks, the exterior walls of the edifice were of pressed brick and sandstone, with Italianate details. Round arches, with stone voussoirs, created contrast in color and texture. A campanile, crowned with a wooden cornice with ornamental brackets, boldly announced the south entry.

[1] *Fort Worth Daily Gazette*, September 24, 1891, p. 5.

Plate 96. First Presbyterian Church, Paris
View of Auditorium

The interior was distinguished by its axial plan and handsome details. Seating was in semicircular form, focusing on the pulpit located on the short axis of the space. On this axis, sliding doors at the back opened to a room on the east, creating more seating space. A second axis, at right angles, directed the eye toward the stained-glass windows located on opposite sides. Overhead, the two apexes of the wooden vaulting, which coincided with the axes, formed a cross.

Enhanced by the warmth of the light transmitted through the intense colors of the stained glass, the interior was predominately finished with wood. Ribs and pendants of wood articulated the ceiling, which was finished with boards with beaded edges. The wainscoting around the auditorium was also of wood.

Plate 97. Channing Methodist Church, Channing, Hartley County (1898)
Architect Unknown   View

Limited means of the builders dictated simple forms, which were spontaneously limited to general effects. Yet, a tower and several lancets communicated a religious function that would not otherwise be apparent. The monolithic quality of these forms was vividly empha-sized by the play of intense light on the white surfaces.

According to the Texas State Historical Survey Committee medallion, this was the oldest church in the Panhandle north of the Canadian River.

Plate 98. Salado Methodist Church, Salado, Bell County (circa 1890)
Architect Unknown   View

The development of the Methodist church at Salado was typical of many throughout the state. God-fearing Methodists there organized at mid-century. In characteristic fashion, they first met at a revival conducted by a circuit rider. Their first meeting places included a brush arbor and then a large log house, which served both ecclesiastical and educational purposes.[1] Later, denominations in the area used the Salado College building (1860) on different Sundays. Finally, near the end of the century, their zeal enabled the Methodists to erect this house of worship, noteworthy for the interesting applications of decorative wood trim.

1 Felda Davis Shanklin, *Salado, Texas: Its History and Its People*, p. 8.

Plate 99. Bethel Methodist Episcopal Church of Hilda, Sixteen Miles Southeast of Mason on FM 783, Mason County (1902)
Architect Unknown   View

Although this edifice was built shortly after the turn of the century, its composition epitomizes many of the earlier churches built by Texas Methodists. With little emphasis on axial composition, it had the typical broad gables, with little overhang, and a corner tower surmounted by a wooden belfry.

This church was erected in a rural region where stone was easily quarried and dressed. The corners were accented by carefully cut quoins contrasting with the hue of the walls. Also noteworthy was the use of brick to span the window openings.

Plate 100. First Baptist Church, Seventh and Houston Streets, Carrizo Springs, Dimmit County (1888–1891)
The Reverend R. H. Brown, Architect   View

Built by a congregation that had been organized in 1878, this was the first Texas Baptist church west of the Nueces River.[1] The designer was pastor of the church, and the congregation furnished the labor for erection. Although not elaborate, it was dignified in the composition of its masses. The wooden cornice, forming a transi-tion between the tower and the steeple, was the chief ornamental feature on the exterior. The entrance was un-usual for a church of this period, since it was not placed in the base of the tower.

[1] Texas State Historical Survey Committee files, Austin.

177

Plate 102. Wesley Brethren Church, Wesley
Interior View

The interior was painted by a pastor, the Reverend Bohuslav Laciak,[1] and displays an interesting array of patterns and details. Walls of wood were colored to represent stone and decorated with representations of Ionic columns. In addition to abstract decorative patterns, sym-bols, such as the chalice, cross, and Solomon's seal—important to Wesley Brethren—appear at various locations.

[1] Charles F. Schmidt, *History of Washington County, Texas*, p. 69.

Plate 101. Wesley Brethren Church, Wesley, Washington County (1866)
Architect Unknown   View

In the 1850's a colony of Czech immigrants settled in Wesley. With them came the religious beliefs of the Moravian Brethren church, a Christian sect organized in 1467 that believed neither in the military nor in social class. Two years after the church was organized in 1864 by the Reverend Joseph Opocensky, work was underway on the new building, a log structure. Beams and plates were hand-hewn timbers, but milled lumber was hauled from Galveston. Finished with clapboards, the exterior form has Classical proportions and roof slope.

Plate 103. Ursuline Academy, 300 Augusta Street, San Antonio, Bexar County (1851–early 1900's)
Jules Poinsard, Francis Giraud, and Others, Architects
View from West: *left to right*, Chapel (1867–1870), Convent (circa 1882–1885)

The Ursuline Academy, a school for the education of girls, was founded in San Antonio in 1851 by the Reverend John M. Odin. The first structure occupied by the nuns was a residential building purchased for the Ursulines by Odin. Poinsard, a Frenchman, had erected the building for his family but sold it when they declined to move to Texas. This was a plain two-story shelter with porches on the south, east, and north and inswinging French windows.

Throughout the last half of the century, new additions were made to accommodate the growth of the institution. In 1866 the cornerstone for a new academic and dormitory building, with a tower and clock, was laid and blessed. The following year the cornerstone for the new chapel was cemented into place.

Plate 104. Ursuline Academy, San Antonio
View of Gate and Convent

As the Academy expanded in the early eighties, this convent was erected. Like the other later buildings, it was built of limestone in Gothic Revival style. Although the random jointing of the masonry in the walls produced a rustic effect, more refinement was apparent in the cut-stone lintels, sills, and drip moldings of the windows. Other interesting features were the dormers and the delicate trefoil ornamental features between them.

In the twentieth century, these buildings were remodeled on numerous occasions. Then, at mid-century, the Academy moved into new quarters. Now owned by the San Antonio Conservation Society, in 1971 the buildings became a State Historical Landmark.

Plate 106. Main Building, Saint Edward's University, South of Austin, Travis County (1885, 1903)
Nicholas J. Clayton, Architect   View

In 1871 a site in the hills near Austin was selected by Father Edward Sorin as the location for a new Catholic institution. Four years afterward Saint Edward's was established, and in 1881 it received a charter from the state legislature. Early in the 1890's the college advertised as a boarding school for boys and young men, in charge of the Fathers of the Holy Cross. Among the advantages claimed by the school were beauty and healthfulness of locale.

In 1903 the Main Building was reerected along the lines of an 1885 structure that had been destroyed by fire earlier that year.[1] Among the spaces included in the rebuilt building were classrooms, dormitories, library, chapel, and refectories. With exterior walls of white limestone, this new edifice, along with another nearby building, was claimed to be absolutely fireproof. The main interior partitions were brick, and floors were concrete. Iron and steel were used in the construction of the stairs and in the roof structure. Throughout the building were located numerous hose connections for fire fighting.

[1] *Houston Daily Post*, July 26, 1903, p. 36.

Plate 105. Main Building, Sam Houston Normal Institute (State College), Huntsville, Walker County (1888–1890)
Alfred Muller, Architect   View

In 1851 the Board of Trustees of Austin College—then located at Huntsville—contracted W. M. Barrett to erect a brick academic building. A two-story structure in Greek Revival style with Tuscan columns, this was completed the following year. After Austin College was removed to Sherman in 1876, the building was transferred to the state for Sam Houston Normal Institute, a college created in 1879.

To accommodate its growth, Sam Houston naturally required additional buildings, among them this splendid work completed after the enrollment had surpassed three hundred. Within the brick structure were twelve rooms and a large auditorium, the latter of which had memorial stained-glass windows, remembering prominent men and events in the history of Texas and Sam Houston Normal. The picturesque structure was particularly noteworthy for the manner in which brick was employed to form a rich variety of decorative details. Among the most dramatic features were the gables, with their corbie steps, and the corner pinnacles.

Plate 107. Saint Ignatius Academy, Fort Worth, Tarrant County (1889)
J. J. Kane, Architect   View

Saint Ignatius opened under the management of the Sisters of Saint Mary, who also had schools in Waco, Sherman, Denison, and Corsicana. Designed by a prominent Fort Worth architect, the building was distinguished by several interesting features, including dormers covered with semicircular hoods and a concave-curved mansard roof. The theme of curves was also repeated by the oval-shaped chimney.

Plate 108. Trinity University (Westminster Bible College), near Tehuacana, Limestone County (1871)
Architect Unknown   View

Located on an eminence overlooking the fertile farm-lands outside Tehuacana, this has been the home of two different church-supported schools. Basically in the secular Second Empire style, but with ecclesiastical Gothic details, the grey stone-walled work, which resembles a courthouse, was erected for Trinity University, a Presbyterian coeducational school founded in 1869. In 1902, Trinity moved to Waxahachie—and later to San Antonio, where it has remained. After the Presbyterian school vacated the building, it was occupied by Westminster

Bible College, a Methodist school founded in 1895 in Collin County.[1] Although originally a four-year institution, in 1916, Westminster became the state's first accredited junior college, with approximately 150 students. Later, after struggling with small enrollments, the administration of the school was assumed by Southwestern University in Georgetown. In 1950, however, the school was closed.

[1] Ray A. Walter, *A History of Limestone County*, p. 119.

Plate 109. Main Building, Baylor University, Fifth Street, Waco, McLennan County (1886)
Larmour and Herbert, Architects   View of Main Façade

After Baylor University—an institution founded in 1845—was moved from Independence to Waco and was consolidated with Waco University, work was commenced on this structure and, shortly thereafter, on Georgia Burleson Hall, a building with similar character. On both, a high central tower was a dominant feature. Comprising the famed "Baylor towers," they were covered by steep-pitched mansard roofs, surmounted by tall belfries. However, these, along with roofs over the corner pavilions, have been removed, completely changing the romantic character of the brick structures.

Plate 110. Administration Building, Southwestern College (University), East Twelfth Street, Georgetown, Williamson County (1898–1900)
Robert Stewart Hyer, Architect   View

In 1854, Rutersville College, which had been chartered in 1840, was moved from Rutersville to Chappell Hill and was renamed Soule University. Less than two decades later it was again relocated, this time permanently at Georgetown, where it became Georgetown College. Prior to the turn of the century, academic activities were housed in several buildings, including one for a college for young ladies (1887). Subsequently, this three-story work, designed by the fourth president of the university at its Georgetown location, was erected to contain administrative offices, classrooms, and an auditorium.

Plate 111. Ashbel Smith Building, University of Texas School of Medicine, 914 Strand, Galveston, Galveston County (1889–1890)
Nicholas J. Clayton, Architect   View

Late in the century, Galveston was selected as the location for the state medical school. Subsequently, this structure was erected to house classrooms, offices, laboratories, and physiology and anatomy amphitheaters. Originally called the Medical College Building and known as "Old Red," in 1949 it was named after Ashbel Smith, a doctor who served the Texas Republic as surgeon general in the army.

Designed by a talented architect, this was a beautiful example of round-arched architecture. Distinguished features were a three-part composition, consisting of a substantial base, a dominant middle range of arches, and a terminal arcade. Textural contrast and polychromatic treatment of the voussoirs and pinnacles both contribute further to the visual impact of the design.

Plate 112. Ashbel Smith Building, Galveston
View of Portal

As attested by this view, the architect devoted considerable attention to the refinement of detail. Each column capital was decorated with a carved likeness of the state arms—the Lone Star encircled by olive and oak branches. Other interesting features, in addition to the variations of pattern, included the anthemions below the cornice.

Plate 113. Saint Mary's Infirmary, 715 Market Street, Galveston, Galveston County (1875)
Nicholas J. Clayton, Architect   View

Erected by contractors Pritchard and Doyle for the Sisters of Charity, this hospital originally contained twenty-seven rooms. Walls and ornamentation were of brick, stuccoed on the exterior. Although several of the archivolts were pointed, suggestive of the Victorian Gothic, the style of the mansard-roofed edifice was termed "Renaissance" by a contemporary.[1]

Only two blocks away, at the corner of Eighth and Strand, was the Galveston City Hospital, also designed by Clayton. A frame building erected at the same time as Saint Mary's, with only eleven rooms in addition to the wards, it was smaller but was claimed to possess all the "modern conveniences."

[1] *Galveston Daily News*, October 3, 1875, p. 1.

The People's Architecture

I F BANKS AND COMMERCIAL BUILDINGS were indicators of material progress, and religious edifices were symbols of spiritual dedication, then the civic buildings of the state were indeed reflections of community pride and wealth. Through monumentality, the people's architecture reflected the confidence of the people in self-government and, through magnitude and style, the tastes and energy of the public. Recognizing these nineteenth-century images, one reporter wrote, "The public buildings of a state are its most pronounced features, and by them the character and genius of the people are largely judged by outsiders."[1]

Aesthetically, the civic buildings were rightfully addressed to the people who built them and were visual, as well as functional, focal points of everyday activities. Public pride in the purpose of these works was expressed through architectural permanence and

exuberance. In substantial jails was embodied the dedication to order; in monumental courthouses were glorified ideals of government.

Public esteem for civic buildings found various outlets. Newspapers printed laudatory descriptions, often acclaiming new edifices as expressions of cultural and economic progress. Further demonstrations of admiration and pride were ceremonious cornerstone levelings for all civic buildings, which were usually preceded by processions and orations and followed by public barbecues. Symbolizing strength and permanence, these stones—hollow, engraved, and highly polished—were laid with pomp and formality and were considered essential for monumental edifices that were intended to endure for many decades.

While most new buildings were undertaken simply in response to needs for new or larger and more permanent facilities, many were replacements for structures that had succumbed to the ravages of flames. Each year every community suffered numerous losses

[1] From the *Houston Daily Post*, printed in the *Fort Worth Daily Democrat*, December 4, 1880, p. 2.

Fig. 38. Perspective of the San Antonio City Hall, San Antonio, Bexar County (1889–1890). O. Kramer, architect. (*Leslie's Illustrated Weekly*, 2d Texas ed., October 4, 1890, p. 9; photo from the University of Texas Library, Austin)

Fig. 39. Perspective of the Galveston City Hall, Galveston, Galveston County (1888). Alfred Muller, architect. (*Harper's Weekly*, November 9, 1895, p. 1066; photo from the Library of Congress)

due to localized blazes, and the history of virtually every town records a major conflagration. According to the press, a fire destroyed four entire blocks of the commercial district in Jefferson in 1868, with an estimated loss of a million dollars. Galveston was ravaged by a holocaust in 1885 that in a few hours laid waste a third of the city, with an estimated loss of over two million dollars. Naturally these losses spurred actions to safeguard public and private property. In response, fire ordinances were enacted in many cities, volunteer fire departments were rapidly organized, and fire engines were purchased, requiring some kind of shelter for them.

These departments were often housed along with the municipal governmental functions in city halls. Although, in small communities these two functions were sometimes contained in separate structures, with the mayor's office and council meeting room located in a small wooden building on the square and the fire-fighting equipment housed nearby, in many towns and cities they were together. Decorated in fashionable style, the city hall occupied a corner of a block or other prominent location in the vicinity of the public square and courthouse.

When the fire department and city offices were in the same building, the mayor's offices and council meeting rooms were often on an upper floor, with the lower given over to housing the firemen, fire engines, and stalls for the horses. The Denison City Hall (1886) was representative of this multifunctional type. On the ground floor, plans called for separate spaces for the fire engine, the fire-hose carriage, the hook and ladder, and stalls for the horses.[2] On the second floor were to be rooms for the firemen and city council. On the outside, on one end of the building, was a high tower, rising above the roof so that signals from the alarm bell would reach the populace. A different example of the multifunctional municipal building was the Georgetown City Hall and Fire En-

[2] *Fort Worth Daily Gazette*, November 22, 1885, p. 7.

gine House (late nineteenth century), where fire-fighting equipment and the city government were in separate wings (plate 114).

In other towns—particularly those with large populations—city government and fire departments were completely separated, as at Victoria (plate 115). Among the finest municipal buildings in the state was the San Antonio City Hall (1889–1890), designed by O. Kramer in French Renaissance (fig. 38). Included in this same mode was the Galveston City Hall (1888), designed by Alfred Muller, which contained a market place in addition to city offices (fig. 39).

In postbellum nineteenth-century Texas towns, market places, such as the one in the Galveston City Hall, were common but were seldom part of a building that housed other functions. Containing stalls in which farmers could sell meat and produce, these were markets usually located in the vicinity of the public square. Before the introduction of refrigeration, such places were considered desirable, not only for the seller's convenience, but also for the public's benefit, since the central market place confined odors to one location and was thought to be more sanitary than having many separate stands or shops scattered about.

While some city halls also had detention facilities, the most substantial jails were built by the counties and state—in many early towns, the sheriff was the only law. Located near the courthouse for the convenience of the sheriff, county jails were often placed upon a corner of the public square but occasionally were situated in a block nearby.

On the primitive frontier, functions for the administration of justice had been allocated to such rude and temporary housing that detention was difficult, and escapes were frequent. But, with advancing civilization, those perishable wooden quarters of frame or logs, many of which frequently burned to the ground, were replaced with structures with thick masonry walls. However, jailbreaks were not uncommon even from these, many of which had been built during the 1850's, when the legislature remitted taxes to the counties for construction of public buildings. In 1873, Governor E. J. Davis disclosed the problems of build-

ing substantial jails capable of keeping prisoners in and the public out: "Our county jails . . . are properly beginning to attract public attention. Our jails are as bad as they can be. When so constructed as to secure the prisoners confined in them they become dense and unfit for habitation of wild beasts. When not made secure, and this is the case in about four-fifths of the counties, the constant escape of the prisoners is made the excuse . . . for the wholesale murder of persons charged with offenses."[3]

In response to these problems, during the last quarter of the century considerable attention was devoted to the design of jailhouses that would make escape difficult, ensure the safety of the jailer, and provide good ventilation and sanitation. The solution to the problem consisted in erecting a masonry shell, designed by an architect or a contractor, and placing within this a patented system of free-standing iron-and-steel cellblocks, which were furnished by a jail-equipment manufacturing specialist. In Texas, cellblocks and sometimes the enclosure were generally supplied by the Pauly Jail Building and Manufacturing Company of Saint Louis.

On the interior the well-designed jails were divided into zones, containing jailer's quarters and cellblocks. As to plan, they might often be square, rectangular, or T-shaped, but sometimes they might even be quite irregular. On the square or rectangular plan, the building was commonly two stories in height, with the residence for the jailer on the ground floor and the cells on the second (plate 116). On the T plan, the jailer's quarters utilized the bar of the T, and cells occupied the stem, as in the Johnson County Jail (1884) in Cleburne, designed by A. N. Dawson. In large jails the detention facilities were designed to segregate prisoners into different cells and cellblocks, according to sex and severity of crime.

Although segregation indicated that the public may have been cognizant of prisoner welfare in the design of nineteenth-century jails, first and foremost in mind was security. In response, inventors contrived various systems of cells and doors to ensure both the detention

[3] *Standard* (Clarksville), February 1, 1873, p. 3.

Fig. 40. Grayson County Jail, Sherman (1887, razed 1936). J. H. Brown, architect. Rotary jail appears at left. (Photo courtesy of Dale Barrick)

of those charged with crimes and the protection of jailers. Among the most formidable developments was the rotary jail, invented by W. H. Brown and Benjamin F. Haugh of Indianapolis and manufactured by the Pauly Jail Building and Manufacturing Company.[4] This system called for a masonry shell, within which was set a circular steel cage with pie-shaped cells, which revolved on a central vertical steel shaft. Access to each cell was gained only by turning a crank to rotate the cage until the cell door was adjacent to the jailer's vestibule. Claimed to be safe and sanitary, several of these rotary jails were constructed in the Midwest,[5] and one each appeared in the Texas towns of Waxahachie (1889) and Sherman (1887). Sherman's Grayson County Jail, designed by J. H. Brown and considered one of the finest prisons in the South, was a multistory building with thirty rotary cells on the second and third floors (fig. 40).

As with other civic buildings, the scale and style of the county jails varied considerably across the state. In the sparsely settled areas, they were usually plain stone cubes with heavy details (plates 117, 118). In

some the impact of the architectural effect developed spontaneously from interesting massing (plate 119). Oftentimes, the most distinctive features in many were symmetrical design and details of the openings and cornice. In the Panola County Jail (1891) in Carthage, brick was used skillfully to relieve the austerity of plain walls (plate 120).

Numerous counties exhibited high regard for their jails by erecting works in fashionable and pretentious architectural styles. The Fayette County Jail in La Grange (1881) was an architectural display of the Victorian Gothic (plate 121). The also popular Romanesque Revival was used in the McCulloch County Jail (1886) in Brady (plate 122).

However, the style of many Texas jails was intended not only to delight the eye, but also to romantically convey to the observer the purpose and concept of the building. In creating an appropriate expression for jails, architects studied the past for fashions that had been produced for special functions and that could be associated with detention. The character of the jail should be that of physical strength, conveyed visually by solidity of construction as well as by designs of antiquity associated with strength. The massive round arches of the Romanesque imparted the quality of strength; machicolations borrowed from the military architecture of antiquity communicated the concept of the object (plate 123). In the larger buildings high picturesque towers, along with other details from military architecture, added to the effect (plate 124). Among the most spectacular was the Comanche County Jail (late nineteenth century), with its collection of Romantic pseudomachicolations, crenellations, and bartizans, many of which have been removed during the twentieth century. However, near the end of the nineteenth century, many of the other large jails were less dramatic and were designed with a sober character (plate 125).

Even though numerous counties had erected substantial and expensive jails before the twentieth century, the most pretentious public buildings were the "temples of justice." Early in 1881 the state legislature passed an act authorizing counties to issue bonds to finance the erection of new courthouses, enabling

[4] *Description of the Patent Rotary Steel Jail*, p. 2.
[5] See Walter A. Lunden, "The Rotary Jail, or Human Squirrel Cage," *Journal of the Society of Architectural Historians* 18, no. 4 (December 1959): 149–157.

Fig. 41. San Marcos and Hays County Courthouse. (Photo from the Texas State Historical Association, Austin)

Fig. 42. Hallettsville and Lavaca County Courthouse. (Photo from the Texas State Historical Association, Austin)

county commissioners' courts to finance elaborate works. During one or the other of the last two decades, most counties built a new temple, many of which are yet in use today, and some counties, such as Wise and Harrison, erected a new courthouse in each decade on the same sites.

The architectural magnificence that had made the palaces of European antiquity the centers of an imperial system made the governmental buildings of Texas the focus of a democratic system. Dominant in most towns, they fulfilled fundamental needs for both monuments and symbols: their strength conveyed assurance; their style, dignity (figs. 41, 42). Prosaic reminders of the role of the courthouse as the seat of justice and the seat of the people's government were imposing statues of the blindfolded Goddess of Justice holding the scales and of the Goddess of Liberty with sword in hand.

In remote and unstable frontier towns, substantial new courthouses were objects not only of beauty and

purpose, but also of hopes for the future. From Seymour, one reporter wrote, "When our $40,500 temple of justice is completed, prospectors and railroads may turn an inquisitive eye to our prosperous Western town."[6] In another expression of confidence in permanent architecture, it was reported from Bellville that a new courthouse would be the advent of a big boom.[7] Moreover, in days when rivalries for the county seat were frequent among towns, a permanent courthouse was likely (although not certain) to assure the location of the seat of justice. After the Bosque County Commissioners' Court ordered a new courthouse for Meridian, an enthusiastic reporter was confident that this would "forever and eternally settle the county seat question."[8]

Throughout the last decades of the nineteenth cen-

[6] *Fort Worth Daily Gazette*, November 23, 1884, p. 4.
[7] Ibid., February 13, 1886, p. 4.
[8] *Galveston Daily News*, February 20, 1886, p. 1.

Fig. 43. Marion County Courthouse, Jefferson (circa 1875). Thomas Hinkle, architect. (Photo from the Marion County Historical Society, Jefferson)

Fig. 44. Harris County Courthouse, Houston (1883–1884, razed 1907). E. J. Duhamel, architect. (Photo from the San Jacinto Museum of History Association, Houston)

tury, the small counties built conservatively. The square and oblong antebellum plans, with the ground-floor rooms separated by cross corridors through the center and with courtroom above, continued to be widely used. On the exterior, façades were similar, although sometimes reflecting the changing times through fashionable stylistic details. For the third Van Zandt County Courthouse (1872–1873, razed 1894), a heavy timber-framed structure, specifications called for a building fifty feet square, having four rooms twenty feet square, separated by cross corridors on the first floor, offices and courtroom on the second, and similar patterns of openings on each elevation.[9] The Floyd County Courthouse in Floydada (1891) was a frame building forty-eight feet square, with hip roof and cupola. As late as 1893 the little county of Somervell erected in Glen Rose a stone-walled edifice of this type (plate 126).

[9] W. S. Mills, *History of Van Zandt County*, pp. 21–22.

Interestingly, because of the requirements for portals on all four sides—to give equal prominence to commercial property on each side of the square—the temple form appeared infrequently in Texas, but, around 1875, the Marion County Courthouse was built in prostyle form with Classical details (fig. 43).

However, during the last quarter of the nineteenth century, in the established and prosperous counties of the Lone Star State, temples of justice became distinguished for their large plans and opulent styles. Increasing population and wealth made county government more active, requiring more massive buildings with larger and more numerous spaces within. At the same time, public taste demanded a character of expression that was forceful and that appropriately glorified the county functions. The architectural style therefore should be bounteous, expressive of the energy and pride of the people, yet orderly and monumental, appropriate to the dignity of purpose associated with the building.

Albeit the impetus of some styles in certain building types was associational—intended to symbolize the function—the choice of style in courthouses was more a matter of changing tastes and the desire for individuality. While designers of churches could draw upon the ecclesiastical architecture of the Medieval period, and designers of jails could borrow details from the military architecture of antiquity to characterize the nature of the function, there were no historic modes of antiquity that had universally communicated the function of self-government. For the most part, styles with elaborate and picturesque details were preferred, since opulence was associated with beauty and the expression of noble purpose. Among those with strong appeal was the Victorian Gothic, ordinarily characterized by pointed arches, turrets, and towers. This was the mode for the Harris County Courthouse in Houston (1883–1884, razed 1907), a large pile with cathedrallike details but with courthouse form and plan—one of the few temples of justice of this style in the state (fig. 44). In the Shelby County Courthouse at Center (1883–1885) turrets, buttresses, ornamental brickwork, and round rather than pointed arches created a verticality and picturesqueness in harmony with the spirit of the Gothic (plate 127). The interior likewise possessed much of the charm so admired during this era (plate 128).

The decorative Victorian Gothic, which was not a particularly good style to "express government," never became as popular for courthouses as did the Classical, originally inspired by the Renaissance. The Gillespie County Courthouse (1881–1882) in the German community of Fredericksburg, with its formal composition and Classical details, conveyed an impression of dignity that was appropriate for civic functions—even in small-scaled works (plate 129). Other early Renaissance Revival temples possessed the same character but were larger and more variegated by virtue of their lack of extensive areas of unbroken surface. The Bell County Courthouse in Belton (1883–1884) was one of the most elegant of these early examples (plate 130). Later and more massive in character but equally rich in appearance was the Milam County Courthouse in Cameron, built in 1891

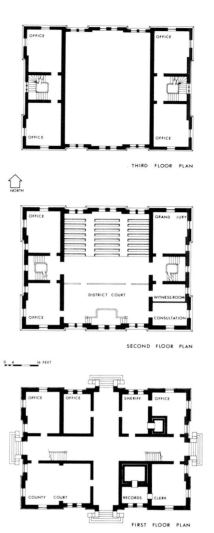

Fig. 45. Floor plans of the Shackelford County Courthouse, Albany (1883–1884). J. E. Flanders, architect. (Drawing by author, from the architect's drawings, Office of the County Clerk, Albany)

(plate 131). A picturesque version of the Classical characterized the Red River County Courthouse (1884–1885) in Clarksville (plate 132), the interior of which maintained the unity of the theme by formal composition and simple Classical details (plate 133).

Many of these built in the 1880's derived their architectural style from Italy, the home of the Renais-

Fig. 47. Perspective of the Travis County Courthouse, Austin (1875–1876). Jacob Larmour and Charles Wheelock, architects. (*Frank Leslie's Illustrated*, May 4, 1889, p. 209; photo from the Library of Congress)

Fig. 46. Perspective of the Dallas County Courthouse, Dallas (1871, remodeled 1880, burned 1890). (*Dallas Morning News*, February 8, 1890, p. 2; photo courtesy of the *Dallas Morning News*)

sance. For instance, the Lampasas County Courthouse in Lampasas (1883), with its rusticated cut-stone quoins and decorative consoles, typified the beauty of the Italianate mode (plate 134). Other excellent examples of similar temples of justice were the Stephens County Courthouse in Breckenridge (1883) and the Shackelford County Courthouse in Albany (1883), both by Dallas architect J. E. Flanders (plate 135).

The plan of the Shackelford edifice was representative of the pretentious courthouses of the 1880's (fig. 45). As an elaboration on the concept of the square plan with cross corridors, the ground floor was divided into four segments by intersecting passages, terminating at doors in the center of each of the four façades. In these quadrants were located various departments of county government. On the second floor, reached by either of two stairways, was the spacious and at-

tractive courtroom. The height of this and the other major rooms was proportioned according to their area, giving a natural variation of outward expression. To relieve the austerity of flat façades, the concept was developed to form projecting pavilions. Although, to a certain extent, this did express the interior configuration of walls and spaces, the main intent of the broken outline was to give a stately appearance and to create contrasting shadow lines. Another example with projecting pavilions, in the Italianate, was the Hood County Courthouse (1889–1891) in Granbury, similar to the one in Lampasas, except that the corner pavilions were covered with mansard roofs (plate 136). This Italianate trend remained popular in Texas until the early nineties.

While, in many instances, the extent of the decoration for Texas courthouses was certainly influenced by budgetary limitations, other determinants for profusion and scale of details were aesthetic. Regardless of the style, most competent nineteenth-century architects certainly recognized that underscaled ornament weakened the statement made by the building and that restraint in the employment of decorative features, such as pediments, consoles, stringcourses, and quoins, increased the importance of the detail that was used; but, in any event, too much ornament destroyed the strength of the form. Generally, the most lavish ornamentation was reserved to emphasize important architectural features, such as exterior doorways and towers and interior courtrooms.

In many Texas courthouses that were similar in plans and scale, it was the variation in detail and style that made each distinctive. When W. C. Dodson planned the Fannin County Courthouse (1888) in Bonham, which has been completely remodeled in the twentieth century, he developed a fine design with profuse, yet well-adjusted ornamental features. Then, when he created the Hill County Courthouse in Hillsboro (1889–1891), he used similar ideas and decorative features, but he crowned the latter with the mansardic roofs of the Second Empire, rather than the gabled roofs of the Italianate, used on the Fannin structure (plate 137). On both, the decoration was robust and creative.

In its capacity to fulfill tastes for architectural exuberance, few styles surpassed the Second Empire, which had been popularized nationally by the State, War, and Navy Building (1871–1875) in Washington, D.C., and by Pennsylvania's huge Philadelphia City Hall (1871–1881). In the 1870's it was adopted for Texas courthouses and remained in vogue, along with contrasting styles, until the 1890's. Early in its development in this state, there was some remodeling with the addition of mansard roofs to existing structures. To an earlier Dallas County Courthouse and a Tarrant County Courthouse, an 1876 building in the octagonal style, were added mansard roofs in the early eighties (fig. 46).

Initial examples of new Second Empire structures were the Travis County Courthouse in Austin (1875–1876; fig. 47)—a large building with multiple straight-sloped and convex-curved mansard roofs, decorated with crestings—and the Lamar County Courthouse in Paris (1874–1875; fig. 48), both of which have been razed. As in the Italianate, the plans for Second Empire works were square or rectangular, with corner pavilions, central first-floor corridors, and a central second-floor courtroom (fig. 49). On the exterior, above the center of the courtroom, rose a wooden-structured tower, as in Weatherford's Parker County Courthouse (1885), a pretentious edifice of

Fig. 48. Perspective of the Lamar County Courthouse, Paris (1874–1875). (Homer S. Thrall, *Pictorial History of Texas*, p. 643; photo from the Texas State Library, Austin)

white stone, designed by Dodson and Dudley (fig. 50).

During the eighties, interesting examples of the mansardic appeared across the state, some of which were more conservative in size and detail than the Hill County and Parker County temples. The Blanco County Courthouse (1885) in Blanco (plate 138) and the Brewster County Courthouse (1888), a small building in Alpine (plate 139), were crowned with mansard roofs.

Although a high central tower was standard on many nineteenth-century courthouses, the visual strength of the dominant mansard roofs allowed successful compositions sans the tower. The Concho County Courthouse (1886) in Paint Rock (plate 140), designed by F. E. Ruffini of Austin, and the Sutton County Courthouse (1891–1893) in Sonora, designed by Oscar Ruffini of San Angelo, were fine examples of this (plate 141). But two of the most elegant late creations were the Caldwell County Courthouse (1893) in

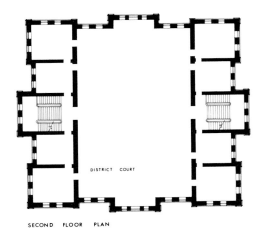

SECOND FLOOR PLAN

DISTRICT COURT

Fig. 50. Perspective of the Parker County Courthouse, Weatherford (1885). Dodson and Dudley, architects. (*Frank Leslie's Illustrated*, October 18, 1890, p. 14; photo from the Library of Congress)

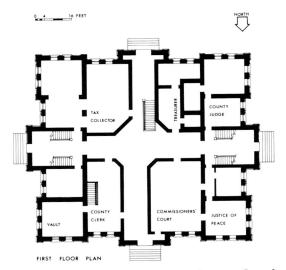

0 4   16 FEET   NORTH

TAX COLLECTOR   TREASURER   COUNTY JUDGE

VAULT   COUNTY CLERK   COMMISSIONERS' COURT   JUSTICE OF PEACE

FIRST FLOOR PLAN

Fig. 49. Floor plans of the Parker County Courthouse, Weatherford (1885). Dodson and Dudley, architects. (Measured and drawn by author)

Fig. 51. El Paso County Courthouse, El Paso (1885–1886, razed 1917). Alfred Giles, architect. (Photo from the Texas State Historical Association, Austin)

Lockhart and the Goliad County Courthouse (1894) in Goliad, both built by Martin, Byrnes, and Johnston and evidently planned by Alfred Giles (plate 142).

Since the Second Empire, with its Classical vocabulary of details, was akin to the Italianate, many courthouses erected near the end of the century bear combinations of stylistic elements that might classify them with either. It is apparent that many architects were not as much concerned with the "purity" of

architectural design as they were with creating imposing effects, a "modern" reflex of the age. Often they composed freely with geometrical, organic, and historical decoration to create an individual expression for each county. Although predominantly Romanesque, the Karnes County Courthouse in Karnes City (1891) featured several mansards.[10] The El Paso

[10] Remodeling has changed considerably the nineteenth-century appearance. For an illustration of the original structure,

Fig. 52. El Paso and El Paso County Courthouse. (Photo from the Texas State Historical Association, Austin)

Fig. 53. Dallas County Courthouse, Dallas (1891–1892), and Dallas Federal Building (late 1800's). (Photo from the Texas State Historical Association, Austin)

County Courthouse in El Paso (1885–1886, razed 1917) and the Presidio County Courthouse in Marfa (1886) successfully combined decorative forms from both the Italianate and mansardic modes (plate 143; figs. 51, 52).

At the time the popularity of these two styles was declining in the Gay Nineties, the Romanesque Revival was rising to fashionableness, following a national trend that had been inspired by the work of prominent Boston architect Henry Hobson Richardson. Perhaps few historic styles were actually more appropriate for nineteenth-century Texas courthouses than the Romanesque, which was at its best when expressed with large units of pitch-faced ashlar masonry, requiring the use of the state's most plentiful building resource—stone. Moreover, in addition to limestone and sandstone, which were easily workable, the quarries of the state yielded material of contrasting colors, allowing richness of polychromy, as in the Erath County Courthouse (1891–1892), Stephenville,

an edifice with walls of contrasting brilliant red and white stone (plate 144).

Picturesque but orderly in composition, Romanesque courthouses were often similar in plan and form to those in other fashions, but they incorporated more romantic features, such as dormers and turrets. The Dallas County Courthouse (1891–1892), one of the largest Romanesque buildings in the state, with its turrets, a large central tower, and a polychromatic masonry presented a most picturesque and memorable monument (plate 145; fig. 53). Less colorful, but equally strong statements were found in the Lavaca County Courthouse in Hallettsville (1897), with its majestic, centrally positioned tower (plates 146, 147), and in the DeWitt County Courthouse in Cuero (1894–1896), with an offset tower (plate 148).

Among the Texas architects who created with the Romanesque, few seemed more confident with or had more sympathy for it than J. Riely Gordon. Extensively using this form-language, he created for many counties in the state charming and attractive temples of justice, such as the **Bexar County Courthouse** (1892–1895), San Antonio (plate 149). The Romanesque decoration of the **Fayette County Courthouse** (1890–1891) in LaGrange (plate 150) and the Victoria County Courthouse (1891–1892) in Victoria (plate

see Hedwig Krell Didear (comp.), *A History of Karnes County and Old Helena.*

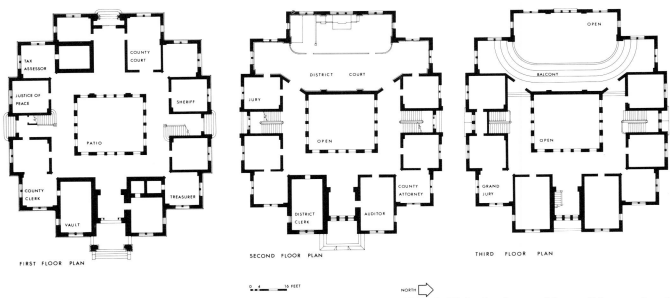

FIRST FLOOR PLAN

SECOND FLOOR PLAN

THIRD FLOOR PLAN

0 4   16 FEET   NORTH

Fig. 54. Floor plans of the Fayette County Courthouse, LaGrange (1891). J. Riely Gordon, architect. (Measured and drawn by author)

151), designed by Gordon along similar lines, included bartizans (ancient military features), a tower, broken massing, and high chimneys.[11] In these buildings, ashlar masonry of contrasting textures further contributed to their distinctive character.

Although the popularity of architectural styles had fluctuated, the concept of courthouse plans had changed little in the seventies, eighties, and nineties. Designs with corridors on the ground floor running in each direction through the center of the building and with the courtroom on the second were virtually universal. When county commissioners and courthouse architects, in preparation for projected buildings, often visited existing temples, they found this to be a workable arrangement and, in emulation, perpetuated it. Since functions changed little, there was little necessity for change in form.

When J. Riely Gordon designed the Fayette and Victoria courthouses, he departed from the traditional cross corridors on the ground floor. Inspired by the de-

sire to develop good natural lighting and a more satisfactory arrangement for natural ventilation of interior spaces, he arranged all the offices and the courtrooms around a thirty-foot-square central courtyard, into which numerous doors opened, providing for cooling breezes through the building (fig. 54).[12] With this arrangement, the basic exterior horizontal profile was rectangular, with projecting pavilions from each side, with doors placed in all four façades, and with corridors leading directly to the open court, which was eventually landscaped with tropical plants.

Retaining this same scheme of a central space surrounded by a gallery and then by adjoining rooms, Gordon subsequently moved the ground-floor offices directly opposite the court, displacing the center-corridor accesses. Providing easy access to all rooms, the stairway was placed in the position of the court, and the tower, with openings for ventilation and light at

[11] The Victoria Courthouse received national attention when its perspective was published in *American Architect and Building News* 54 (1896): pl. 1086.

[12] It would appear that this was a daring departure from convention, since a special resolution was passed by the Fayette Commissioners' Court authorizing the open court at the time Gordon's plans were accepted (see Commissioners' Court Minutes, Fayette County, III, 419).

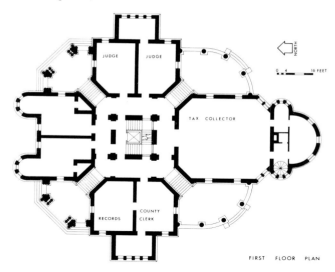

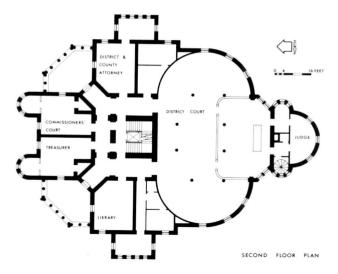

FIRST FLOOR PLAN

SECOND FLOOR PLAN

Fig. 55. Floor plans of the Ellis County Courthouse, Waxahachie (1894–1896). J. Riely Gordon, architect. (Measured and drawn by author)

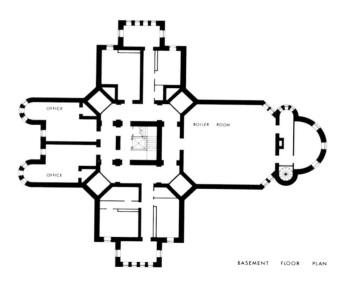

BASEMENT FLOOR PLAN

the top, rose above the court (fig. 55). On the ground floor all this produced the form of a Greek cross, the four accesses to which were at the reentrants. On the second floor this architectural form plastically responded to the spatial requirements for the courtroom and other rooms, producing quite dramatic compositions. One of the earliest examples of this style was the Brazoria County Courthouse in Brazoria (1893–

1894), a red pressed-brick edifice with granite columns and red sandstone trim.[13] This example was followed by the Ellis County Courthouse (1894–1896) in Waxahachie (plate 152).

Using this scheme, in competition with other architects and contractors, Gordon won numerous courthouse commissions. Among these, in addition to the Waxahachie temple, were the Van Zandt County Courthouse in Canton (1894–1896, razed 1935), a brick structure, and the Wise County Courthouse in Decatur (1895–1897), a granite building (plate 153). The picturesqueness of massing produced by Gordon's cruciform plan was readily accommodated by the Romanesque Revival. The circular-form vocabulary of this mode made it ideal for the required plasticity. To heighten the effect, turrets containing offices or stairways were added, along with balconies and dormers, exemplified by the Hopkins County Courthouse (1894–1895) in Sulphur Springs (plate 154) and the Gonzales County Courthouse (1894–1896) in

[13] Sadly, this four-story building, in addition to basement—a very expensive work—was vacated only a few years after it was completed. At the end of the decade, the county seat was moved to Angleton.

Gonzales (plate 155). Even though the plans of Gordon's courthouses were similar, individuality resulted from variations in materials and in the design of the details.

As evident in the Lee County Courthouse in Giddings (1898), another advantage of Gordon's cruciform plan was that it allowed a composition of forms with a central tower of masonry, creating unity between the elements (plate 156). Since the majority of courthouses were located in the center of the public square, the pressure to make the tower equally prominent from all viewpoints demanded that it rise from the center of the mass. It had not been possible to build towers of masonry over the traditional central second-floor courtroom. Because of the weight-bearing limitations of wooden trusses to support the roof and the tower directly over the center of the courtroom, only wooden structures covered with light sheet-metal details could be used overhead, but with the cruciform, the walls enclosing the core were available for bearing the weight of a heavy tower.

Although the cruciform concept was developed originally for any courthouse that was located in the middle of the public square, Gordon even employed modified versions of it in different situations. At New Braunfels the Comal County Courthouse (1898) was situated on a corner, diagonally across the street from the public square, requiring some changes to accommodate the entrances (plate 157). The Hopkins County Courthouse was likewise across from the square and had a modified plan to accommodate the situation.

While the Romanesque Revival adopted for many of his courthouses declined in popularity near the end of the century, Gordon continued to employ the cruciform scheme. The Harrison County Courthouse (1899–1900) in Marshall was based on this concept (plate 158), but since the building was designed in the Renaissance Revival, the romantic picturesqueness of the Romanesque gave way to Classical repose.

Near the end of the century, architect W. C. Dodson, a prominent figure in Central Texas architecture, also modified the traditional plan to allow the erection of a high central masonry tower. In the Denton

Fig. 56. Perspective of the Houston Federal Building, Houston, Harris County (1888–1889). Will A. Ferret, supervising architect. (*Harper's Weekly*, May 19, 1888, p. 366; photo from the Library of Congress)

County Courthouse in Denton (1895–1896) the large spaces, including the courtroom, were placed on either side of a single main corridor, allowing the supporting walls for the tower to pass through the center of the mass (plate 159). Planning for the Coryell County Courthouse in Gatesville (1897–1898) was similarly directed, with an oval-shaped courtroom, resembling some of Gordon's designs, flanked by the tower-supporting walls (plate 160).

The trend away from the picturesque character toward the Classical that appeared in the Harrison and Coryell courthouses was epitomized by the Tarrant County Courthouse in Fort Worth (1893–1895), a beautiful Renaissance Revival monument (plate 161). A more severe Classicism was evident several years later in Galveston County's new temple of justice (1897–1898) in Galveston (plates 162, 163).

The architects for these two courthouses were selected through national design competitions—across the nation, this method of selecting architects for public buildings had been common since the first national capitol competition in 1792. As in the case of most Texas courthouses, county commissioners published notices in newspapers inviting the submission of plans for projected courthouses. Frequently both architects

Fig. 57. Perspective of the Galveston Federal Building, Galveston, Galveston County (circa 1888). Will A. Ferret, supervising architect. (*Harper's Weekly*, May 19, 1888, supplement, p. 366; photo from the Library of Congress)

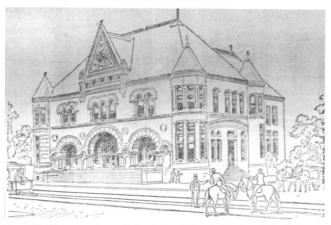

Fig. 58. Perspective of the Fort Worth Federal Building, Fort Worth, Tarrant County (1892–1896). W. J. Edbrooke, supervising architect. (*Fort Worth Daily Gazette*, May 29, 1892, p. 2; photo from Microfilm Service and Sales, Dallas)

Fig. 59. Perspective of the San Antonio Federal Building, San Antonio, Bexar County (1888). Will A. Ferret, supervising architect. (*Harper's Weekly*, May 19, 1888, supplement, p. 367; photo from the Library of Congress)

and contractors responded, although small buildings sometimes attracted only the attention of local builders. On large works, however, submissions came from a wide geographical area.

Although for state, county, and city public buildings architects were usually selected through competition, all federal government structures in Texas were designed in Washington, D.C., in the office of the supervising architect of the Treasury. Consequently, although the styles of post offices and federal courthouses in Texas generally conformed to national trends, they were commonly "designed . . . with embellishments for securing certain architectural effects,"[14] occasionally intended to relate them to their region. The Houston Federal Building (1888–1889; fig. 56) was designed with Moresque character, while the one in Galveston (circa 1888) possessed a quality that might have been found in the Mediterranean architecture of Spain (fig. 57). Romanesque characterized the Fort Worth Federal Building (1892–1896; fig. 58) and the San Antonio Federal Building (1888;

14 Percy Clark, "New Federal Buildings," *Harper's Weekly* (supplement), May 19, 1888, p. 368.

fig. 59)—quite in accord with national taste. It was also employed for the Jefferson Federal Courthouse and Post Office (1888–1890), created during William A. Ferret's tenure as supervising architect (plate 164).

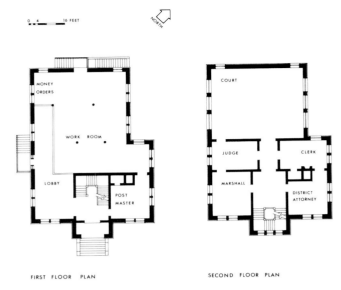

FIRST FLOOR PLAN   SECOND FLOOR PLAN

Fig. 60. Floor plans of the Jefferson Federal Courthouse and Post Office, Jefferson, Marion County (1888–1890). Will A. Ferret, supervising architect. (Drawings by author, from an engraving in the Jefferson County Historical Society Museum)

The plan of the Jefferson building was characteristic of the federal architecture in the state (fig. 60). The post office occupied the ground floor, while the courtroom and related spaces were on the second. As was common, it was located on a corner lot, since a design concept—sometimes called the "double front" —was developed with separate entrances on different streets for the two basic functions.

Near the end of the nineteenth century, formality, rather than picturesqueness, customarily characterized governmental architecture of the military at the Texas forts. Particularly for prestigious buildings, architectural compositions were balanced and dignified, appropriate to the formality of the army (plate 165). Thus, Classical details supplied ideal contributions to the discipline of design.

While many federal buildings rivaled the magnificence and character of some of the county temples of justice, no nineteenth-century edifice in Texas (and few elsewhere) could compete with the grandeur of the state Capitol (1882–1888) in Austin, the pride of all Texans (plate 166). As early as 1876 land had been officially set aside to finance the building, and late in 1880—a few months before the antebellum Capitol was consumed by flames—architects across the nation were invited to participate in a design competition to develop projected plans. Selected as the winner of the competition, in which eleven firms participated for a $1,700 prize, was Elijah E. Myers of Detroit, a self-made architect and designer of capitols for Michigan, Idaho, Colorado, and Utah.[15]

The most massive and complete nineteenth-century state capitol in America,[16] this colossal edifice was designed in Renaissance Revival, with Doric, Ionic, and Corinthian orders. Modeled after the national Capitol in Washington, D.C., it had a symmetrical plan, approximating the form of a Greek cross, with an imposing dome over the crossing, which unified the composition (plates 167, 168).[17] Its south, or main, entrance was distinguished by a monumental, triumphal arch.

The interior of this tour de force was as beautiful as the exterior (plates 169, 170). The accommodations that were provided on the separate floors for the departments of government—executive, legislative, and judicial—were all appropriately enhanced with Classical details. In the public areas the architecture was glorified by sculpture, paintings, and decorations, featuring prominent men and events in Texas history —reminders of the proud heritage of the Republic and state (plate 171).

Certainly, the state Capitol, a statement of magnificence, forms a fitting climax to nineteenth-century public architecture in Texas. It, together with the capitols preceding it, represents several stages in the development of the art of building in the Southwest.

[15] Allen Stross, *The Michigan State Capitol*, p. 38.

[16] Texas Capitol Building Commission, *Report of the Capitol Building Commission upon the Completion of the New Capitol*, p. 5.

[17] While the new Capitol was under construction, a temporary capitol was erected nearby, at the head of Congress Avenue, across from the Travis County Courthouse. Completed early in 1883 and built of cut stone, the three-story building housed the three departments of government until the permanent edifice was completed. Unfortunately, in 1899, the interior of the temporary building was consumed by flames.

The People's Architecture

During the century, this was an architecture with a broad spectrum. Under six flags, it advanced from a primitive and indigenous type to a sophisticated and pretentious level of expression. Early architecture, whether Spanish colonial, Mexican provincial, or republican, was essentially building of necessity and for shelter, while the antebellum years of statehood were identified by the dignified architecture of the Greek Revival style. Although the character of industrial and military works erected during the war between the states may have reflected the somberness of the times, the years following Reconstruction witnessed a delightfully Romantic age, in which there was con-siderable pride in architectural sophistication and character. Buildings became meaningful in the sense that they were associational, representational, and ornamental. The edifices that were most highly esteemed were not only opulent but also designed to exhort and astound.

In all eras, the architecture had a warmth and a human scale that is missing from much of today's austere precision. Unfortunately, innumerable significant buildings have disappeared, but enough have survived to preserve the past for the appreciation of future generations.

Plate 114. Georgetown City Hall and Fire Engine House, Georgetown, Williamson County (late 1800's)
Architect Unknown   View

Located at a street intersection, this was representative of many multifunctional civic buildings erected at the end of the nineteenth century. Containing both municipal offices and fire department, the construction was typical. Exterior walls were substantially built of coursed ashlar masonry. The cornices terminating each main façade and the window caps over the large doors were galvanized iron.

Plate 115. Victoria City Hall, Victoria, Victoria County (1900, razed 1965)
Architect Unknown   View

In the early nineties, after the Victoria County commissioners refused to provide space in their new courthouse, the City Council voted to erect a small frame building on the public square to house their governmental functions.[1] A few years later the cornerstone for this permanent brick edifice was laid.

Built by S. M. Bailey, the City Hall, although small, was distinguished by its details. Brick of contrasting colors was used in the walls and to form the quoins, stringcourses, and arches. Sheet metal, a popular material during the latter part of the century, was used on the mansard roof, the dormers, and the cupola.

[1] Roy Grimes (ed.), *300 Years in Victoria County*, p. 473.

Plate 116. Burnet County Jail, Burnet (1884)
F. E. Ruffini, Architect   View

Early in 1884, Burnet County commissioners advertised in the *Galveston Daily News* for bids on a projected jail. On the work that was subsequently contracted, the masonry detail was remarkable. In contrast with the walls of pitch-faced stone, the corner pilasters on both the main mass and the projecting pavilion—which boldly announced the entrances—were formed with stone blocks with tooled margins. Cut stone was employed for the sills, the round and stilted arches, and the entrance features.

Plate 117. Bosque County Jail, Meridian (circa 1885)
Architect Unknown   View from Northwest

Typical of many jails of this period, this was orig-inally a two-story cube. On the ground floor of the mas-sive work was the residence for the sheriff or jailer, and above were the cages. The design was simple, but visual-ly strong. The blocks of white limestone in the thick walls were subtly reduced in size in proportion to the height of the structure, producing a structural repose that fulfilled intuitive senses for weight and support.

The annex was added around 1895.

Plate 118. Mason County Jail, Mason (1894)
Architect Unknown   View from Northwest

Located across the street from the public square, this substantial work had walls of rust-colored native sandstone and white mortar. The heavy mass was characterized by straightforward details but was accented with a tower, emphasizing the entrance. The only ornamental features appeared in the tympanums of the metal-roofed tower.

Plate 119. Hood County Jail, Granbury (1885)
J. N. Haney, Architect   View from Southwest

In May 1885, Hood County commissioners passed a resolution to build a new jail. Haney's plans and specifications, which included the Pauly Jail Building and Manufacturing Company's system of cells, were subsequently accepted, and he was awarded the contract to build the structure.[1] The work was evidently completed that year. The following year, Haney added a 17-by-21-foot kitchen to the building.

[1] Commissioners' Court Minutes. Hood County, vol. B, p. 350.

213

Plate 120. Panola County Jail, Public Square, Carthage (1891)
Architect Unknown   View

Characterized by the formal composition that was considered so essential in the nineteenth century, this structure was noteworthy for its integral decorative details. Brick was used in relief to define stilted and round arches over the openings and to form the stringcourse around the building. The ornamental pattern of the cornice provided additional interest.

In 1956 this building was transferred to the city of Carthage for a city jail. Less than a decade later, the Panola County Historical Society leased it for a museum.

Plate 121. Fayette County Jail, South Main and West Crockett Streets, LaGrange (1881)
Andrewarthe and [James] Wahrenberger, Architects   View from Southwest

Early in 1881 the Fayette County Commissioners' Court authorized advertisement for plans and specifications for a new jail. Several months later, the contract to erect the structure was awarded to Fritz Schulte.

Built of stone, it was a picturesque work containing jailer's quarters and cells. Wings formed angular projections from the corners of the main mass, creating interesting architectural effects. A picturesque tower and lancet openings also contributed to the richness.

The incongruous second-story porch is obviously a later addition, and it has recently been removed

Plate 122. McCulloch County Jail, Brady (1886)
Architect Unknown   View from Northeast

This structure was remarkable for its picturesque features. Above the upper story, which was decorated only with stringcourses and arches, rose towers, parapets, and battlements, all inspired by the architecture of antiquity. The corbeled ornamental work recalled machicolations of ancient castles. These, along with the arches and stringcourses, were then emphasized by contrasting color.

The Erath County Jail in Stephenville was quite similar in form and detail.

Plate 123. Bandera County Jail, Bandera (1881)
Alfred Giles, Architect   View

Designed by an architect who also planned jails for
the counties of Presidio, Kerr, El Paso, and Uvalde, this
picturesque work was built of native stone. The water
table, window caps, and quoins were noteworthy details.
In addition to these, the battlements created impressions
of ancient architecture for defense.

In 1938 a new jail was erected. During subsequent
years the 1881 structure was used for various purposes,
including offices for the Bandera County Historical Survey Committee, which is restoring the building.

Plate 124. Milam County Jail, Cameron (late 1800's)
Architect Unknown   View

Located near the courthouse, this building was distinguished by its crenellated parapet and prominent turrets,
all of which recall the military architecture of antiquity.
In addition to these picturesque details, the cut-stone
voussoirs that span the openings, the carved turret corbels, and stringcourses were significant features. The austerity of the massive walls was relieved at the parapet by
delicate ornamental features.

This building was virtually identical in design with
the Austin County Jail in Bellville.

Plate 125. Bastrop County Jail, Public Square, Bastrop (1891–1892)
Martin, Byrnes, and Johnston, Architects and Builders   View

Unlike many who planned jails during this era of romanticism, the designers of this structure made no attempt to symbolically represent the function. Rather, with the contrasting brick in the pilasters and stilted arches, the intent was to create a dignified and interest-ing building. For this composition, the metal cornice and mansard roofs then formed an appropriate crown.

In 1925 the building was extensively remodeled by the Southern Steel Company of San Antonio.

Plate 126. Somervell County Courthouse, Glen Rose (1893)
John Cormack, Builder   View

Located in what was then, and still is, the third smallest county in the state (formed in 1875), this courthouse
was quite modest in scale, costing only $13,500. It re-
placed the first courthouse, erected in 1882, which was
destroyed by fire. The walls were of local limestone, layers of which lie near the surface of the ground, or above
it, in the vicinity. Details were simple, yet strong.

Plate 127. Shelby County Courthouse, Public Square, Center (1883–1885)
J. J. E. Gibson, Architect　　　　View

Shortly after an earlier wooden courthouse had burned, work was commenced on this imposing structure. Designed by an Irish immigrant, ponderous turrets, buttresses, and round arches gave it the character of a Norman castle of the eleventh or twelfth century. The composition of the contrasting round and rectangular elements was unified by decorative brick stringcourses and the cornice.

Plate 128. Shelby County Courthouse, Center
View of Courtroom

The decorative and functional use of wood makes this interior distinctive. The windows, which were provided with shutters, were handsomely finished with wood paneling. A bar enclosure with ornamental newels and balusters was provided, further contributing to the beauty of the interior. However, the most interesting features were structural. Trusses, with their pendant posts, corbels, and braces, were clear expressions of load-bearing function. Chamfered edges on these and the purlins revealed refinement of craftsmanship.

Plate 129 Gillespie County Courthouse, Public Square, Fredericksburg (1881–1882)
Alfred Giles, Architect   View

Designed by a San Antonio architect and built by John Heiner and James A. Courtney, this courthouse, with its formal balance, heavy decorative consoles, and Classical roof slopes, possessed the dignity that was characteristic of Renaissance Revival buildings. The cut-stone work at the corners and around the openings contributed to the stateliness of the edifice. Although it no longer houses county governmental functions, its survival seems assured as a public library.

Included among Giles's other public works were the Bexar County Courthouse of 1882 and the Llano County Courthouse of 1884, both of which served only for a short period of time.

Plate 130. Bell County Courthouse, Public Square, Belton (1883–1884)
J. N. Preston and Son, Architects   View from Southwest

Although the exterior retains much of its original character, remodeling has removed many of the salient features of this handsome three-story courthouse, leaving an incomplete composition.[1] At the time of completion, a magnificent tower 125 feet high was terminated by a statue of the Goddess of Justice, with sword and balance in hands. This tower was supported by a wide base, surrounded by a colonnade.

Stone of a golden hue from a nearby quarry further distinguished the exterior. The base was of pitch-faced ashlar, the upper portion of cut stone. On each of the four façades an entry was announced by a portico supported by cut-stone columns with carved capitals and bases.

Sheet-metal details manufactured in Fort Worth were employed extensively in the original design. Galvanized iron and spun zinc were used to form the cornices, balusters, urns, and window pediments, many of which have been removed. The roof was of tin in a pattern imitative of slate.

Elegant materials also contributed to the beauty of the interior. Corridor and portico floors were marble. Wood finished in natural colors was used throughout, and the courtroom had a paneled ceiling supported by fluted pilasters with paneled pedestals and carved capitals and bases.

[1] For an early view of the courthouse, see Temple Junior Chamber of Commerce, *Bell County History*, p. 21.

Plate 131. Milam County Courthouse, Public Square, Cameron (1890–1891)
J. Larmour and A. O. Watson, Architects   View

This edifice was erected on the site of an earlier courthouse, which it replaced. Although it has been remodeled extensively on the interior, and changed some on
the exterior, the walls yet retain most of their original
charm. However, a tower that once rose above the mass

has been removed, along with an ornate galvanized-iron
cornice.

The Comanche County Courthouse in Comanche
(1890–1891, razed 1939), also designed by Larmour and
Watson, was virtually identical in appearance.

Plate 133. Red River County Courthouse, Clarksville
View of Courtroom

This courtroom still retains much of its original interest. A handsome paneled bench was emphasized by an arched recess, and the wooden ceiling was decorated with pendants—rich contrast with the plastered walls. The bar enclosure was of ornamental iron, while the jury box was enclosed with wooden balusters and railing.

W. H. Wilson, in association with another architect, a Mr. Tozer, also designed the Clay County Courthouse in Henrietta (1884). The exterior of that edifice, with some variations, was similar to the Red River house. The interior, which has been vastly remodeled, was also on a similar plan.

Plate 132. Red River County Courthouse, Clarksville (1884–1885)
W. H. Wilson, Architect   View

Although, because of cost, the size of the courthouse was reduced from the original plan, it nonetheless was a monumental work with Classical details. The walls were white limestone from Honey Grove, while the cornice and tower were sheet metal, manufactured in Dallas, the home town of the architect. The columns and their bases, projecting obliquely from the corners, were chief features of interest.

The agreement with the builder, P. C. Livingston, excluded the clock, but before construction had far advanced, citizens pressed the commissioners to add it. Manufactured in Boston, the clock struck the rounds on a two-thousand-pound bell and was the official regulator of county activities.

Plate 134. Lampasas County Courthouse, Public Square, Lampasas (1883)
W. C. Dodson, Architect　　　View from Southwest

This edifice, the cornerstone for which was laid in September by the Saratoga Lodge, AF&AM, was only the second temple of justice in the county's history. It was built of native limestone with plans and form similar to those employed by Dodson on several other Texas courthouses of the 1880's. The tower and roof were covered with light sheet-metal components, into which were stamped geometrical designs. The walls were noteworthy for the beauty of the cut stone around the entrances and other openings.

Plate 135. Shackelford County Courthouse, Public Square, Albany (1883–1884)
J. E. Flanders, Architect　　　View from South

A courthouse of hewn cedar pickets, set up in 1875, was replaced by this temple. Designed by a Dallas architect, the plan accepted by the commissioners' court was lauded for its "qualities of safety, durability and grandeur."[1] Due to errors in estimation, work on the new courthouse was suspended in September 1883 by the contractors, Harris and Company, when they were financially unable to continue. Subsequently, the county assumed the contract, and the county attorney, Edgar Rye, superintended the completion of the work.

It was built with buff-colored stone, quarried on a ranch three miles southwest of Albany and cut and laid up by Scottish masons. The north and south elevations consisted of five-part massing, while the east and west had only three. Each of the dominant masses was terminated with a large sheet-metal cornice decorated with large consoles, and the roof was covered with metallic shingles. Delicate wrought-iron railings, contracted from the firm of Huey and Philip in Dallas, added interest to the composition.

As was common, several items were supplied by Eastern manufacturers. The Howard Clock Company of Boston furnished the timepiece. A. H. Andrews and Company of Chicago manufactured and installed the furniture, much of which is still in use.

[1] *Fort Worth Daily Gazette*, March 20, 1883, p. 2.

Plate 136. Hood County Courthouse, Public Square, Granbury (1889–1891)
W. C. Dodson, Architect   View

As early as 1885, Hood County commissioners had considered a new courthouse, but the official resolution had failed. Four years later, the county judge wrote, "Owing to the exposure of Public Records & Papers of this County I believe it to be imperative duty of the Commissioners Court to build a new Court House for the Safe-keeping preservation of same,"[1] after which the decision to build was made. Following a tour of inspection of other courthouses in the state and reception of plans from several architects, the court adopted the proposal of Dodson.

The old courthouse was sold and razed, the stones reappearing in commercial buildings on the north and west sides of the public square.[2] As was usual, county offices were moved into a two-story stone commercial building fronting on the square, pending construction of the new courthouse. Erected by Moodie and Ellis of Greenville, the new building had walls of Granbury limestone from a nearby quarry.

[1] Commissioners' Court Minutes, Hood County, vol. C, p. 162.
[2] *Fort Worth Daily Gazette*, February 7, 1890, p. 1.

Plate 137. Hill County Courthouse, Public Square, Hillsboro (1889–1891)
W. C. Dodson, Architect   View from East

To replace a two-story brick courthouse that had been erected in 1874, the Hill County commissioners selected the plans of a Waco architect. In December 1889 the contract for construction was awarded to the firm of Lovell, Miller, and Hood for $83,000. Nearly two years later, the edifice was received from the contractors.

The ninety-two–foot–square building contained three stories. On the first floor, corridors through the center each way provided access to the offices. The main courtroom, a two-story space, along with several other rooms, was on the second floor, and additional offices occupied the third floor, adjacent to the upper courtroom space.

Built of white limestone, the four façades were similar, but only opposite ones were identical in detail and composition. Contrasting with the rough coursed ashlar walls, the smooth-cut ornamental features had remarkable intricate carving.

Rising above the courtroom, the tower, which supported a clock and large bell, was of wood and metal. Bearing on the courtroom trusses, the tower consisted of a heavy timber framework enclosed with wooden sheathing covered with light sheet-metal components.

Plate 138. Blanco County Courthouse, Public Square, Blanco (1885)
F. E. Ruffini, Architect   View

In the mid-eighties Blanco County commissioners authorized the construction of this substantial structure,
apparently confident that the county seat would remain
in Blanco. However, only five years after construction
commenced, citizens petitioned for an election to deter-
mine whether the county seat should be moved to Johnson City. In an election highlighted by a shooting affray,
Johnson City won, and within hours all the records were
loaded on wagons and moved to the new county seat.
After the county vacated the temple, it became a bank
and then later served as a hospital.

Several towns and their courthouses suffered similar
fates in the spirited competition over seats of justice.
Among these were Frio City, whose stone courthouse
(1876) was vacated when the seat was moved to Pearsall
in 1883—resulting in the demise of the town—and Sher-
wood, whose courthouse (1900) was vacated when the
seat was moved to Mertzon in 1937.

The specifications for the Blanco temple called for a
variety of masonry techniques. Quarry-faced ashlar was
required below the water table. Above this line, quarry-
and pitch-faced ashlar was specified for the walls; smooth
rubbed stone was used for the moldings, door caps, and
pilaster caps. Cut stones with bush-hammered centers
and margin drafts were specified for pilaster faces,
friezes, door sills, window caps, and jambs on the interior. Bricks were required for the walls and roof of the
vaults as well as for the chimneys. Limestone flagstones
were specified for the vault floors.[1]

[1] F. E. Ruffini, "Specifications for the Erection and Completion of Court House for Blanco County to be Built at Blanco,
Texas," Texas State Library, Austin.

Plate 139. Brewster County Courthouse, 200 Sixth Street, Alpine (1888)
Architect Unknown　　　View

This small edifice is the seat of justice for the largest county in Texas—the area of the mountainous county is greater than the state of Connecticut. Although on a conservative scale, simple details created a statement of dignity. The brick walls, on a foundation of stone, were articulated by pilasters and by a corbeled stringcourse. Prominent accents were provided by semicircular window caps and an entrance pediment. All these were surmounted by a sheet-metal cornice and a mansard roof with triangular dormers.

Plate 140. Concho County Courthouse, Public Square, Paint Rock (1885–1886)
F. E. Ruffini and Oscar Ruffini, Architects   View from Southeast

Built by contractors J. B. Kane and John Cormack, this native-stone structure was planned by F. E. Ruffini of Austin. Shortly before construction commenced, his brother, Oscar Ruffini, a native of Cleveland, Ohio, who did considerable architectural work in West Texas, was hired to supervise construction. The edifice was erected on conventional plans, with corridors that divided the ground floor into four equal quadrants, and with a central courtroom on the second.

Metal was extensively used for the decorative features. The cornices, pediments, and dormers were galvanized iron. Malleable iron was used for the crestings. On the interior, the ceilings were finished with stamped sheet-metal panels.

In addition to this edifice, F. E. Ruffini designed the main academic building at the University of Texas in Austin, and Oscar Ruffini designed the Tom Green County Courthouse in San Angelo, where he lived.

Plate 141. Sutton County Courthouse, Public Square, Sonora (1891–1893)
Oscar Ruffini, Architect   View from West

This small but charming courthouse was built on the traditional scheme with corridors running through the center of the building each way. As was typical, the courtroom was in the center of the second floor of the symmetrical arrangement.

For his plans and specifications, Ruffini received the sum of 3.5 percent of the contract price of the building, which was $27,706;[1] for supervision, 1.5 percent was paid. These were the commissions that were generally awarded to architects for their services on nineteenth-century courthouses.

This was the only courthouse built by Sutton County, an unusual situation.

[1] Commissioners' Court Minutes, Sutton County, vol. I, p. 8.

Plate 142. Goliad County Courthouse, Public Square, Goliad (1894)
Alfred Giles, Architect [?]; Martin, Byrnes, and Johnston, Builders   View

The excitement accompanying the commencement of work on this courthouse was characteristic. Excursion trains to historic Goliad were run from Houston and other South Texas towns. These brought interested individuals to the cornerstone laying, on March 2, 1894, which was celebrated with a barbecue and formal orations.

The stone masonry was outstanding. Openings on the various floors were spanned by round, flat, or segmental arches, with subtle contrasts of color. Below these, a con-

trasting stringcourse accented the walls. Other noteworthy features were the cut-stone pilasters of the corner and center pavilions.

Originally the building was virtually identical with the Caldwell County Courthouse in Lockhart. However, a central tower was removed from the Goliad courthouse after it was damaged by a storm in 1942 and a large wing was added on the south in 1964, both of which actions considerably changed the character.

236

Plate 143. Presidio County Courthouse, Public Square, Marfa (1886)
Attributed to Alfred Giles, Architect   View

Despite difficulties over the sale of county bonds that were claimed to have been illegally issued, construction began on this large courthouse. Although smaller and considerably less ornate, it was quite similar in form and massing to the courthouse that Giles designed for El Paso County (1885–1886, razed 1917). It was erected by J. H. Britton of Sherman, who also built the El Paso temple.

Plate 144. Erath County Courthouse, Public Square, Stephenville (1891–1892)
J. Riely Gordon and D. E. Laub, Architects   View

Early in the summer of 1891, the Erath County commissioners ordered the construction of a new courthouse. However, work was delayed, pending the results of an election over the question of moving the county seat to Dublin. After the vote finally determined that the seat would remain in Stephenville, work was commenced on the Romanesque Revival structure.

With typical pride, it was boasted in the press, "No

expense in the way of architectural design will be spared to make it beautiful and substantial."[1] Fulfilling this ambition, the exterior was of white limestone from the nearby hills, with trim of Pecos red sandstone. Built by S. A. Tomlinson of Fort Worth, the interior had marble floors and ornamental iron stairs.

[1] *Fort Worth Daily Gazette*, June 14, 1891, p. 14.

Plate 145. Dallas County Courthouse, Houston and Commerce Streets, Dallas (1891–1892)
Orlopp and Kusener, Architects   View from Northeast

As was the case with many counties, Dallas suffered large losses from fires. In 1880 flames consumed the third Dallas County Courthouse, leaving only the walls. It was subsequently repaired, only to succumb again to flames early in 1890.

Rather than again renovating, commissioners determined to build an entirely new temple of justice, and late in 1890 the huge blue granite cornerstone was cemented into place with appropriate ceremonies. But before the work was completed, the builder was released

from his contract (and his name removed from the cornerstone). Retaining M. A. Orlopp of Little Rock, Arkansas, as a supervisor, the county commissioners then completed construction. The walls of the massive structure were built of contrasting blue granite and red Pecos sandstone. On the interior a wainscot of marble enhanced the work. Originally, a massive stone bell tower, with clocks on each side, rose from the center of the building. However, in 1919 structural problems necessitated removal of the 205-foot-high work.

Plate 146. Lavaca County Courthouse, Public Square, Hallettsville (1897)
Eugene T. Heiner, Architect   View

Designed by a prominent Houston architect, this three-story building was a fine example of the Romanesque Revival. A lofty tower, large openings spanned by heavy arches, and numerous pinnacles and gables all contributed to the picturesque yet orderly composition.

To conveniently accommodate the various county functions, a modified T-shaped plan, 100 by 106 feet, was developed, with offices on the first floor. Heiner placed the spacious district courtroom on the second floor (within the left-hand mass with arched openings in this view). The office of the county clerk and the jury rooms were conveniently adjacent. The upper story was used for additional offices. C. H. and J. Stadtler were the contractors for the fireproof work.

Plate 147. Lavaca County Courthouse, Hallettsville
Detail of Portal

Intricate details and warm materials enhanced both the exterior and the interior. Elaborate carving appeared on the tower and pinnacles. In this view the imposts of the broad arch were supported on columns with sculptured capitals. Cut stone was used also for the cornice and archivolt.

On the interior a floor with mosaic patterns and ornamental iron stairs delighted visitors. Throughout the public spaces paneled wooden wainscots, deep brown in color, enriched the walls.

Plate 148. DeWitt County Courthouse, 307 North Gonzales Street, Cuero (1894–1896)
A. O. Watson, Architect   View

With exterior walls of red sandstone, this temple had a frontal composition that was reminiscent of the Allegheny County buildings in Pittsburgh, Pennsylvania (1884–1888), designed by influential architect Henry Hobson Richardson. Although much smaller and more simple, the central tower, flanked by pavilions on either side, and the triple-arched arcade, as well as the steep-pitched roofs, were similar to Richardson's work. Interesting features that were not, however, on the paradigm were the balconies and the third-story engaged columns on the corners of the pavilions.

Plate 149. Bexar County Courthouse, 20 Dolorosa Street, San Antonio (1892–1895)
J. Riely Gordon and D. E. Laub, Architects   View from Northwest

In 1891, Bexar County commissioners determined to erect a new temple of justice to replace the county edifice that had been designed by Alfred Giles and built less than a decade earlier. The commission to design the building was won by J. Riely Gordon in association with D. E. Laub, a partnership that was severed shortly after construction was commenced. Gordon was retained as supervising architect.

Each contractor bidding on the new courthouse submitted with his proposal samples of the stone that he intended to use. The contract was awarded to George Dugan and Otto P. Kroeger for a building with exterior walls of pink granite and red Pecos sandstone. Specifications called for concrete footings and sandstone for foundations not exposed to view.[1] Pitch-faced granite was employed up to the first-story sills, and polished granite was used for stringcourses, steps, and columns. Above, the red sandstone walls terminated under a terra-cotta frieze, with foliated design.

Additions to the south of the building were made in 1914–1915 and 1925–1928.

[1] Commissioners' Court Minutes, Bexar County, vol. C, p. 519.

Plate 151. Victoria County Courthouse, 101 North Bridge Street, Victoria (1891–1892)
J. Riely Gordon and D. E. Laub, Architects   View

Located across from De Leon Plaza, this was another fine example of Romanesque Revival design. Built of stone with subtle contrasts in color, it featured arches with voussoirs that were smoothly finished and heavily molded archivolts. Features resembling bartizans decorated the corners of the large masses, while each of the corners of the projecting pavilions was terminated with a molded arris.

Characteristic of good Romanesque design, below the cornice appeared a wide billet, comprised of square-faced stones in checkerboard pattern. Also appearing on the building were open arcades, uncommon features in Texas courthouses. Other interest was added by the decorative chimneys.

In recent years a new courthouse has been built, but this excellent nineteenth-century building still stands.

Plate 150. Fayette County Courthouse, Public Square, LaGrange (1890–1891)
J. Riely Gordon, Architect   View from East

In March 1890, Gordon's plans for a courthouse with an open court in the center were adopted by the Fayette County commissioners. Several months later, after bids from seven contractors were opened, the firm of Martin, Byrnes, and Johnston of Colorado City, builder of numerous Texas courthouses, was selected as the contractor.

Handsome materials were used throughout. The exterior walls were of Belton white limestone and blue sandstone, the latter quarried at nearby Muldoon. Red Pecos sandstone stringcourses and pink Burnet granite columns and steps formed rich accents. On the tower was a large stone slab on which was carved an American eagle. Above this, at the corners, were the likenesses of griffins. The roof was covered with slate and Spanish tile.

The materials on the interior were equally elegant. Black and white marble tile covered the hallway floors, in checkerboard pattern. Woodwork throughout was Texas curly pine. The main courtroom, equivalent to two stories in height, was provided with carpeting and opera chairs, seating a total of approximately five hundred on the main floor and gallery.

It is indeed unfortunate that in the 1940's the need for additional space necessitated converting the open court into a vault and offices.

Plate 152. Ellis County Courthouse, Public Square, Waxahachie (1894–1896)
J. Riely Gordon, Architect   View from Southwest

This was among the most controversial Texas courthouses of the nineteenth century. Unlike many counties that were forced to erect new temples of justice to replace earlier ones that had been consumed by flames, Ellis County had had a substantial two-story stone building, dating from 1874. However, the commissioners, when a tie vote was affirmatively broken by the county judge, decided that it was not commensurate with their needs and moved to erect a new building on the site of the old. After voluminous public petitioning, the matter of taxes to finance the work came before the commissioners' court. However, according to law, the levying of taxes required that all members of the court be present, and one commissioner who was opposed to the project had mysteriously disappeared, stalling any action. After an extensive search failed to produce the missing commissioner, another was appointed by the district judge, after which the tax measure was passed, permitting the sale of bonds.

Late in 1894 the contract was let to Otto P. Kroeger of San Antonio. However, even after the old courthouse was razed, other delays were caused by litigations created by the opposition.

Typical of Gordon's designs, this was a splendid work, enhanced by a variety of stone. Above a base of grey granite, rose walls of pink granite and Pecos red sandstone. Voussoirs and stringcourses were sandstone, while polished columns were of both sandstone and granite. The porch floors were paved with marble tiles of two different grains.

While Gordon designed the building, the firm of Messer, Sanguinet, and Messer of Fort Worth supervised construction and prepared plans and specifications for the furniture. Although evidently finished at the end of 1896, the edifice was not accepted by the commissioners until 1897.

Plate 153. Wise County Courthouse, Public Square, Decatur (1895–1897)
J. Riely Gordon, Architect   View from Southeast

On January 8, 1895, flames destroyed the second courthouse (1881–1882) in Wise County's history—a stone building that had been designed by architect R. F. Sayers. During the next several months, while using a building belonging to the Wise County National Bank as a temporary seat, county commissioners journeyed to several towns across the state, inspecting temples of justice, which included the Bexar County Courthouse.

After the commissioners had examined the plans submitted by eight architects, Gordon's design—which was similar to but not identical with the Ellis County Courthouse—was selected. He was subsequently directed to develop details and specifications and to superintend the work.

Built by contractor J. A. White, the edifice was an outstanding work of masonry. Exterior walls were of pink pitch-faced Texas granite, and the main columns were pink polished granite. Terra cotta was used extensively in the frieze, turrets, and dormers. For the roof, light-blue Bangor slate was specified. The beauty of the interior

matched the exterior: floors of the porches, halls, lobbies, and rest rooms were finished with marble tiles of contrasting colors. The base and wainscoting of the halls, lobbies, and stairwell were also marble.

Although the building was remodeled in 1960, it yet retains most of its original character on the outside.

Plate 154. Hopkins County Courthouse, Church and Jefferson Streets, Sulphur Springs
(1894–1895)

J. Riely Gordon, Architect   View from Southwest

Located on a corner across from the public square, this edifice was erected by
Sonnefield and Emmins of Dallas. Although there were no entries on the northeast
or southeast, the plans were similar to other courthouses designed by Gordon on the
concept of the Greek cross.

Plate 155. Gonzales County Courthouse, Saint Joseph Street, Gonzales (1894–1896)
Attributed to J. Riely Gordon, Architect   View

Built by Otto P. Kroeger, this edifice, the second erected by Gonzales County, replaced an antebellum courthouse that had been consumed by flames in 1893. Following the fire, county commissioners advertised for plans and specifications for a new structure. In competition with a group of architects that included W. C. Dodson of Waco, Eugene T. Heiner of Houston, Elijah E. Myers of Detroit, and several others, T. S. Hodges of Lockhart, Texas, won the commission. However, for unknown reasons, his plans and specifications were later rejected and the court decided not to employ an architect. Subsequently, contractors were invited to submit plans and specifications, and those of Otto P. Kroeger were selected. Because of the similarity between the Gonzales temple and courthouses designed during the mid-1890's by J. Riely Gordon, credit for the design must go to the San

Antonio architect, even though he is not officially credited. Either Kroeger hired Gordon to prepare the plans, or he used plans from one of Gordon's other courthouses, which he had built.

The Gonzales courthouse was erected on the cruciform plan, with entries at the reentrants of the arms of the cross. On the ground floor of the brick structure were the various county offices. On the second floor was the district courtroom, with offices for district and county attorneys and the district clerk. On the third floor were offices for grand and petit juries. The core, enclosed by the tower-bearing walls, contained the only stairway. The massive tower, which held a Seth Thomas clock and bell, served to ventilate the building through openings at the top.

Described as a "very neat, clean design, conveniently arranged and substantial in its general construction" by architect A. O. Watson, who officially inspected the work early in 1895, the building was distinguished on the exterior by beautiful polychromy. Walls were of pink granite with rough texture, while columns and steps were blue polished granite. Producing vivid contrast, cut red sandstone was employed for voussoirs, lintels, and stringcourses. In the center of the north and south façades, below the small balconies, appeared delightful carvings, which include florid designs and human visages—common features of the Romanesque Revival. Cartouches, elaborately decorated with carving, bear the date of construction.

Unsympathetic remodeling unfortunately detracts from the beauty of the original design.

Plate 156. Lee County Courthouse, Public Square, Giddings (1898)
J. Riely Gordon, Architect   View

Replacing an 1878 courthouse that was destroyed by fire, this structure was built by Sonnefield, Emmins, and Albright of San Antonio. It was located on a public block that, unlike most squares in towns throughout the state, was surrounded by residential rather than commercial buildings.

The exterior walls were red brick, trimmed with white sandstone, creating brilliant contrast. Blue granite was employed for the steps and polished columns. The interior décor of the building was characteristic of many designed by Gordon in this style. On the ground level the floor was finished with marble tile, border, and base, all of a different color. Attractive woodwork enhanced the courtrooms. The district courtroom had the usual high ceiling and gallery, supported by iron columns, and a stamped-metal ceiling.

Plate 157. Comal County Courthouse, San Antonio and Seguin Streets, New Braunfels (1898)
J. Riely Gordon, Architect   View from Southwest

Rather than on the square, this edifice was located on a street across from it. The public space, which was centered on Seguin Street, was then reserved for a garden, fountain, and bandstand. Only the southwest entrance to the native-limestone structure was prominent in this situation. Although twentieth-century additions have been developed with details that harmonize, the massing nonetheless detracts from the original composition.

Plate 158. Harrison County Courthouse, Public Square, Marshall (1899–1900)
J. Riely Gordon and C. G. Lancaster, Architects
View from East

Late in 1899 the Harrison County commissioners' court issued bonds to finance a new courthouse to replace an 1888 edifice with Renaissance details of pressed brick and sandstone that had been gutted by fire. The replacement was designed by J. Riely Gordon, and construction was supervised by C. G. Lancaster, a Marshall architect. This was among Gordon's last Texas works before he moved to New York in 1904.

With walls of buff-colored pressed brick of local manufacture on a pink granite base, the form and details presented a grandiose appearance. In Renaissance Revival style, the cornice and balustrade were of galvanized iron, while the arcade was of terra cotta and the columns of blue granite. To fulfill the sovereign image, eagles with six-foot wing spreads, fabricated from zinc, deco-

rated the balustrade around the dome and the apexes of the pediments. A statue of the Goddess of Justice crowned the dome.

Among the most remarkable features was the rotunda, which, like the other parts of the building, had an iron structure. On the interior a coffered ceiling and windows glazed with colored glass created an imposing design.

Several twentieth-century remodelings have changed the appearance. In 1924 and 1927, Lancaster planned additions in which the east and west porticoes were moved out and new rooms added between these and the main part of the building. In 1964, after a new courthouse was completed, this became the Harrison County Museum.

Plate 159. Denton County Courthouse, Public Square, Denton (1895–1896)
W. C. Dodson, Architect   View

The third courthouse for Denton County, this replaced a brick building designed and built by J. H. Britton in 1876–1877. After the county commissioners determined to build a new temple, on July 3, 1895, they ordered "the Romanesque style of Architecture for the Denton County Court House as shown in the design prepared by Architect J. R. Gordon."[1] However, subsequent study of Gordon's plans, for some unrecorded reason, resulted in his discharge and in the award of the commission to W. C. Dodson for the preparation of plans, specifications,

and details, as well as supervision of construction.

Masonry of harmonizing hues produced an imposing work. Walls were sandstone; the column capitals were carved from stone from the Ganzer quarry, while the shafts of pink granite came from Burnet. These pillars, eighty in number, were polished in Fort Worth and were among the first to be finished with electrically powered equipment.

[1] Commissioners' Court Minutes, Denton County, vol. C, p. 503.

253

Plate 160. Coryell County Courthouse, Public Square, Gatesville (1897–1898)
W. C. Dodson, Architect   View from Southeast

In the summer of 1897 the limestone temple of justice that had been erected in 1872 was razed to make room for this new courthouse, built by contractor Tom Lovell. Plans called for a building in Italian Renaissance Revival style, but with walls of Romanesque character, out of cream-colored limestone and red sandstone. On October 2, 1897, the hollow granite cornerstone was set into place with solemn Masonic ceremonies.

Imbued with symbolism, the cornerstone leveling was typical of those of highly esteemed buildings. The stone was placed on the northeast corner, symbolic of light. Following appropriate orations, it was slowly lowered into place by machinery to the accompaniment of music, after which it was sprinkled with corn, wine, and oil, emblematic of plenty, health, and peace. Among the inscriptions on the stone were the dates, both anno Domini and *anno lucis*, the latter the Masonic date.

Into the hollow cornerstone was deposited a box of articles intended to represent to future generations something of the life of the society that erected the building. Among the deposits in the Coryell County Courthouse stone were a photo of the old courthouse, two boxes of medicine, a copy of the *Dallas Morning News*, an 1897 five-cent piece, a bottle of whiskey, a list of WCTU officers, a Columbian half dollar, and a Masonic lodge Bible.[1]

[1] Frank E. Simmons, *History of Coryell County*, p. 102.

Plate 161. Tarrant County Courthouse, Public Square, Fort Worth (1893–1895)
Gunn and Curtiss, Architects   View from Southeast

Due to the magnitude of the projected work, the courthouse to replace an 1876 structure received national attention from architects and contractors. Responding to the design competition were eighteen architects from eight states—although one firm was eliminated when it offered to divide the $2,500 prize with the county judge, if selected as the winner. Among the competitors were J. Riely Gordon, designer of numerous Texas courthouses, and Elijah E. Myers, designer of the Texas state Capitol. A Kansas City firm won the competition.

On the plans of Gunn and Curtiss, contractors from

several states submitted bids based on sandstone, lime-stone, or granite exterior walls. Although not the lowest bid, the proposal from the Probst Construction Company of Chicago—builders of the famous Chicago Auditorium, designed by Adler and Sullivan—for $408,240 for a pink-granite edifice was accepted.

Built of the same granite used in the state Capitol, in Renaissance Revival style, the massive structure was 230 feet long and 150 feet wide. The tower, an iron structure covered with copper, was 198 feet high. Intended to last indefinitely, the walls of the front projection were five feet thick.

The exterior of the monumental edifice was beauti-fully detailed. The portico columns were polished granite. On the front gable, cut in granite, appeared

the shield of Texas—the Lone Star with its wreath of oak and laurel. Artisans attracted the continuous at-tention of the residents when they erected scaffolding and carved the county name and date into the frieze.

The interior of the building was functionally zoned. On the ground floor, separated by 20-foot-wide cross-ing corridors, were four large rooms and sixteen small offices for the county commissioners, clerk, assessor, tax collector, sheriff, and other officials. On the second floor, surrounded by galleries, were located four coun-ty and district courtrooms—two great spaces with 34-foot ceilings and two with 21-foot ceilings. On the upper floor were located the court of appeals, law library, and grand jury rooms. Two elevators and a grand stair provided communication between floors.

Plate 162. Galveston County Courthouse, Galveston (1897–1898)
N. J. Clayton and Company, Architects   View

Twenty-six architects responded to the invitation for plans and specifications for a proposed new courthouse published nationally in the *American Architect and Building News*.[1] After the commissioners' court and a committee of citizens appointed by the chamber of commerce narrowed the field of competitors to seven, the proposal of Nicholas J. Clayton—one of three local architects—was accepted. Previously he had remodeled the old courthouse, but it had been finally consumed by fire.

Although revealing many Renaissance Revival features, the edifice may be appropriately identified with the Beaux-Arts Classicism that prevailed nationwide at the turn of the century as a result of the influence of the esteemed French school, the École des Beaux-Arts in Paris. Without tower, dome, or other picturesque features, and with restrained ornamentation, the design was relatively plain, even severe in form and character. The broad steps and large columns both contributed to the heavy monumentality of the brick, granite, and terra-cotta work.

[1] *American Architect and Building News* 55 (January 1897): xv.

Plate 163. Galveston County Courthouse, Galveston
View of Stairway

This shaft penetrated the center of the courthouse, providing light and ventilation to county offices on the first floor and to the various courtrooms on the upper two floors of the three-story work. The space also contained the stairway, on which the decorative potential of iron was exploited with elaborate patterns. The bridge, emphasized by marble tiles of contrasting color, created an interesting spatial penetration.

Plate 164. Jefferson Federal Courthouse and Post Office, 224 West Austin Street, Jefferson, Marion County (1888–1890)

William A. Ferret, Supervising Architect of the Treasury, Architect   View from South

With walls and trim of brick, this was a representative example of federal architecture in Texas. On the first floor was the post office, with its entrance off South Market Street, and on the second were the federal courtroom and offices, served directly by an entrance in the base of the tower off West Austin Street. On the third floor were additional offices, and in the basement was located the grand jury room.

The roof drainage system was designed to collect rainwater for drinking. Galvanized-iron gutters and downspouts conducted the runoff into cisterns. The draining surfaces, which were originally covered with slate shin-

gles, have been recently changed to asphalt. Among other changes, much of the original ornamental cresting has been removed.

In 1964 the post office was closed, and the following year the federal court was discontinued. Subsequently, the building was purchased by the Jefferson Historical Society and was converted into a museum.

Numerous records exist on the structure. The original drawings were deposited in the National Archives. In 1966 it was recorded by the Historic American Buildings Survey with photographs and measured drawings.

Plate 165. Quadrangle Tower, Fort Sam
Houston, Quadrangle, San Antonio,
Bexar County (1876)
Architect Unknown   View

In 1875 construction was commenced
on the Quadrangle, a large building
499 feet wide by 624 long and 30 deep,
with a sallyport on the south. Containing storerooms and offices, all of which
opened only to the court, this structure
was designed to serve as a supply depot
and was later named Fort Sam Houston. Enclosed in the center of the Quadrangle, erected at the same time, was
this 87-foot-high tower.

In addition to beauty, the tower had
several functions. At the top was a
30,000-gallon water tank,[1] which was to
be used for fire protection. Early in the
1880's the tank, along with a short arcade, was removed, and a large bell and
Seth Thomas clock were installed. The
tower also served as a watch station; a
plaque near the top contains an inscription, which begins:
San Antonio Quartermaster Depot
Erected by Act of Congress—1876
IN PEACE PREPARE FOR WAR

[1] Mary Olivia Handy, *A History of Fort
Sam Houston*, p. 43.

Plate 166. Texas State Capitol, North Congress Avenue, Austin, Travis County (1882–1888)
Elijah E. Myers, Architect   Overall View from Southeast

To finance the new Capitol, the legislature had earlier appropriated 3,050,000 acres of land, located in ten counties in the Panhandle, adjoining New Mexico. Fifty thousand of these were to pay the cost of surveying, while the remainder was offered as payment to the contractors bidding upon Elijah E. Myers's plans, the contract to be awarded to the one accepting the smallest quantity of the public domain in exchange for the building. Of only two bids submitted, that of Mattheas Schnell of Rock Island, Illinois, was low. After Schnell was awarded the contract early in 1882, he assigned his interest to the firm of Taylor, Babcock, and Company, which was represented by Abner Taylor of Chicago, who, in turn, sublet the work to Gus Wilke. The company, with the assistance of English capital, subsequently developed their land into the famous XIT Ranch.

After Myers's design was selected for the Capitol, architect Napoleon LeBrun of New York, who had been hired by the Building Commission to consult on the competition, suggested several modifications, which were accepted. These included changes in the rotunda, the addition of an elevator, increasing the thickness of interior walls, and refinements of proportions, to all of which Myers consented before preparing working drawings.[1]

In addition to its monumental composition, the exterior was distinguished by the beauty of its materials. The massive walls were of pink granite. Although the dome gave the impression of stone, it was actually metal, with cast-iron Corinthian columns. Galvanized iron was used for the cornice of the colonnade and the shell of the dome. Originally, cast iron had been specified for these elements, but difficulties in casting, as well as conservation of weight, necessitated the use of the lighter material. Above the apogee of the dome rose the lantern, supporting a zinc statue of the Goddess of Liberty with glass star in hand.

The cupolas functioned as ventilating devices.

[1] See Texas Capitol Building Commission, *Report of January 1, 1883*, p. 19, for LeBrun's recommendations, and page 21 for Myers's consent.

Plate 167. Texas State Capitol, Austin
View of Dome

Numerous controversies accompanied the construction of the Capitol, among them disputes over the stonework in the exterior walls. Originally, it was intended that sand-rubbed, rustic ashlar from the Oatmanville quarry near Austin, a light-grey-colored material, be used. However, it was discovered that neither this quarry nor any other in the state would yield a sufficient quantity of stone in uniform color to complete the edifice, which required an estimated fifteen thousand carloads of rock, three thousand of which were on the exterior. Moreover, it was found that iron in the stone oxidized when exposed to the elements, causing objectionable staining. Subsequently, the contractor's proposal to use a high quality limestone from Bedford, Indiana, was approved by the Capitol Building Commission, but Texan pride and loyalty would not accept nondomestic material. Following numerous offers of stone from various parts of the state, it was determined that pink granite from Burnet would

be used outside and limestone on the inside. Much harder and more difficult to cut than limestone or marble, the igneous rock was considerably more expensive. As compensation to the contractor for the additional cost, the state agreed, despite many protests, to furnish convict labor and a quarry, the stone from which was finally donated. Later, other problems developed between the contractor and the International Association of Granite Cutters, resulting in a boycott against construction.[1] The upshot of this conflict was that stone cutters were imported from Scotland to work on the building. A lawsuit followed but construction continued.

As additional compensations to the contractor, other modifications were made in the design. Among these, porticoes on the east and west were eliminated. In addition, the florid Corinthian order originally proposed by the architect for the capitals of the exterior pilasters was changed to the simpler Doric.

[1] For an account of this controversy, see Texas Capitol Building Commission, *Third Biennial Report of the Capitol Building Commission*, pp. 7–41.

Plate 168. Texas State Capitol, Austin
View of Rotunda

Numerous structural problems were encountered in the erection of the Capitol. Myers's plans contained a number of deficiencies, which created doubts over the safety and permanent stability of the building. Requests of the Capitol Building Commission to furnish amended plans and answer questions relative to points in doubt, which included walls of inadequate thickness and a weak dome, received only evasive answers. Subsequently, the commissioners threatened suit against the bond that Myers had been obliged to provide, terminating his association with the building.

In 1887 expert architects B. A. Harrod of New Orleans,

Nicholas J. Clayton of Galveston, and Eugene T. Heiner of Houston were appointed to investigate the building and make recommendations to correct such deficiencies as they discovered.[1] Included in their proposals, which were accepted, was the strengthening of the dome with a series of horizontal steel beams connecting the steel ribs that supported it. The lantern, they further advised, should be made stronger with both steel uprights and steel braces.

[1] For their report, see Texas Capitol Building Commission, *Report of the Capitol Building Commission upon the Completion of the New Capitol*, pp. 68–73.

Plate 169. Texas State Capitol, Austin
View of First-Floor Corridor

Handsome finishes and details characterized the interior. The original flooring was encaustic tile, a material harder than marble. Yellow pine was used to finish the basement walls. The governor's offices were decorated with mahogany, his second-floor reception room with cherry, and his consultation room with walnut. Elsewhere, including the corridors and legislative halls, oak was employed.

The legislative halls possessed an elegance appropriate for their function. Galvanized-iron cornices with decora-tion in the Corinthian order contributed to the stately appearance of these, and ornamental iron columns enhanced the wooden rostra. Natural lighting penetrated from the sides through two tiers of windows and from overhead through stained plate glass, over which were skylights.

The contract called for 3,200 gas light fixtures to be used throughout, although the building was wired for electricity before it was finished.

Plate 170. Texas State Capitol, Austin
View of Grand Stair

Located immediately east and west of the rotunda were the grand stairways, furnishing communication to vestibules of the legislative halls on the second floor and their galleries on the third. The stairways, along with interior columns, were also cast iron. Although structural wrought iron was reportedly imported from Belgium, this stairway and other ornamental iron work were cast in the East Texas Penitentiary at Rusk, using convict labor.

Plate 171. Texas State Capitol, Austin
View of South Lobby

The Texas statehouse was an immense structure, second in size only to the national Capitol. It was 566 feet long and 288 feet wide, covering an area of two and a quarter acres. From the base line of the building to the star in the hand of the statue of the Goddess of Liberty was 311 feet.

The main entry to the building was through this lobby. On the first floor were executive offices, on the second were the two legislative halls—the Senate in the east wing, the House of Representatives in the west—and on the third level was the judicial department.

In 1935 funds were appropriated for terrazzo floors on the executive level. These were installed with designs incorporating the names of famous battles of Texas's military heritage.

GLOSSARY OF ARCHITECTURAL TERMS

adobe: sun-dried earth blocks incorporating straw or grass as a binder.

antefix: ornamental feature placed at the edge of a tile roof to cover the ends of the tiles.

anthemion: ornamental form in low relief derived from the honeysuckle or palmette, common in ancient Greek architecture.

apse: projecting space located at the altar end of a church, usually semicircular in plan.

arabesque: decorative panel containing patterns derived from foliage, animal, or geometrical forms.

arcade: series of arches and their supports.

architrave: lowest section of the entablature of a Classical order, located below the frieze and above the column capitals.

archivolt: decorative molding around the upper edge of an arch.

arris: projecting edge of an angle.

ashlar: type of masonry employing stones with square or rectangular faces.

baluster: vertical support for a handrail or other decorative rail.

balustrade: series of balusters and their rail.

Baroque: late Renaissance style of architecture characterized by richness of decoration.

bartizan: projecting cylindrical form, usually located high upon a corner of a structure; in ancient military architecture it was a watch (or ward) station.

base: lower member or section of a column or wall.

basilica: ancient Roman edifice with a semicircular apse at one end; this type of building, containing side aisles formed by columns, was also used by early Christians for worship and became a common church plan.

battlement: parapet with multiple slots at the top; in ancient military architecture it was used for defense; in the nineteenth century it was used for decoration.

bay: repetitive division of a building based on openings or the structural system.

beam: horizontal structural member supported by columns or walls.

Beaux-Arts Classicism: academic style of design employing Greek, Roman, or Renaissance details and composition originally taught at the national school of fine arts in Paris.

belfry: small bell tower.

billet: decorative band comprised of a pattern of small square or rectangular blocks, located below the cornice of Romanesque buildings.

board-and-batten construction: type of wall finish consisting of thin wide planks nailed to a framework in vertical pattern, with the interstices covered with thin narrow members.

boss: projecting ornamental stud or block.

brace: structural member applied on an angle to stabilize a building framework against horizontal movement.

bracket: projecting decorative or structural member employed to support an overhanging part of a building.

bull's-eye window: circular window with a disk-shaped sash.

bushhammer: tool for dressing the faces of stones, consisting of cutting plates with channels bolted between.

buttress: structural component, usually of masonry, designed to reinforce a wall or to absorb thrust from another member.

campanile: tall bell tower.

cap: crowning feature of a wall, a post, or another architectural detail.

capital: upper feature of a column or pilaster.

cartouche: flat or convex panel, often with an inscription, surrounded by an elaborate decorative frame.

chamfer: beveled edge.

chancel: in churches, the space at the end of the nave where the clergy conducts services.

chancery: record offices for church or ambassadorial business activities.

chautauqua: building used for entertainment and lectures.

chord: upper or lower member of a truss.

Churrigueresque: Baroque style characterized by an elaborate decorative vocabulary originating in Spain.

clapboards: boards with tapered cross section installed with overlaps to form an exterior wall surface.

Classical style: mode of design based upon decorative features of ancient Greek, Roman, or Renaissance Europe.

coffered: pattern of square or rectangular recessed panels in a ceiling or vault.

colonnade: line of columns at repetitive spacing with a common entablature.

console: ornamental bracket attached to a wall to support a cornice or other feature.

coping: continuous cap on a wall, used to protect the top of the wall from weather.

corbel: overhanging form in masonry created by successively stepping outward individual courses of bricks or stones as the wall rises in height.

corbie: one of the offsets in a stepped gable of a building.

Corinthian order: type of column and entablature in Classical architecture incorporating acanthus leaves as primary decorative features.

cornice: projecting component at the top of a wall; in Classical architecture, the upper section of the entablature.

crenellation: parapet wall with a repetitive pattern of slots or embrasures, open at the top.

cresting: decorative member capping the ridge of a roof.

cruciform plan: arrangement of spaces with a layout in the form of a cross.

cupola: small structure rising above the apex of a roof, used for ventilation and/or decoration.

dentil: one of a row of small blocks forming a part of the cornice located immediately below the soffit in Classical architecture.

dog-trot cabin: dwelling or other building type consisting of two rooms, separated by an open breezeway, all under a single continuous roof.

dome: roof consisting of a hemispherical shell, or some other section of a sphere.

Doric order: systemic arrangement of decorative features in Classical architecture, characterized by simplicity.

dormer: small roofed feature, usually with a window, projecting from a large inclined roof.

double-hung window: window containing two sashes that slide vertically.

drip molding: projecting part of a cornice or window designed to convey rainwater clear of parts below.

English Perpendicular style: system of structural and decorative features developed in Medieval England during the fourteenth century, characterized by vertical forms and proportions.

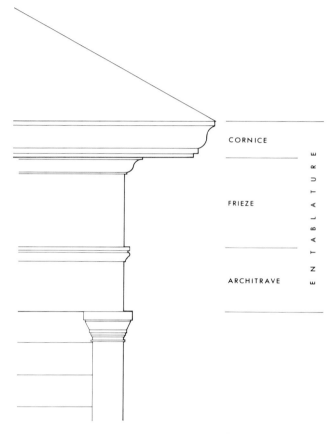

entablature: in Classical architecture, the group of members in the upper section of a wall, consisting of cornice, frieze, and architrave.

façade: exterior face of a building, usually a front.

fanlight: semicircular or semielliptical window with muntins radiating from a center.

fascia: long vertical member in a cornice.

fieldstone: rough undressed rocks.

finial: ornament placed at the apex of a roof, a spire, or another high point.

flat arch: structural component constructed with voussoirs that form a horizontal line.

French doors: pair of doors with rectangular glass and/

or wood panels extending full height, placed in a single opening.

fresco: decorative colored surface of a wall or ceiling finished with lime plaster and pigments that were applied while the plaster was still wet.

frieze: middle section of a Classical entablature located between the cornice and architrave.

gable: upper section of a wall just below the roof edge at the end of a building, or the upper section of a wall extending above a roof plane.

garland: in architecture, a decorative feature resembling a wreath.

Georgian style: Classical English mode of architecture, popular during the eighteenth and early nineteenth centuries during the reigns of Anne and the four Georges.

Gothic Revival style: mode of architecture popular in the nineteenth century that revived spatial and decorative forms that had originated in Medieval Europe.

Greek Revival style: mode of architecture employing forms and ornamental details that had originated in ancient Greece.

hip roof: roof with inclined planes sloping up from all four sides of a building.

hood: ornamental molding over a door or window.

horseshoe arch: structural component constructed with voussoirs placed in the form of a horseshoe—the curvature begins rising opposite the direction of the span.

impost: upper part of a pier from which an arch springs.

interstice: open space between logs or boards.

intrados: bottom or inner curve of an arch.

Ionic order: Classical mode of architecture in which the volute forms a prominent feature of the capitals.

Islamic style: mode of architecture developed by the Islams in ancient Syria, Palestine, and Persia, characterized by horseshoe arches and elaborate surface decoration.

Italianate style: mode utilizing decorative features from the architecture of Renaissance Italy.

jacal: primitive shelter with walls of pickets or sticks planted vertically into the ground, then plastered with mud and covered with a thatched roof.

jamb: side of a window or door opening.

joist: light wooden or metal floor or ceiling structural member.

keystone: center wedge-shaped voussoir of an arch—when an arch is constructed, it is the last component to be set into place.

lancet form: narrow opening terminating in a pointed arch, in which the radii of curvature are commonly equal to or greater than the span of the opening.

lantern: small cylindrical form with windows crowning a dome.

lintel: beam spanning an opening or a space.

machicolation: in an overhanging parapet, an opening in the floor, through which the wall below could be defended.

mansard roof: roof with each side comprised of two pitches; a steep slope near the edge of a building and a low slope toward the center—named for François Mansart, a seventeenth-century French architect.

Medieval style: mode of building of the Middle Ages of Europe, generally characterized by steep roofs, pointed arches, and often buttresses and battlements.

mezzanine: story of a building with a large section open to the floor below.

minaret: slender tower, especially a tower of a mosque from which are issued calls to prayer.

molding: thin continuous functional or decorative member with a curved and/or rectangular profile, projecting from a surface.

Moorish style: mode of architecture belonging to the Moors; Islamic.

muntin: thin division bar in a window sash.

narthex: entrance or foyer to a church.

nave: main interior space in churches where the lay worshippers are seated.

newel: terminal post for the handrail at the foot, head, or landing of a stair.

order: stylistic design vocabulary of Classical architecture.

paradigm: model or prototype.

parapet: low wall, usually rising above a roof or deck.

paterae: circular ornaments in Classical architecture.

pavilion: projecting mass of a building, usually with a separate roof line; also, a building for temporary use in an exhibition.

pedestal: short pier on which a column, pilaster, or statue bears.

pediment: ornamental geometrical form, usually triangular but sometimes in segmental or other form, located at a roof or gable or over a colonnade, wall, door, or window.

pendant: suspended ornamental feature.

pendentive: support for a dome that rises from the corner of a square or polygonal room to make a transition for a circular ring at the base of the dome.

pilaster: rectangular structural pier projecting from a wall, with design features resembling a column.

pinnacle: terminal architectural feature generally ending with a spire; a masonry detail used in Gothic architecture to weight a buttress.

pitch face: rough ashlar stone face texture resulting from fresh splitting in the quarry but with edges defined by lines cut with a pitching chisel.

plate line: line of support for a floor or roof system; in

wood frame construction, the line on which the horizontal support is placed over the studs.

portico: entrance porch with a colonnade.

prostyle: Classical term indicating columns placed only across the front of a building.

purlin: secondary roof structural member spanning between beams or trusses and supporting roof joists or decking.

quarry face: ashlar face texture resulting from a fresh split face, as made in the quarry.

quatrefoil: four-lobed figure, like a cloverleaf.

Queen Anne style: mode of architecture first evolving in England during the early eighteenth century, then in the last half of the nineteenth century; in America, characterized by picturesque massing, brick walls, shingled wall panels, and high brick chimneys.

quoin: stone in the corner of a wall, usually larger, of different texture, and always more precisely cut than the intermediate stones.

Renaissance Revival style: nineteenth-century mode incorporating decorative features revived from the Renaissance architecture of Europe.

Renaissance style: form and decorative vocabulary of architecture that developed in various countries of Europe beginning in the fifteenth century, characterized by the re-use of ancient Roman Classical elements. The term includes many variations, all of which have specific designations.

revetment: facing on a sloping earthwork.

rock face: weathered quarry face stone texture.

Romanesque style: mode of architecture based on Roman forms in use in Western Europe during the eleventh century through the thirteenth century, characterized by stone construction and round arches.

Romantic style: any architectural fashion embodying symbolic or emotional meanings.

rose window: round window with radiating ribs and tracery, usually containing stained glass.

rotunda: space under a dome, usually defined by circular walls.

round arch: arch in which the voussoirs form a semicircle; a Roman arch.

rubble: rough undressed stones used in masonry walls.

rusticated: stonework with beveled or rebated edges to make the joints stand out.

sallyport: technically, a passageway from a fortification designed to allow for sorties on an attacking enemy; the term is now often used to identify any open passageway through a building.

sanctuary: most sacred space of a church or cathedral.

scrollwork: ornamental features fabricated from wood boards or planks with a scrollsaw or jigsaw.

Second Empire style: style of architecture named for the French Second Empire of Napoleon III, which was developed in France during the nineteenth century, characterized by mansard roofs, dormers, and Classical decorative details.

segmental arch: arch in which the voussoirs form a segment of a circle, less than a semicircle.

sill: bottom member of a door or window opening; also the lowest member of a frame wall, supported by the foundation.

soffit: surface on the bottom of an architectural member, such as a cornice or an arch.

spandrel: wall panel below a window; also the surface enclosed by the archivolt of an arch, a horizontal line extending from the crown, and a vertical line from the base of the archivolt.

spindle column: thin round vertical shaft, often turned on a lathe, with numerous bands and flanges.

spire: tapered terminal feature of a tower.

springline: level from which an arch ordinarily begins its curvature.

stilted arch: arch with springlines above the level of the imposts.

stringcourse: decorative horizontal molding projecting from the exterior wall of a building.

Syrian arch: round arch supported on short columns or piers.

tongue-and-groove: technique of joining boards where the edge of one is milled with a continuous recess, and the adjoining board with a continuous rib to fit into the groove.

tooth molding: continuous decorative strip incorporating features with sections radiating from a raised point, common in Early Gothic architecture.

trace: layout or plan of a fortification.

tracery: thin, curvilinear decorative work in interlocking and repetitive patterns in Gothic or Gothic Revival buildings.

transept: space in either of the projecting arms of a cruciform plan.

transom: hinged window above a door; also a horizontal bar over a door and under a window.

trefoil: three-lobed decorative figure, like a cloverleaf.

truss: floor or roof structural member comprised of thin members arranged in triangular patterns.

Tudor style: late Gothic architectural mode of England, characterized especially by the prevalent use of arches with four centers of curvature.

turret: cylindrical towerlike architectural form, originally used in ancient military architecture for defensive purposes.

Tuscan style: simplest ancient Classical mode of architecture, developed by the Etruscans.

tympanum: area enclosed by the upper and lower cornices of a pediment; also the space enclosed by a door or window lintel and an arch over the lintel.

urn: in architecture, an ornamental figure in the form of a vase.

vault: arched structure of masonry spanning between the walls or beams of a building or bridge; also a room in which the documents and valuables are placed for security.

vestibule: small space forming a transition between the exterior and interior space of a building.

Victorian Gothic style: late-nineteenth-century architectural fashion employing a variety of Medieval stylistic elements, rendered in a variety of materials and proportions to achieve richness and solidity.

volute: spiral scroll-shaped ornament.

voussoir: one of the wedge-shaped stones of an arch or a vault.

wainscoting: paneling that rises only several feet in height, applied to an interior wall.

water table: molding or offset of the exterior of a wall located several feet above ground level.

BIBLIOGRAPHY

UNPUBLISHED MATERIALS

Allen, Winnie. "The History of Nacogdoches, 1691–1830." M.A. Thesis, University of Texas, 1925.

Anderson, Garland. "The Courthouse Square: Six Case Studies in Texas Evolution, Analysis, and Projections." M.S. Thesis, University of Texas, 1968.

Commissioners' Court Minutes. Individual Texas counties.

Connally, Ernest Allen. "The Ecclesiastical and Military Architecture of the Spanish Province of Texas." Ph.D. Dissertation, Harvard University, 1955.

Goeldner, Paul. "Temples of Justice: Nineteenth-Century Courthouses in the Midwest and Texas." Ph.D. Dissertation, Columbia University, 1969.

Historic American Buildings Survey. Microfilm of drawings, photos, and data sheets. Library of Congress, Washington, D.C.

National Archives. Cartographic Branch, and Textual Records Branch, Washington, D.C.

Ruffini, Elise. Letter to James Day, August 29, 1961, Texas State Library, Austin.

Ruffini, F. E. "Specifications for the Erection and Completion of Court House for Blanco County to be Built at Blanco, Texas." Texas State Library, Austin.

Texas State Historical Association. Collection of photographs, Austin.

Texas State Historical Survey Committee, files, Austin.

Texas State Library. Archives Division, files, Austin.

University of Texas at Austin. Barker History Center, Texas Collection, lithograph collection.

Wallace, Percy Everett. "The History of Austin College." M.A. Thesis, Austin College, 1924.

Walsh, Sister Natalie. "The Founding of Laredo and St. Augustine Church." M.A. Thesis, University of Texas, 1935.

GOVERNMENT DOCUMENTS

Laws and Decrees of the State of Coahuila and Texas, in Spanish and English. To Which is Added the Constitution of Said State: Also, the Colonization Law of the State of Tamaulipas, and Naturalization Law of the General Congress. Translated by J. P. Kimball. Houston: Telegraph Power Press, 1839.

Laws of Texas 1822–1897. Compiled and arranged by H. P. N. Gammel. Austin: Gammel Book Co., 1898.

Texas Capitol Building Commission. *Final Report of the Capitol Building Commissioners upon the Completion of the New Capitol.* Austin, 1888.

————. *Report of January 1, 1883.* Austin, 1883.

————. *Report of the Capitol Building Commission to the Governor of Texas.* Austin, 1885.

————. *Report of the Capitol Building Commission upon the Completion of the New Capitol.* Austin, 1888.

————. *Third Biennial Report of the Capitol Building Commission.* Austin, 1886.

Texas Legislative Council. *The Texas Capitol: Building a Capitol and a Great State.* Austin, 1967.

U.S. Congress. House. *Condition of Texas.* H. Ex. Doc. 35, 24th Cong., 2d Sess., 1836.

————. *Frontier Defense in Texas.* H. Ex. Doc. 27, 35th Cong., 2d Sess., 1859.

————. *General Order No. 1.* H. Ex. Doc. 2, 32d Cong., 1st Sess., 1851.

————. *Report of the Chief of Engineers.* H. Ex. Doc. 1, 46th Cong., 3d Sess., 1880, II.

————. *Report of the Chief of Engineers.* H. Ex. Doc. 2, 57th Cong., 1st Sess., 1901.

————. *Report of the Committee on Awards of the World's Columbian Commission.* H. Doc. 510, 57th Cong., 1st Sess., 1901, pp. 5–25.

————. *Report of First Lieutenant N. C. Givens.* H. Ex. Doc. 2, 32d Cong., 1st Sess., 1851.

————. *Report of First Lieutenant J. B. Plummer, R. Quartermaster.* H. Ex. Doc. 2, 32d Cong., 1st Sess., 1851.

————. *Report of Lieutenant A. Jackson.* H. Ex. Doc. 2, 32d Cong., 1st Sess., 1851.

————. *Report of Lieutenant Haldeman.* H. Ex. Doc. 2, 32d Cong., 1st Sess., 1851.

————. *Report of Lieutenant Turnley, Acting Assistant Quartermaster.* H. Ex. Doc. 2, 32d Cong., 1st Sess., 1851.

————. [C. M. Conrad.] *Report of the Secretary of War.* H. Ex. Doc. 2, 32d Cong., 1st Sess., 1851.

U.S. Congress. Senate. *Report of the Secretary of War.* S. Ex. Doc. 2, 36th Cong., 1st Sess., 1859.

————. *Report to J. G. Totten.* S. Doc. 443, 28th Cong., 1st Sess., 1846, vol. 10.

U.S. National Park Service. *Historic American Buildings Survey.* Washington, D.C.: Government Printing Office, 1941.

U.S. Quartermaster General's Office of the War Department. *Outline Descriptions of Southwestern Military Posts and Stations, 1871.* Washington, D.C.: Government Printing Office, 1872.

U.S. Surgeon General's Office. *Circular No. 4: Plan for a Post Hospital of Twenty-Four Beds.* Washington, D.C.: Government Printing Office, April 27, 1867.

————. *Circular No. 4: A Report on Barracks and Hospitals with Descriptions of Military Posts.* Washington, D.C.: Government Printing Office, 1870.

————. *Circular No. 8: A Report on the Hygiene of the United States Army with Descriptions of Military Posts.* Washington, D.C.: Government Printing Office, 1875.

Utley, Robert M. *Fort Davis National Historic Site, Texas.* National Park Service Historical Handbook Series, no. 38. Washington, D.C.: Government Printing Office, 1965.

Works Progress Administration. *Beaumont: A Guide to the City and Its Environs.* Houston: Anson Jones Press, 1939.

————. *Houston: A History and Guide.* Houston: Anson Jones Press, 1942.

————. *Old Villita.* San Antonio: Clegg Co., 1939.

————. *Port Arthur.* Houston: Anson Jones Press, 1940.

————. *San Antonio: A History and Guide.* San Antonio: Clegg Co., 1938.

————. *Texas: A Guide to the Lone Star State.* New York: Hastings House, 1940.

BOOKS AND JOURNALS

American Architect and Architecture. 1876–1937.

American Architect and Building News. 1876–1917.

American Institute of Architects, Dallas Chapter. *The Prairie's Yield.* New York: Reinhold Publishing Co., 1962.

American Institute of Architects, San Antonio Chapter. *Historic San Antonio, 1700–1900.* San Antonio, 1963.

Anderson, Garland. "Coryell County Courthouse." *Texas Architect* 17, no. 2 (February 1968): 24–25.

Andrews, Wayne. *Architecture, Ambition and Americans: A Social History of American Architecture.* New York: Harper & Brothers, 1955.

Ashcraft, Allan C. "Fort Brown, Texas, in 1861." *Texas Military History* 3, no. 4 (Winter 1963): 243–247.

"Austin, the Capital of Texas." *Frank Leslie's Illustrated Newspaper,* May 22, 1880, pp. 196–197.

Bancroft, Hubert Howe. *The Works of Hubert Howe Bancroft.* Vols. 15 and 16, *History of the North Mexican States and Texas.* San Francisco: A. L. Bancroft Co., 1884, 1889.

Barkley, Mary Starr. *History of Travis County and Austin, 1839–1899.* Waco: Texian Press, 1963.

Barnstone, Howard. *The Galveston That Was.* New York: Macmillan, 1965.

Battle, William James. "A Concise History of the University of Texas." *Southwestern Historical Quarterly* 54, no. 4 (April 1951): 391–411.

Baxter, Sylvester. *Spanish-Colonial Architecture in Mexico.* 12 vols. Boston: J. B. Millet, 1901.

Beecher, Catharine E., and Harriet Beecher Stowe. *The American Woman's Home: or, Principles of Domestic Science, Being a Guide to the Formation and Maintenance of Economical, Healthful, Beautiful, and Christian Homes.* New York: J. B. Ford & Co., 1869.

Berglund, Ernest, Jr. *History of the First Methodist Church, Marshall, Texas.* Marshall, Tex.: Demmer Co., 1964.

Biesele, Rudolph Leopold. *The History of the German Settlements in Texas, 1831–1861.* Austin: Von Boeckmann-Jones, 1930.

Blake, R. B. *Historic Nacogdoches.* Nacogdoches, Tex.: Nacogdoches Historical Society, 1939.

Bollaert, William. *William Bollaert's Texas.* Edited by W. Eugene Hollon and Ruth Lapham Butler. Norman: University of Oklahoma Press, 1956.

Bolton, Herbert Eugene. *Texas in the Middle Eighteenth Century: Studies in Spanish Colonial History and Administration.* New York: Russell and Russell, 1962.

Bonnell, George W. *Topographical Description of Texas.*

Bibliography

To Which Is Added an Account of the Indian Tribes. Austin: Clark, Wing, & Brown, 1840.

Bowler, George. *Chapel and Church Architecture, with Designs for Parsonages.* Boston: J. P. Jewett, 1856.

Bowman, Jon. "Gethsemane Lutheran Church: Our Legacy." *Texas Architect* 18, no. 4 (April 1968): 4–6.

Bracht, Viktor. *Texas in 1848.* Translated by Charles Frank Schmidt. San Antonio: Naylor Printing Co., 1931.

Brady, Donald V. "The Theatre in Early El Paso." *Southwestern Studies* 4, no. 1 (1966): 1.

Browning, Webster E. "Joseph Lancaster, James Thomson, and the Lancasterian System of Mutual Instruction, with Special Reference to Hispanic America." *Hispanic American Historical Review* 4 (February 1921): 49–98.

Burchard, John, and Albert Bush-Brown. *The Architecture of America: A Social and Cultural History.* Boston: Atlantic Monthly Press, 1961.

Burk, Gary. "The First Christian Church of Menard, Texas." *Texas Architect* 19, no. 9 (September 1969): 23–25.

Burke, James, Jr. *Burke's Texas Almanac and Immigrants' Handbook.* Houston: American News Co., 1882–1883.

Bywaters, Jerry. "More about Southwestern Architecture." *Southwest Review* 18, no. 3 (April 1933): 234–264.

Calleros, Cleofas. *El Paso, Then and Now.* El Paso: American Printing Co., 1954.

Camara, Kathleen da. *Laredo on the Rio Grande.* San Antonio: Naylor Co., 1949.

Carroll, B. H., ed. *Standard History of Houston, Texas, from a Study of Original Sources.* Knoxville, Tenn.: H. W. Crew & Co., 1912.

Castañeda, Carlos E. *Our Catholic Heritage in Texas: 1519–1936.* 7 vols. Austin: Von Boeckmann-Jones Co., 1936–1950.

Chabot, Frederick C. *The Alamo: Mission, Fortress and Shrine.* San Antonio: Privately printed, 1936.

———. *San Antonio and Its Beginnings; Comprising the four numbers of the San Antonio Series with Appendix.* San Antonio: Artes Graficas, 1936.

Chatfield, W. *The Twin Cities.* New Orleans: E. P. Brandoo, 1893.

Clark, Joseph L. *The Texas Gulf Coast: Its History and Development; Family and Personal History.* 2 vols. New York: Lewis Historical Publishing Co., 1955.

Clark, Percy. "New Federal Buildings." *Harper's Weekly* (supplement), May 19, 1888, pp. 365–368.

Clopper, J. C. "Journal and Book of Memoranda for

1828, Province of Texas." *Quarterly of the Texas Historical Association* 13 (1909–1910): 44–80.

Collins, Peter. *Changing Ideals in Modern Architecture 1750–1950.* Montreal: McGill University Press, 1967.

Conger, Roger Norman. *Highlights of Waco History.* Waco: Hill Printing and Stationery Co., 1945.

———. *Historic Log Cabins of McLennan County, Texas.* Waco: Heritage Society of Waco, 1954.

———. *A Pictorial History of Waco.* 2d ed. Waco: Texian Press, 1965.

———. "The Waco Suspension Bridge." *Texana* 1, no. 3 (Summer 1963): 181–224.

Connally, Ernest Allen. "Architecture at the End of the South: Central Texas." *Journal of the Society of Architectural Historians* 11, no. 4 (December 1952): 8–12.

Connor, Seymour V. "Log Cabins in Texas." *Southwestern Historical Quarterly* 53, no. 2 (October 1949): 105–116.

Convention of Ministers and Delegates of the Congregational Churches in the United States. *A Book of Plans for Churches and Parsonages.* New York: D. Burgess and Co., 1853.

Cooke, Philip St. George. *Exploring Southwestern Trails, 1846–1854.* Glendale, Calif.: Arthur H. Clark Co., 1938.

Cosby, Hugh E., ed. *History of Abilene.* Abilene, Tex.: Hugh E. Cosby Co., 1955.

Cotton, Fred R. "Log Cabins of the Parker County Region." *West Texas Historical Association Year Book* 29 (October 1953): 96–104.

Coursey, Clark. *Courthouses of Texas.* Brownwood, Tex.: Banner Printing Co., 1962.

Cox, I. J. "Educational Efforts in San Fernando de Bexar." *Quarterly of the Texas State Historical Association* 6, no. 1 (July 1902): 27–63.

Cox, Mamye. *Sam Houston Normal Institute and Historic Huntsville.* Dallas, 1899.

Creese, Walter. "Fowler and the Domestic Octagon." *Art Bulletin* 27, no. 2 (June 1946): 89–102.

Crocket, George Louis. *Two Centuries in East Texas: A History of San Augustine County and Surrounding Territory from 1865 to the Present Time.* Dallas: Southwest Press, 1932.

Croff, G. B. *Progressive American Architecture, Presenting in Illustration an Extensive Collection of Original Studies for Dwelling, Bank, School and Office Buildings Costing from One Thousand to One Hundred Thousand Dollars; Also Details of Every Feature, Exterior and Interior.* New York: Orange Judd Co., 1875.

Crouch, Carrie J. *A History of Young County, Texas.* Austin: Texas State Historical Association, 1956.

Cuervo, Tienda de. "Tienda De Cuervo's Ynspección de Laredo." Translated by Herbert Eugene Bolton. *Quarterly of the Texas State Historical Association* 6, no. 3 (January 1903): 187–203.

Dabb, A. N. *Practical Plans for District Schoolhouses for the Use and Guidance of School Boards and Officers.* Philadelphia: J. A. Bancroft, 1874.

"Dallas, Texas: The Marvel of the Lone Star State." *Frank Leslie's Illustrated Newspaper,* October 6, 1888, pp. 129–131.

De Cordova, Jacob. *The Texas Immigrant and Traveller's Guide Book.* Austin: De Cordova & Frazier, 1856.

Description of the Patent Rotary Steel Jail. Chicago, n.d.

Dexter, Henry Martin. *Meeting Houses Considered Historically and Suggestively.* Boston: J. E. Tilton, 1859.

Didear, Hedwig Krell, comp. *A History of Karnes County and Old Helena.* Austin: Jenkins Publishing Co., 1969.

Downing, A. J. *The Architecture of Country Houses; including Designs for Cottages, Farm Houses and Villas; with Remarks on Interiors, Furniture, and the Best Modes of Warming and Ventilating.* New York: D. Appleton and Co., 1856.

Eastlake, Charles L. *Hints on Household Taste in Furniture, Upholstery, and Other Details.* Boston: J. R. Osgood, 1872.

Eastman, Seth. *A Seth Eastman Sketchbook, 1848–1849.* Austin: University of Texas Press, 1961.

Eichenroht, Marvin. "Fredericksburg." *Texas Architect* 10, no. 2 (February 1960): 8–9.

————. "The Kaffee-Kirche at Fredericksburg, Texas, 1846." *Journal of the Society of Architectural Historians* 25, no. 1 (March 1966): 60–63.

Estill, Harry F. "The Old Town of Huntsville." *Quarterly of the Texas State Historical Association* 3, no. 4 (April 1900): 265–278.

Everts, William W. *The House of God: Or Claims of Public Worship.* New York: American Tract Society, 1872.

Ewell, Thomas T. *History of Hood County Texas from Its Earliest Settlement to the Present.* Granbury, Tex.: Granbury News, 1895.

Falconer, Thomas. *Notes on a Journey through Texas and New Mexico in the Years 1841 and 1842.* London, 1842 [?].

Ferguson, Dan. "Austin College in Huntsville." *Southwestern Historical Quarterly* 53, no. 4 (April 1950): 386–403.

Field, M. *City Architecture: Designs for Dwelling Houses, Stores, Hotels, etc.* New York: G. P. Putnam and Co., 1853.

Fisher, Orceneth. *Sketches: Texas in 1840, Designed to Answer, in a Brief Way, the Numerous Enquiries Respecting the New Republic, as to Situation, Extent, Climate, Soil, Productions, Water, Government, Society, Religion, Etc.* Reprint. Waco: Texian Press, 1964.

Fitch, James Marston. *American Building: The Historical Forces That Shaped It.* 2d ed. Boston: Houghton Mifflin Co., 1966.

Freeman, W. G. "W. G. Freeman's Report on the Eighth Military Department." Edited by M. L. Crimmins. *Southwestern Historical Quarterly* 51, no. 1 (July 1947): 54–58; no. 2 (October 1947): 167–174; no. 3 (January 1948): 252–258; no. 4 (April 1948): 350–357; 52, no. 1 (July 1948): 100–108; no. 2 (October 1948): 227–233; no. 3 (January 1949): 349–353; no. 4 (April 1949): 444–447; 53, no. 1 (July 1949): 71–77; no. 2 (October 1949): 202–208; no. 3 (January 1950): 308–319; no. 4 (April 1950): 443–473.

Fuermann, George. *The Face of Houston.* N.p., 1963.

Gallaher, James. *The Western Sketch Book.* Boston: Crocker and Brewster, 1850.

Galveston: The Commercial Metropolis and Principle Seaport of the Great Southwest; Its Geographical Position, Extent, and Resources. Galveston: Land and Thompson, 1885.

"Galveston Harbor." *Frank Leslie's Illustrated Newspaper,* May 31, 1890, pp. 365–368.

Giedion, Sigfried. *Space, Time and Architecture: The Growth of a New Tradition.* 5th ed. rev. Cambridge: Harvard University Press, 1967.

Graham, Roy Eugene. "Federal Fort Architecture in Texas during the Nineteenth Century." *Southwestern Historical Quarterly* 74, no. 2 (October 1970): 165–188.

Gray, Andrew B. *Survey of a Route for the Southern Pacific Railroad, on the 32nd Parallel.* Cincinnati: Wrightson & Co.'s Print., 1856.

Grimes, Roy, ed. *300 Years in Victoria County.* Victoria, Tex.: Victoria Advocate Publishing Co., 1968.

Habig, Marion A. *The Alamo Chain of Missions: A History of San Antonio's Five Old Missions.* Chicago: Franciscan Herald Press, 1968.

Hagner, Lillie May. *Alluring San Antonio, through the Eyes of the Artist.* San Antonio: Naylor, 1940.

Haley, J. Evetts. *Fort Concho and the Texas Frontier.* San Angelo, Tex.: San Angelo Standard-Times, 1952.

Hamlin, Talbot. *The American Spirit in Architecture.* Vol. 13 of *Pageant of America.* New Haven: Yale University Press, 1926.

————. *Greek Revival Architecture in America.* New York: Dover Publications, 1944.

Hammond, William J., and Margaret W. Hammond. *La*

Bibliography

Réunion: A French Settlement in Texas. Dallas: Royal Publishing Co., 1958.

Handy, Mary Olivia. *A History of Fort Sam Houston*. San Antonio: Naylor Co., 1951.

Harris, August Watkins. *Minor and Major Mansions in Early Austin*. Austin: Privately printed, 1958.

Hart, Herbert M. *Old Forts of the Southwest*. Seattle: Superior Publishing Co., 1964.

Hart, J[oseph] Coleman. *Designs for Parish Churches in the Three Styles of English Church Architecture; with an Analysis of Each Style, a Review of Nomenclature of the Periods of English Gothic Architecture, and Some Remarks Introductory to Church Building, Exemplified in a Series of Over One Hundred Illustrations*. New York: Dana and Co., 1857.

Hasskarl, Robert A., Jr. *Brenham, Texas, 1844–1958*. Brenham, Tex.: Banner-Press Publishing Co., 1958.

Hatcher, Mattie Austin, trans. "Instructions which the Constitutional Ayuntamiento of the City of San Fernando de Bexar Draws Up in Order that Its Provincial Deputy May Be Able to Make Such Representations, Take Such Steps, and Present Such Petitions as May be Conducive to the Happiness, Development, and Prosperity of Its Inhabitants." *Southwestern Historical Quarterly* 23 (July 1919): 61–68.

Hermansen, David R. "Indiana County Courthouses of the Nineteenth Century." In *Ball State University Faculty Lecture Series, 1967–68*, pp. 13–37. Muncie, Ind., 1968.

Hitchcock, Henry-Russell. *Architecture: Nineteenth and Twentieth Centuries*. Baltimore: Penguin Books, 1958.

————. *The Architecture of H. H. Richardson and His Times*. Cambridge: MIT Press, 1966.

Hogan, William Ransom. *The Texas Republic: A Social and Economic History*. Norman: University of Oklahoma Press, 1946.

Holland, G. A. *History of Parker County and the Double Log Cabin*. Weatherford, Tex.: Herald Publishing Co., 1937.

Holley, Mary Austin. *Letters of an Early American Traveller, Mary Austin Holley: Her Life and Her Works, 1784–1846*. Edited by Mattie Austin Hatcher. Dallas: Southwest Press, 1933.

————. *Texas*. Lexington, Ky.: J. Clarke and Co., 1836.

Hooten, Charles. *St. Louis' Isle, or Texiana, with Additional Observations Made in the United States and Canada*. London: Simmonds and Wards, 1847.

Hudgens, William M. "St. Marienkirche Zu Friedrichsburg, Texas." *Texas Architect* 19, no. 10 (October 1969): 19–23.

Hulme, F. Edward. *Principles of Ornamental Art*. London: Cassell Potter and Galpin, 1875.

Hunt, Richard S., and Jesse F. Randel. *A New Guide to Texas: Consisting of a Brief Outline of the History of Its Settlement, and Colonization and Land Laws; A General View of the Surface of the Country; Its Climate, Soil, Productions, etc. With a Particular Description of the Counties, Cities, and Towns*. New York: Sherman and Smith, 1845.

Hunter, J. Marvin. *Pioneer History of Bandera County: Seventy-Five Years of Intrepid History*. Bandera, Tex.: Hunter's Printing House, 1922.

Ikin, Arthur. *Texas: Its History, Topography, Agriculture, Commerce, and General Statistics. To Which is Added a Copy of the Treaty of Commerce Entered Into by the Republic of Texas and Great Britain. Designed for Use by the British Merchant, and as a Guide to Emigrants*. 1841. Reprint. Waco: Texian Press, 1964.

Inland Architect and Builder. 1883–1900.

Irwin, Jack C. "Dallas County Courthouse: Texas Historical Architecture." *Texas Architect* 18, no. 4 (April 1968): 25–27.

Jackson, J. B. "The Almost Perfect Town." *Landscape* 2 (Spring 1952): 2–8.

Jobson, F. J. *Chapel and School Architecture, as Appropriate to the Buildings of Nonconformists, Particularly to Those of the Wesleyan Methodists; with Practical Directions for the Erection of Chapels and School-Houses*. London: Hamilton, Adams and Co., 1850.

Johonnot, James. *School-Houses*. New York: J. W. Schermerhorn and Co., 1871.

Julian, Ralph. "A Recent Journey through the West." *Harper's Weekly*, November 9, 1895, p. 1064.

Jutson, Mary Carolyn Hollers. *Alfred Giles: An English Architect in Texas and Mexico*. San Antonio: Trinity University Press, 1972.

Kennedy, William. *Texas: The Rise, Progress, and Prospects of the Republic of Texas*. 2d ed. London, 1841. Reprint. Fort Worth: Molyneaux Craftsmen, 1925.

Kerr, Hugh. *A Poetical Description of Texas, and Narrative of Many Interesting Events in That Country, Embracing a Period of Several Years, Interspersed with Moral and Political Impressions: Also an Appeal to Those Who Oppose the Union of Texas with the United States, and the Anticipation of That Event. To Which is Added, the Texas Heroes, No. 1 and 2*. New York: Privately printed, 1838.

Kimball, Fiske. *American Architecture*. New York, 1928. Reprint. New York: AMS Press, 1970.

Kirkpatrick, A. Y. *Early Settlers Life in Texas and the Organization of Hill County*. Hillsboro, Tex., 1909. Reprint. Waco: Texian Press, 1963.

Knight, Oliver. *Fort Worth, Outpost on the Trinity*. Norman: University of Oklahoma Press, 1953.

Lancaster, Clay. *Architectural Follies in America, or Hammer, Saw-Tooth and Nail*. Rutland, Vt.: Charles E. Tuttle Co., 1960.

———. "Oriental Forms in American Architecture, 1800–1870." *Art Bulletin* 29, no. 3 (September 1947): 183–193.

———. "Some Octagonal Forms in Southern Architecture." *Art Bulletin* 27, no. 2 (June 1946): 103–111.

Landolt, G. L. *Search for the Summit: Austin College through XII Decades, 1849–1970*. Austin: Von Boeckmann-Jones Co., 1970.

Lathrop, Barnes F. *Migration into East Texas, 1835–1860: A Study from the United States Census*. Austin: Texas State Historical Association, 1949.

Lawrence, A. B. *Texas in 1840, or the Emigrant's Guide to the New Republic by a Resident Emigrant Late from the United States*. New York: Nafis and Cornish, 1845.

Leclerc, Frédéric. *Texas and Its Revolution*. Translated by James L. Shepherd III. Facsimile. Houston: Anson Jones Press, 1950.

Lindsley, Philip. *A History of Greater Dallas and Vicinity*. 2 vols. Chicago: Lewis Publishing Co., 1909.

Linn, John Joseph. *Reminiscences of Fifty Years in Texas*. New York: D. and J. Sadlier and Co., 1883.

Lockwood, Frances B. *Comanche County Courthouses*. N.p., 1969.

"The Lone Star State." *Frank Leslie's Illustrated Newspaper*, September 27, 1890 (supplement), pp. 1–16; October 4, 1890 (supplement), pp. 1–20; October 18, 1890 (supplement), pp. 1–16.

Lotto, F. *Fayette County: Her History and Her People*. Schulenburg: Sticker Steam Press, Tex., 1902.

Lunden, Walter A. "The Rotary Jail, or Human Squirrel Cage." *Journal of the Society of Architectural Historians* 18, no. 4 (December 1959): 149–157.

Lynes, Russell. *The Tastemakers*. New York: Grosset and Dunlap, 1954.

Maass, John. *The Gingerbread Age: A View of Victorian America*. New York: Rinehart and Co., 1957.

McCalla, William Latta. *Adventures in Texas, Chiefly in Spring and Summer of 1840, with a Discussion of Comparative Character, Political, Religious and Moral; Accompanied by an Appendix, Containing an Humble Attempt to Aid in Establishing and Conducting Literary and Ecclesiastical Institutions*. Philadelphia: Privately printed, 1841.

McClintock, William A. "Journal of a Trip through Texas and Northern Mexico in 1846–1847." *Southwestern Historical Quarterly* 34, no. 1 (July 1930): 20–37;
no. 2 (October 1930): 141–158; no. 3 (January 1931): 231–256.

McConnell, H. H. *Five Years a Cavalryman; or, Sketches of Regular Army Life on the Texas Frontier Twenty Years Ago*. Jacksboro, Tex.: J. N. Rogers and Co., 1889.

McDonald, M. Lynn. "Millett Opera House." *Texas Architect* 20, no. 6 (June 1970): 16–21.

McKenna, Rosalie Thorn. "James Renwick, Jr., and the Second Empire Style in the United States." *Magazine of Art* 44, no. 3 (March 1951): 97–101.

M'Laughlin, Charles N. *Complete Guide to the Texas Capitol, in Brief, in Detail and by Departments . . .* Austin: M'Laughlin, 1888.

McLeod, William A. *Story of the First Southern Presbyterian Church, Austin, Texas*. N.p., 1939.

Mahan, D[ennis] H[art]. *An Elementary Course in Civil Engineering for the Use of Cadets of the United States' Military Academy*. 4th ed. rev. New York: John Wiley, 1848.

Mansfield, J. K. F. "Colonel J. K. F. Mansfield's Report of the Inspection of the Department of Texas in 1856." Edited by M. L. Crimmins. *Southwestern Historical Quarterly* 42, no. 2 (October 1938): 122–148; no. 3 (January 1939): 215–257; no. 4 (April 1939): 351–387.

Marryat, Frederick. *The Travels and Adventures of Monsieur Violet, in California, Sonora, and Western Texas*. London: G. Routledge and Sons, 1843.

Martínez, Antonio. *The Letters of Antonio Martínez*. Translated and edited by Virginia H. Taylor. Austin: Texas State Library, 1957.

Meeks, C. L. V. "Form beneath Fashion: 19th Century Depots." *Magazine of Art* 39, no. 8 (December 1946): 378–380.

———. *The Railroad Station: An Architectural History*. New Haven: Yale University Press, 1956.

———. "Romanesque before Richardson in the United States." *Art Bulletin* 35, no. 1 (March 1953): 17–33.

A Memorial and Biographical History of Dallas County. Chicago: Lewis Publishing Co., 1892.

A Memorial and Biographical History of Ellis County, Texas. Chicago: Lewis Publishing Co., 1892.

A Memorial and Biographical History of Johnson and Hill Counties. Chicago: Lewis Publishing Co., 1893.

A Memorial and Biographical History of Navarro, Henderson, Anderson, Limestone, Freestone, and Leon Counties. Chicago: Lewis Publishing Co., 1893.

"Methodist Church Architecture." *National Magazine, Devoted to Literature, Art and Religion* 7 (December–January 1855): 497–512; 8 (February–March 1856): 220–225.

Mills, W. S. *History of Van Zandt County*. Canton, Tex.: Privately printed, 1950.

Bibliography

Moore, Francis, Jr. *Map and Description of Texas, Containing Sketches of Its History, Geology, Geography and Statistics; With Concise Statements, Relative to the Soil, Climate, Productions, Facilities of Transportation, Population of the Country; and Some Brief Remarks Upon the Character and Customs of Its Inhabitants.* Philadelphia, 1840. Reprint. Waco: Texian Press, 1965.

Morfi, Juan Agustín. *History of Texas, 1673–1779.* Translated with biographical introduction and annotations by Carlos Eduardo Castañeda. Albuquerque: Quivira Society, 1935.

Morgan, Charles D. "The Comanche County Courthouse, 1890–1939." *Texas Architect* 19, no. 12 (December 1969): 18–21.

Morgan, Jonnie R. *The History of Wichita Falls.* Oklahoma City: Economy Co., 1931.

Morgan, William Manning. *Trinity Protestant Episcopal Church, Galveston, Texas, 1841–1953: A Memorial History.* Houston: Anson Jones Press, 1954.

Morphis, J. M. *History of Texas from Its Discovery and Settlement, With a Description of the Principal Cities and Counties, and the Agricultural, Mineral, and Material Resources of the State.* New York: United States Publishing Co., 1874.

Morrell, A. N. *Flowers and Fruits from the Wilderness; or Thirty-Six Years in Texas and Two Winters in Honduras.* 3d ed. St. Louis: Commercial Printing Co., 1882.

Morrison, Hugh. *Early American Architecture: From the First Colonial Settlement to the National Period.* New York: Oxford University Press, 1952.

Mumford, Lewis. *The Brown Decades: A Study of the Arts in America, 1865–1895.* New York: Harcourt, Brace and Co., 1932.

———. *Roots of Contemporary American Architecture: A Series of Thirty-Seven Essays Dating from the Mid-Nineteenth Century to the Present.* New York: Reinhold Publishing Co., 1952.

———. *Sticks and Stones: A Study of American Architecture and Civilization.* New York: Dover Publications, 1955.

Murphy, DuBose. "Early Days of the Protestant Episcopal Church in Texas." *Southwestern Historical Quarterly* 34, no. 4 (April 1931): 293–316.

Neumann, Ray. *A Centennial History of St. Joseph's Church and Parish, 1868–1968, San Antonio, Texas.* San Antonio: Clemens Printing Co., 1968.

Neville, A. W. *The History of Lamar County (Texas).* Paris, Tex.: North Texas Publishing Co., 1937.

Newcomb, Rexford. *Spanish-Colonial Architecture in the United States.* New York: J. J. Augustin, 1937.

Newell, Chester. *History of the Revolution in Texas, Particularly of the War of 1835 & '36; Together with the Latest Geographical, Topographical and Statistical Accounts of the Country from the Most Authentic Sources.* New York: Wiley and Putnam, 1838.

"Notes on Texas. By a Citizen of Ohio." *Hesperian; or, Western Monthly Magazine* 1, no. 5 (September 1838): 350–360; 1, no. 6 (October 1838): 428–440; 2, no. 1 (November 1838): 30–39; 2, no. 2 (December 1838): 109–118; 2, no. 3 (January 1839): 189–199; 2, no. 4 (February 1839): 288–293; 2, no. 5 (March 1839): 359–367; 2, no. 6 (April 1839): 417–426.

Nuttall, Zelia. "Royal Ordinances concerning the Laying Out of New Towns." *Hispanic-American Historical Review* 4 (November 1921): 743–753.

O'Connor, Kathryn Stoner. *The Presidio La Bahía del Espíritu Santo de Zúñiga 1721 to 1846.* Austin: Von Boeckmann-Jones Co., 1966.

Olmsted, Frederick Law. *A Journey through Texas; or, A Saddle-Trip on the Southwestern Frontier: With a Statistical Appendix.* New York: Dix, Edwards and Co., 1857.

Parisot, P. F., and C. J. Smith. *History of the Catholic Church in the Diocese of San Antonio, Texas.* San Antonio: Carrico and Bowen, 1897.

Parker, A[mos] [Andrew]. *Trip to the West and Texas, Comprising a Journey of Eight Thousand Miles, through New-York, Michigan, Illinois, Missouri, Louisiana and Texas, in the Autumn and Winter of 1834–5. Interspersed with anecdotes, incidents and observations. With a Brief Sketch of the Texian War.* Concord, N.H.: White and Fisher, 1835.

Patterson, W. M. *A Manual of Architecture: For Churches, Parsonages and Schoolhouses, Containing Designs, Elevations, Plans, Specifications, Form of Contract, Rules for Estimating Cost of Buildings, With Suggestions on Acoustics, Ventilating, Heating, Lighting, Painting, Etc.* Nashville, Tenn.: Methodist Episcopal Church South, 1875.

Pevsner, Nikolaus. *An Outline of European Architecture.* 5th ed. rev. London: Penguin Books, 1957.

A Plea for the Use of the Fine Arts in the Decoration of Churches. New York: J. F. Trow, 1857.

Polk, Stella Gipson. *Mason and Mason County, Texas: A History.* Austin: Jenkins Publishing Co., 1966.

Power, Tyrone. *Impressions of America; during the Years 1833, 1834 and 1835.* Philadelphia: Carey, Lea & Blanchard, 1836.

Price, Edward T. "The Central Courthouse Square in the American County Seat." *Geographical Review* 58, no. 1 (1968): 29–60.

Rankin, Melinda. *Texas in 1850*. Reprint. Waco: Texian Press, 1966.

Rathjen, Frederick W. "The Texas State House: A Study of the Building of the Texas Capitol Based on Reports of the Capitol Building Commissioners." *Southwestern Historical Quarterly* 60, no. 4 (April 1957): 433–462.

Reps, John W. *The Making of Urban America: A History of City Planning in the United States*. Princeton: Princeton University Press, 1965.

———. *Town Planning in Frontier America*. Princeton: Princeton University Press, 1969.

Richardson, Rupert Norval. *The Frontier in Northwest Texas, 1846 to 1876, Advance and Defense by the Pioneer Settlers of the Cross Timbers and Prairies*. Glendale, Calif.: Arthur H. Clark Co., 1963.

———. *Texas: The Lone Star State*. New York: Prentice-Hall, 1943.

Rister, Carl Coke. *Fort Griffin on the Texas Frontier*. Norman: University of Oklahoma Press, 1956.

Roach, Dennis B. "Culberson County Courthouse." *Texas Architect* 20, no. 5 (May 1970): 14–19.

Robinson, Willard B. "The Public Square as a Determinant of Courthouse Form in Texas." *Southwestern Historical Quarterly* 75, no. 3 (January 1972): 339–372.

Roemer, Ferdinand. *Texas, with Particular Reference to German Immigration and the Physical Appearance of the Country, Described Through Personal Observation*. Translated by Oswald Mueller. San Antonio: Standard Printing Co., 1935.

Rose, Victor M. *Some Historical Facts in Regard to the Settlement of Victoria, Texas: Its Progress and Present Status*. Laredo, Tex.: Daily Times, 1883.

"San Antonio, Texas." *Frank Leslie's Illustrated Newspaper*, November 2, 1878, p. 141.

Sánchez, José María. "A Trip to Texas in 1828." Translated by Carlos Eduardo Castañeda. *Southwestern Historical Quarterly* 29, no. 4 (April 1926): 249–288.

Sanford, Trent Elwood. *The Architecture of the Southwest: Indian, Spanish, American*. New York: W. W. Norton and Co., 1950.

———. *The Story of Architecture in Mexico: Including the Work of the Ancient Indian Civilizations and That of the Spanish Colonial Empire Which Succeeded Them Together with an Account of the Background in Spain and a Glimpse at the Modern Trend*. New York: W. W. Norton and Co., 1947.

Schmidt, Charles F. *History of Washington County, Texas*. San Antonio: Naylor Co., 1949.

Schmitz, Joseph William. *Texas Culture in the Days of the Republic, 1836–1846*. San Antonio: Naylor Co., 1960.

Scott, Zelma. *A History of Coryell County, Texas*. Austin: Texas State Historical Society, 1965.

Scully, Vincent J., Jr. "Romantic Rationalism and the Expression of Structure in Wood: Downing, Wheeler, Gardner, and the 'Stick Style,' 1840–1876." *Art Bulletin* 35, no. 2 (June 1953): 121–142.

———. *The Shingle Style: Architectural Theory and Design from Richardson to the Origins of Wright*. New Haven: Yale University Press, 1955.

Sealsfield, Charles. *The Cabin Book; or, Sketches of Life in Texas*. New York: J. Winchester, 1844.

Shanklin, Felda Davis. *Salado, Texas: Its History and Its People*. Belton, Tex.: Peter Hansbrough Bell Press, 1960.

Sheridan, Francis C. *Galveston Island; or a Few Months off the Coast of Texas: Journal of Francis C. Sheridan, 1839–1840*. Edited by Willis W. Pratt. Austin: University of Texas Press, 1954.

Sheridan, Philip H. *Personal Memoirs of P. H. Sheridan, General, United States Army*. 2 vols. New York: Charles L. Webster and Co., 1888.

Shurtleff, Harold R. *The Log Cabin Myth: A Study of the Early Dwellings of the English Colonists in North America*. Cambridge, Mass.: Harvard University Press, 1939.

Sibley, Marilyn McAdams. *Travelers in Texas, 1761–1860*. Austin: University of Texas Press, 1967.

Simmons, Frank E. *History of Coryell County*. Belton, Tex.: Coryell County News, 1936.

Simpson, Harold B., ed. *Frontier Forts of Texas*. Waco: Texian Press, 1966.

Sleeper, John, and J. C. Hutchins. *Waco and McLennan County, Texas; Containing a City Directory of Waco, Historical Sketches and Notices of Prominent Citizens. Information with Regard to Our Various Institutions, Organizations, Etc.* Waco: Examiner Steam Press, 1876.

Smith, Edward. *Journey through Northeastern Texas, Undertaken in 1849 for the Purposes of Emigration Embodied in a Report: to Which are Appended Letters and Verbal Communications, from Eminent Individuals; Lists of Temperature; of Prices of Land, Produce, and Articles of Merchandize and the Recently Adopted Constitution of Texas, With Maps from the Last Authentic Survey*. London: Hamilton, Adams, and Co., 1849.

"Stagecoach Inn, Winedale." *Texas Architect* 16, no. 6 (June 1966): 7–14.

Stanislawski, Dan. "Early Spanish Town Planning in the New World." *Geographical Review* 37 (1947): 94–105.

———. "The Origin and Spread of the Grid-Iron Pat-

Bibliography

tern Town." *Geographical Review* 36 (1946): 105–120.

Stieghorst, Junann. *Bay City and Matagorda County: A History.* Austin: Pemberton Press, 1965.

Stiff, Edward. *The Texan Emigrant; being a Narrative of the Adventures of the Author in Texas, and a Description of the Soil, Climate, Productions, Minerals, together with the Principal Incidents of Fifteen Years Revolution in Mexico: And Embracing a Condensed Statement of Interesting Events in Texas, From the First European Settlement in 1692, Down to the Year 1840.* Waco: Texian Press, 1968.

Stross, Allen. *The Michigan State Capitol.* Lansing: Michigan Historical Commission, 1969.

Tallmadge, Thomas E. *The Story of Architecture in America.* New York: W. W. Norton and Co., 1936.

Temple, Texas, Junior Chamber of Commerce. *Bell County History: A Pictorial History of Bell County, Texas, Covering Both the Old and the New.* Fort Worth: University Supply and Equipment Co., 1958.

Texas Almanac. Galveston: Galveston News, 1857–1872.

Texas in 1840, or the Emigrant's Guide to the New Republic being the Result of Observation, Inquirey and Travel in that Beautiful Country by an Emigrant, Late of the United States. With an Introduction by the Rev. A. B. Lawrence of New Orleans. New York: William W. Allen, 1840.

"Texas in the Union." *Antiques* 53, no. 6 (June 1948): 447–452.

Texas State Gazetteer and Business Directory. Vol. 4. Detroit: R. L. Polk and Co., 1892.

Thrall, Homer S. *History of Methodism in Texas.* Houston: E. H. Cushing, 1872.

———. *A History of Texas, from the Earliest Settlements to the Year 1885, with an Appendix Containing the Constitution of the State of Texas, adopted November, 1875, and the Amendments of 1883.* New York: University Publishing Co., 1885.

———. *The People's Illustrated Almanac, Texas Handbook and Immigrant's Guide, for 1880; Being an Index to Texas, Her People, Laws, State and Local Governments, Schools, Churches, Railroads, and other Improvements and Institutions with Chronological History of the State for 1879.* St. Louis: N. D. Thompson and Co., 1880.

———. *A Pictorial History of Texas, From the Earliest Visits of European Adventurers, to A.D. 1879. Embracing the Periods of Missions, Colonization, the Revolution, the Republic and the State; also, a Topographical Description of the Country, Together with Its Indian Tribes and Their Wars, and Biographical Sketches of Hundreds of Its Leading Historical Characters. Also, a List of the Counties, with Historical and Topical*

Notes, and Descriptions of the Public Institutions of the State. 5th ed. rev. St. Louis: N. D. Thompson and Co., 1879.

Turnley, Parmenas Taylor. *Reminiscences of Parmenas Taylor Turnley, From the Cradle to Three-score and Ten; by Himself, from Diaries Kept from Early Boyhood. With a Brief Glance Backward Three Hundred and Fifty Years at Progenitors and Ancestral Lineage.* Chicago: Donohue & Henneberry, Printers, 1892.

Tyler, George W. *The History of Bell County.* Edited by Charles W. Ramsdell. Belton, Tex.: Kelley, 1966.

Upjohn, Everard M. *Richard Upjohn, Architect and Churchman.* New York: Columbia University Press, 1939.

Upjohn, Richard. *Upjohn's Rural Architecture. Designs, Working Drawings and Specifications for a Wooden Church, and Other Rural Structures.* New York: G. P. Putnam, 1852.

A Visit to Texas: Being the Journal of a Traveller through Those Parts Most Interesting to American Settlers with Descriptions of Scenery, Habits, C.&C. New York, 1834. Facsimile. Austin: Steck Co., 1952.

Walter, Ray A. *A History of Limestone County.* Austin: Von Boeckmann-Jones, 1959.

Waugh, Julia Nott. *Castro-Ville and Henry Castro, Empresario.* San Antonio: Standard Printing Co., 1934.

Webb, Walter Prescott, ed. *The Handbook of Texas.* 2 vols. Austin: Texas State Historical Association, 1952.

Weisman, Winston. "Commercial Palaces of New York: 1845–1875." *Art Bulletin* 36, no. 4 (December 1954): 285–302.

Wellman, Rita. *Victoria Royal: The Flowering of a Style.* New York: Charles Scribner's Sons, 1939.

Weyand, Leonie Rummel, and Houston Wade. *An Early History of Fayette County.* LaGrange, Tex.: LaGrange Journal Plant, 1936.

Whiffen, Marcus. *American Architecture since 1780: A Guide to the Styles.* Cambridge: MIT Press, 1969.

———. "The Early County Courthouses of Virginia." *Journal of the Society of Architectural Historians* 18, no. 1 (March 1959): 2–10.

White, Raymond E. "Cotton Ginning in Texas to 1861." *Southwestern Historical Quarterly* 61, no. 2 (October 1957): 257–269.

———. "The Texas Cotton Ginning Industry, 1860–1900." *Texana* 5, no. 4 (Winter 1967): 344–358.

Wilcox, Seb. "Fort McIntosh." *Epic-Century Magazine* 5, no. 8 (September 1938): 7–9.

———. "Laredo during the Texas Republic." *Southwestern Historical Quarterly* 42, no. 2 (October 1938): 83–107.

Withey, Henry F., and Elsie Rathburn Withey. *Bio-*

graphical Dictionary of American Architects Deceased. Los Angeles: Hennessey and Ingalls, 1970.

Wodehouse, Lawrence. "Ammi Burnham Young, 1798–1874." *Journal of the Society of Architectural Historians* 25, no. 4 (December 1966): 268–280.

———. "The Custom House, Galveston, Texas, 1857–1861, by Ammi Burnham Young." *Journal of the Society of Architectural Historians* 25, no. 1 (March 1966): 64–67.

Woldert, Albert. *A History of Tyler and Smith County, Texas.* San Antonio: Naylor Co., 1948.

Woodman, David, Jr. *Guide to Texas Emigrants.* Boston: M. Hawes, 1835.

Wortham, Louis J. *History of Texas, from Wilderness to Commonwealth.* 5 vols. Ft. Worth: Wortham-Molyneaux, 1924.

Yoakum, Henderson King. *History of Texas from Its First Settlements in 1685 to Its Annexation to the United States in 1846.* 2 vols. New York: Redfield, 1855.

Young, Samuel O. *A Thumb-Nail History of the City of Houston, Texas, from its Founding in 1836 to the Year 1912.* Houston: Rein and Sons Co., 1912.

Zucker, Paul. *Town and Square: From the Agora to the Village Green.* New York: Columbia University Press, 1959.

NINETEENTH-CENTURY TEXAS NEWSPAPERS

Abilene Reporter.
Austin Record.
Brazos Courier.
Daily Bulletin (Austin).
Dallas Morning News.
Dallas Weekly Herald.
Fort Worth Daily Democrat.
Fort Worth Daily Democrat-Advocate.
Fort Worth Daily Gazette.
Galveston Daily News.
Houston Daily Post.
Matagorda Bulletin.
Northern Standard (Clarksville).
Redlander (San Augustine).
San Antonio Express.
Standard (Clarksville).
Telegraph and Texas Register (San Felipe de Austin and Houston).
Texas Gazette (San Felipe de Austin).
Texas Republican (Brazoria).
Texas Republican (Marshall).

INDEX

Abilene, 106
academies, 18, 144–145, 180–181, 184
Adler and Sullivan: architects, 255
adobe buildings, 53–54, 95; Mexican, 8; at military posts, 41, 43, 46
aesthetics: of courthouses, 198–199; of ecclesiastical architecture, 136–137; of iron construction, 60; of public buildings, 191; of towns, 17–18, 107
Agricultural and Mechanical College of Texas (College Station), 17, 145
Alamo. *See* Mission San Antonio de Valero
Alamo Baptist Church (San Antonio), 143
Alamo Iron Works (San Antonio), 93
Albany, 197, 198, 228
Albright: builder, 250
Allert, Robert: builder, 102
Almonte, Col. Juan Nepomuceno, 12
Alpine, 199, 233
Alvarez de Piñeda, Alonzo, 4
American Colonial Revival style, 114–115
Anáhuac, 13
Anderson, 24, 25
Anderson's Mill, 56
Andrewarthe and Wahrenberger: architects, 214
Andrews, A. H., and Co., 228
Angleton, 203 n
Annie Riggs Hotel (Fort Stockton), 63, 95
Annie Riggs Memorial Museum, 95
Annunciation, Church of (Houston), 137–138, 152–153
antebellum architecture, 19–29
architects: biographies of, 107, 108; ethical standards of, 108; military, 45, 53–54; professional qualifications of, 107–108
architecture: character of, as basis for judgment, 107; as enticement to attract investment, 113; as expression of

energy and pride, 196; as fulfillment of needs for monuments, 195; impact of Civil War on, 55; importance of, 107; as indication of cultural advancement, 16, 64, 146; indigenous, 3–4, 41, 207; influence of, on moral character, 16; and life and times of society, 3; reflection of Eastern trends in, 60, 62; as reflection of nature of religion, 138–140, 142–143; as reflection of pride and wealth, 191; as reflection of region, 3–4, 13, 50–51, 59, 64; regulation of practice of, 108; as symbol of progress, 61; symbolism (associationalism) in, 16, 21, 64, 137, 194–195, 197
—Mexican, 8–9, 11–13, 207
—military: Mexican, 9; in Republic of Texas, 39–40; Spanish colonial, 6, 8; U.S., 40–50
Arlington Heights Hotel (Fort Worth), 115
Armstrong, A. J.: architect, 112–113
Armstrong and Messer: architects, 112, 113
Arnim and Lane Building (Flatonia), 58–59, 76–77
arsenal, 19
Ashbell Smith Building (U.T. School of Medicine), 146, 188–189
Austin, Moses, 10
Austin, Stephen F., 10, 11
Austin: Capitol (1839) in, 18, 20; Capitol (1852–1854) in, 27; Capitol (1882–1888) in, 206, 260–265; churches in, 25, 137, 138, 149, 158; courthouse in, 198–199; described, 19, 20; General Land Office in, 28, 34–35; Governor's Mansion in, 28; hotel in, 111, 128–130, 131; mill near, 56; opera house in, 111, 131; plat of, orientation of, 19; university buildings in, 17, 144, 145, 158, 183
Austin College (Huntsville and Sherman), 17, 182–183

Austin County Jail, 218

Bailey, S. M.: builder, 208
Ball, George, 126
Ball High School (Galveston), 146
Ballinger, 18, 106
Bandera, 138, 155, 217
Bandera County Historical Survey Committee, 217
Bandera County Jail, 217
bandstands, 107, 117
bank buildings, 58, 74, 232; architectural character of, 64; Beaux-Arts, 126; highrise, 113; in historical styles, 64, 101–102; Islamic, 110, 124–125; with native materials, 64, 99–100; Renaissance Revival, 110, 119; Romanesque Revival, 63–64; sites for, 64
Bankers' and Merchants' National Bank (Dallas), 63
Baptist Church (Anderson), 24, 25
Baptist church buildings, 24, 25, 142–143, 177
Baroque style, 6, 115
barracks, 43, 45–49 and n. 34; at Anáhuac, 13; cavalry, 52; design of, 49; in Fort Worth, 41; Spanish colonial, 8–9
Barrett, W. M.: master builder, 183
bars, sites for, 18
Baskin Building (Cameron), 88–89
Bastrop, 11, 219
Bastrop County Jail, 219
Baunach, Father Peter, 155
Bay City, 64, 102
Bay City Bank, 64, 102
Baylor University, 17, 145, 186
Beach Hotel (Galveston), 114–115
Beaumont, 26
Beaux-Arts style, 126, 256
Bell County Courthouse, 27, 197, 224
Bell County Jail, 21
Bellville, 195, 218
Belton: commercial building in, 58, 72; courthouses in, 27, 197, 224; jail in, 21

Index

Index